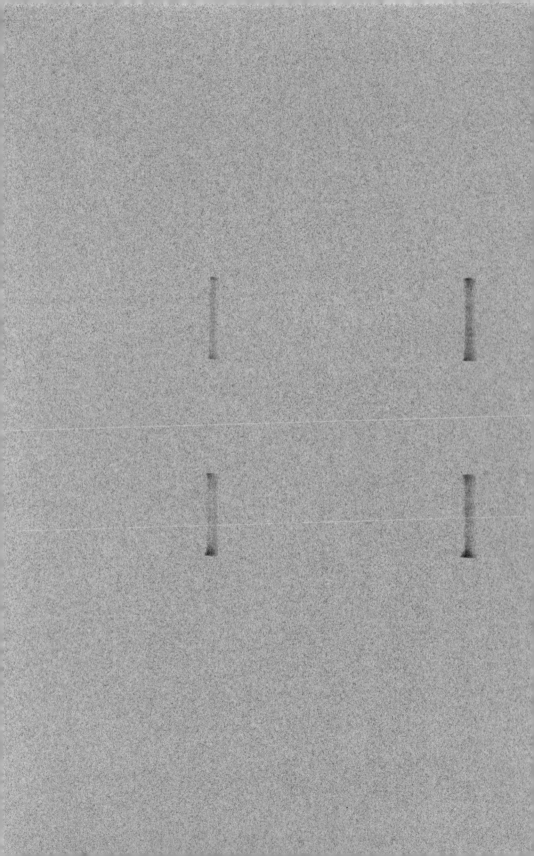

THE THINGS THAT WERE SAID OF THEM

THE THINGS THAT WERE SAID OF THEM

Shaman Stories and Oral Histories of the Tikiġaq People

TOLD BY ASATCHAQ

Translated from the Iñupiaq by

Tukummiq and Tom Lowenstein

Introduction and Commentaries by

Tom Lowenstein

UNIVERSITY OF CALIFORNIA PRESS   BERKELEY   LOS ANGELES   OXFORD

DOUGLAS & McINTYRE   VANCOUVER   TORONTO

University of California Press
2120 Berkeley Way
Berkeley, California 94720

University of California Press, Ltd.
Oxford, England

Published in Canada by Douglas & McIntyre Ltd.
1615 Venables Street
Vancouver, British Columbia V6L 2H1

The masks on the cover, frontis, and pages facing
part openings were produced in Tikiġaq during the
mid-nineteenth century and are typical of Point
Hope wood carving. Photographs courtesy of the
University of Alaska Museum.

Library of Congress and Canadian Cataloging-in-
Publication data appear on the last page of the book.

Printed in the United States of America

9 8 7 6 5 4 3 2 1

The paper used in this publication meets the
minimum requirements of American National
Standard for Information Sciences—Permanence
of Paper for Printed Library Materials,
ANSI Z39.48-1984. ♾

*This book is dedicated to
the memory of Asatchaq (1891–1980)
and to the community of
Point Hope, Alaska*

*Also to my mother and to
the memory of my father,
E. H. Lowenstein*

CONTENTS

ACKNOWLEDGMENTS

To have lived and worked for many years in an Iñupiaq community has been a privilege that is impossible to acknowledge adequately. Tikiġaq (Point Hope) was and remains a second home for me, and the friends I lived with became, as I was drawn into their families, my own family. For its hospitality and tolerance, I extend my gratitude to the whole community. I hope that this book, whose audience starts with Tikiġaq, will approximate what I blindly promised when I started.

In addition to my own fieldwork, the entire book flows from pioneering work done by previous ethnographers. As I mention in the Introduction, the basis of this project was information recorded in 1940–41 by Froelich Rainey. Without Rainey's monograph and unpublished field notes on Tikiġaq, my work would have been out of the question. Rainey interviewed Tikiġaq elders who lived a good part of their lives within an almost unfragmented tradition. These men and women, born between 1870 and 1880, had firsthand, adult experience of precontact ceremonial and thought. Thus, behind almost every commentary here lie the recollections of the following Tikiġaġmiut: Aġviqsiiña (Frank), Ququk (Dives), Peter Kunuyaq, Nasugluk, Nasugruk, Uyaġaq (Sam Rock), Aivatchiq, Quwana, and Niġuvana (Asatchaq's mother, 1875–1942). Asatchaq, the main storyteller of this book, also worked with Rainey. But it would have been impossible to comprehend Asatchaq's stories without a record of his parents' generation.

In addition to Asatchaq, Tukummiq, Umigluk, and Aviq, whose stories and translations are presented here, I worked during the course of many field trips with other Tikiġaq elders, whose insight and information I have woven continually into my commentaries. I therefore thank Augustus and Walter Kowunna, Solomon Killigivuk, Donald and Lily Oktollik, Patrick Attungana, Kirk Oviok, and Alec Millik. Also, I remember with gratitude George Omnik, Charles and Lucy

Jensen, Laurie Kingik, Beatrice Vincent, Bob Tuckfield, and Herbert Kinneavauk, all of whom have died over the past decade. I should especially like to thank the following friends, with whom I lived, worked, ate, went whaling, or traveled: Rex and Piquk Tuzroyluk, Joe and Lucy Towkshjea, Elijah and Dorcas Rock, Henry Nashookpuk, Konrad Killigivuk, Isaac Killigivuk, Peter Lisbourne, and Willy Omnik.

I gratefully acknowledge my principal Iñupiaq teacher, Lawrence Kaplan, who has supplied a transcription of one of the stories in the book and has, over the past fifteen years, unstintingly provided linguistic help. Without his constantly available expertise regarding a language I was very far from fluent in, this work would not have been possible. And many thanks to the excellent teaching of Edna Ahgeak MacLean, who also painstakingly checked many of the story translations.

The late Don Charles Foote, who lived in Tikiġaq between 1960 and 1961, also left notes of great importance, which tragically he did not live to use in their entirety. These, along with Rainey's notes, are in the archives of the University of Alaska. I am likewise indebted to Ernest Burch and John Bockstoce: Burch's historical work and Bockstoce's publications on whaling have been indispensable.

I am also particularly grateful to Patricia Partnow, who first brought me to Alaska and who has been a continuing support to this work, and to the librarians and archivists of the Elmer Rasmusen Library of the University of Alaska in Fairbanks and the archives of the Episcopal Church, Austin, Texas. Help and encouragement of many kinds came from Brigid MacCarthy, Richard Nelson, James Vanstone, Irene Reed, John Bockstoce, John O'Neil, Eric Smith, Pamela Herman, Armand Schwerner, Selima Cavanagh, Rafael and Jacintha Nadal, the late Geoffrey Vickers, and Helge Larsen. I am especially grateful to Richard Bready, whose advice and encouragement have been a constant.

Fieldwork scattered over fifteen years was made possible by the following foundations, to whom grateful acknowledgment is made: the Alaska Historical Commission, the Arctic Institute of North America, the American Philosophical Society, the North Slope Borough, the John Simon Guggenheim Memorial Foundation, the Nuffield Foundation, and the Leverhulme Trust. Radio programs based on these stories were funded by the Maniilaq Association in Kotzebue and the National Endowment for the Arts (Folks Arts Division).

These acknowledgments would be incomplete without thanks to my editors at the University of California Press, in particular Pamela MacFarland Holway, Dan Gunter, Jeanne Sugiyama, and Doug Abrams, for patient help in bringing a tangled manuscript to its present shape. It goes without saying that in a work of reconstruction like this there will be errors of fact and interpretation; all of them will be mine.

Tom Lowenstein

Iñupiaq names and terms are given in the standard orthography, which is in general use throughout the Alaskan Iñupiaq region. Phonetically, Iñupiaq is quite different from English, even though its sounds are represented by symbols from the same Latin alphabet. For a more detailed discussion of Iñupiaq pronunciation, see MacLean 1981.

VOWELS

Iñupiaq has three short vowels, which are partially similar to those of English: *a* is pronounced *uh*, something like the *u* in English "cut"; *i* is pronounced *ee*, as in "see"; *u* is pronounced *oo*, as in "boot." There are also three long vowels, written *aa, ii,* and *uu.* The long vowel *aa* is pronounced *ah,* as in English "father"; long *ii* and *uu* are roughly similar to their short counterparts, but the sound is lengthened accordingly.

Any two short vowels may occur in a cluster, giving six possibilities: *ai, ia, au, ua, iu,* and *ui.* In Point Hope *ai* is pronounced like a long [e:], something like the vowel in English "say"; *au* is pronounced like a long [o:], approximately as in "so." Other vowel clusters simply sound like a combination of the two short vowels they contain.

All vowel sounds may be modified somewhat by surrounding consonants, notably uvulars (*q, ġ*), which tend to lower the sound of the vowel. Thus, for example, in the vicinity of *q* or *ġ* an *i* is closer to the *e* in English "let," while a *u* approximates the *o* in the British pronunciation of "box."

CONSONANTS

Most of the consonants of Iñupiaq correspond closely to their English equivalents. However, Iñupiaq contains a number of sounds which do not occur in English:

q	a uvular or back *k*, pronounced in the upper throat
ġ	a uvular or back *g*, like a French or German *r*
ḷ	a palatal *l*, similar to the *ll* in "million"
ñ	a sound like the Spanish *ñ*, or the first *n* in "onion"
ŋ	a sound like the *ng* in "singer"

As with vowels, consonants (with the exception of *s*) also occur long. Long, or geminate, consonants are written double: *tt* (*tuttu*, "caribou"), *ll* (*qulliq*, "oil lamp"), etc. Long *ch*, though, is written *tch*.

STRESS

Iñupiaq words containing only short vowels are stressed on the initial syllable: *nu*-na, "land"; *Ti*-ki-ġaq, "Point Hope"); *qal*-gi, "ceremonial house." (Words of more than three short syllables are usually stressed on the antepenultimate syllable.) Syllables containing a long vowel or a vowel cluster receive stress: u-nip-*kaaq*, "legend"; U-tua-*ġaa*-luk (a name).

QUICK PRONUNCIATION GUIDE TO PRINCIPAL NAMES AND TERMS

Aliŋnaq	*Uh*-ling-nuk
aŋatkuq	*ung*-ut-kok
Aniŋatchaq	Uh-*ning*-ut-chuk
Aqsaqauraq	Uk-suh-*koh*-ruk
Asatchaq	*Uh*-sut-chuk
Ataŋauraq	Uh-tung-*oh*-ruk
Ayagiiyaq	Uh-yuh-*gay*-yuk
Iḷaŋiaqpak	I-*lyung*-iuk-puk
iḷiappaq	i-*lyiup*-puk
iḷitqusiq	i-*lyit*-koo-sek
iñua	i-*nyoo*-uh

Iñupiaq	I-nyoo-*pyuk*
Iqiasuaq	Eh-*keah-suohk*
Kiḷigvak	*Ki*-lyig-vuk
Killigivuk	*Ki*-lyig-vuk
Kinnaq	*Kin*-nuk
maktak	*muk*-tuk
Niġuvana	Neh-roo-*vuh*-nuh
Nuyagruaq	Noo-yuh-*gruohk*
Paniunayuk	Pun-*nyoo*-nuh-yook
Pisiktaġaaq	Pi-sik-tuh-*rahk*
qalgi	*kul*-gi
qattaq	*kut*-tuk
Qaunnaiḷaq	*Kohn-nay*-lyuk
Qipuġaluatchiaq	Keh-poh-ruh-*loouh*-chyuk
quġvik	*kor*-vik
qulliq	*kol*-lek
Tikiġaġmiu	Ti-keh-rur-*myoo*
Tikiġaq	*Ti*-keh-ruk
Tuluŋigraq	Too-*loong*-ig-ruk
tuunġaq	*toon*-ruk
uiḷuaqtaq	uee-*lyuahk*-tuk
umialik	oo-*may*-lik
unipkaaq	oo-nip-*kahk*
uqaluktuaq	oo-kuh-look-*tuohk*
Utuaġaaluk	Oo-toouh-*rah*-look

"True story," the old man says, and lapses into the silence that follows each telling. I make tea; we eat crackers. The wind shakes the cabin. "North wind," says Asatchaq, sliding one hand off the wrist of the other and gesturing north. "Good for polar bear hunting." Asatchaq is eighty-five; two strokes and arthritic knees have lamed him. All day he sits and rehearses stories he will tell the next evening. The stories arrive in a confident, slow series. "No. I can't tell that one," he says one windy morning. "I want to tell it. But I can't remember that boy *aŋatkuq*'s name." A few days later, as I enter the cabin, his sharp voice hits me, crying out the boy's name. "Tigguasiña! Tigguasiña! Write it down! Where's it been? I don't know . . ." The name of the *aŋatkuq*—the shaman—has surfaced. The story emerges. "*Real* story. *True* story."

The idea of the genuine is essential to the Iñupiaq, a north Alaskan Inuit people. "Iñupiaq" itself means "real people": *iñuk*, "person," + *piaq*, "real." The animal meat (*niqi*) at the center of Iñupiaq existence is called *niqipiaq*, "real meat." The suffix *-piaq* ("authentic, real") is matched by its opposite, *-ŋŋuaq* ("to pretend to be, false"). There was plenty in nature and traditional Tikiġaq culture to deceive. To maintain one's self-possession, to see clearly in high winds and blizzards, to orient the eye and body in twilight, in fog, in drifting snow and shifting ice—these skills were a condition of survival.

Likewise, Iñupiaq people, especially the shamans, had to know their way in the metaphysical realm, the world of spirits. The spirits would otherwise destroy them or would simply not manifest themselves. In the story of Tigguasiña, a deceiving shaman is unmasked by a child initiate:

"Did you meet a spirit [*tuunġaq*] yesterday?" Tigguasiña asks a boy who
has been tricked.
"Yes," says the boy.

"A real spirit [*tuuŋapiaq*]?" Tigguasiña asks.

"A real one," says the boy.

Tigguasiña points to an iglu. Its skylight is lit.

"You see that skylight? That's where your spirit lives."

And then he tells the boy about the man who has pretended to be the spirit. At the end of the story, the deceiving shaman kills himself in disgrace.

To consort with spirits was never to deny materiality. The Iñupiaqs' grip on the present and the concrete was hard and comprehending. But the present was just one aspect of reality. Adept at split-second timing, calculation, and trajectory, Iñupiaq hunters also lived within a temporal frame that extended deep into myth and history. The ancestors had established the way things should be done. The present was an extension of what the ancestors had started. The more accurately this past could be realized in rituals, songs, and stories, the more present action acquired meaningful context and justification. Asatchaq could have invented a name for the boy in the story of the false *tuuŋaq,* and I, as collector, would have been no wiser. But the story was neither complete nor true without the name Tigguasiña.

All but three of the stories in this collection were told by Asatchaq (Jimmie Killigivuk) in Point Hope, Alaska, during the winter and spring of 1976. Asatchaq's twenty-one stories begin with the creation of the Tikiġaq peninsula, take in the world of legend and nineteenth-century village history, and end with the saga of the strongman or "chief" Ataŋauraq, who was slain in 1889. Recorded in Iñupiaq and translated by Tukummiq (Carol Omnik)—a bilingual Tikiġaq woman—and myself, these texts make up about a quarter of the legends and histories that Asatchaq and other elders recorded for me during field trips between 1973 and 1988. The last two tales in the collection, told in English by Umigluk and Aviq, postdate Ataŋauraq's assassination and lead us to the conversion and death in the Kotzebue clinic of the shaman Pisiktaġaaq. To Aviq's account of Pisiktaġaaq's renunciation of shaman power I have added an anecdote about Masiiñ, the last Tikiġaq shaman, who in March 1953 claimed to have killed Stalin. Opening in mythic time, the collection thus ends with the final gestes of shamans in the modern era. Between these extremes are legends and histories that offer a unique panorama of Iñupiaq shamanism in its social, intellectual, and spiritual context.

Asatchaq (1891–1980) was born to powerful and ambitious parents at a time when Tikiġaq society was threatened with extinction. From

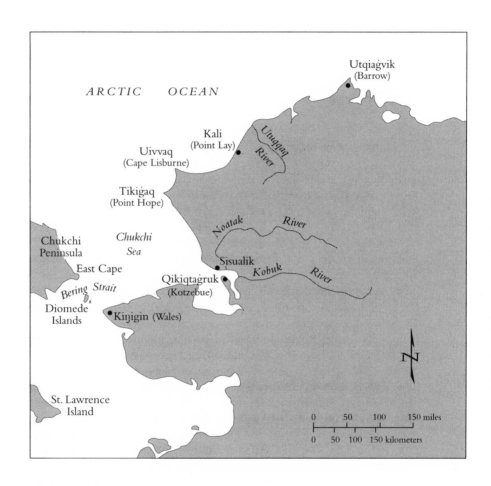

Northwest Alaska

an estimated population of thirteen hundred in 1800, this ancient, vigorous community had shrunk by the end of the nineteenth century to little more than a hundred. The immediate cause lay in contact with white culture following the entry, around 1850, of American commercial whalers and traders to the western Arctic. The first casualty was the bowhead whale, which was hunted for its baleen ("whalebone"), the flexible black krill-straining plates that hang from the whale's upper jaw. Baleen met the contemporary American and European demand for corset stays and other luxury goods; however, by 1915 baleen had been replaced by tensile steel. By the mid-1870s the bowhead—and, incidentally, the walrus, too—had been hunted almost to extinction, thus robbing Tikiġaq, like all the northwest Alaskan coastal communities, of its essential subsistence. At the peak of this crisis, in the 1880s, the caribou herds on which Tikiġaq depended for meat and skins went into cyclic decline. Along with the whaling ships came the other inevitable ills of contact—influenza, tuberculosis, measles, venereal disease, and liquor—against which Tikiġaq was defenseless. As starving families fled north in search of livelihood, a society that had extended over thousands of square miles and along two hundred miles of coast shrank to a scattering of demoralized villages.

Compounding the misery of the 1880s was the rise of Ataŋauraq, a tyrannical shaman who monopolized Tikiġaq's ivory and baleen trade with the big ships and abused his position to exercise a decade of terror over the remnant population. The watershed in Tikiġaq's fortunes came in 1889 with the murder of Ataŋauraq. In the decade that followed, wretched as it continued to be, a peaceful, albeit temporary, balance between local tradition and imported ways evolved.

In the meantime, commerce between Tikiġaq and the Yankee whalers intensified when, in 1887, a motley of Americans and Europeans abandoned their ships to establish a shore-based whaling station five miles south of Tikiġaq. Within five years, Jabbertown—so called for the babel of languages and Iñupiaq dialects spoken there—had a population of two hundred people. Most of these were southern Iñupiaqs who came to work the commercial dinghies during the spring hunt. Many stayed year-round; and as the Caucasians and the new Iñupiaqs mingled, intermarried, and traded with Tikiġaq, the unique character of the local culture began to change. Centralized intervention soon followed. As a result of a Coast Guard report on the epidemics of imported diseases and alcohol abuse that were sweeping northwest Alaska, Tikiġaq received its first missionary in the summer of 1890. This was John D. Driggs, an Episcopalian and medical doctor. By 1910 Tikiġaq's population was beginning to stabilize, and both a school and a church had been established.

The birth of a healthy boy during this period was little short of a miracle. A party of some fifteen relatives attended Asatchaq's arrival, in June 1890, sixty miles north of the village. There, remote from Tikiġaq, in his mother's birth hut, he was inducted with due ceremony into Tikiġaq society. The naming of an infant was of prime importance, since name (*atiq*) was part of a person's soul and linked the newborn with the spirit of the recently dead bearer of the name.[1] Asatchaq was named after the last great Tikiġaq shaman, who died around 1890 (story 19); he also received the name Kamik ("boot") after a paternal uncle (story 20).[2] Equally important were the amulets presented to Asatchaq: a squirrel skin and a bracelet of rifle shells. Tikiġaq people were divided into two mutually opposed amulet classes: those whose amulets could be activated by grave goods (*quŋuqtuqtuq*) and those whose charms had to touch umbilical cords, pregnant women, or placentas (*igñiruaqtuqtuq*, "has an amulet empowered by birth things"). Asatchaq was affiliated with the latter; but like much of Tikiġaq's arcane theory, the amulet system was already eroding. Perhaps the most important social and ceremonial tie was the infant's ceremonial house (*qalgi*) membership. At the height of Tikiġaq's prosperity there had been six or seven qalgis in the village, but by the 1890s the number had been reduced to three. Asatchaq joined his father's qalgi, Uŋasiksikaaq.

Asatchaq's generation was the last to be brought up by elders who identified completely with precontact life. Like all Tikiġaq children, Asatchaq played, traveled, and was educated within an extended family. His father, Kiḷigvak ("mastodon"), taught him the rudiments of hunting and made him the toy weapons with which he caught his first squirrels and ptarmigan. Niġuvana and Samaruna, his mother and maternal uncle, taught him dancing, singing, storytelling, and the ceremonial traditions. He spent autumns and winters with his grandparents in their tiny iglus on the Kuukpak River. But Asatchaq (baptized "Jimmie Killigivuk" by Driggs, who created a surname from Kiḷigvak) also learned to read, write, and do figures at the mission school. And he grew up

1. The word *atiq* has several connotations: "name," "namesake," and "inherited soul residing in a name." Any living or dead person called "Asatchaq" would be an atiq to Asatchaq. Depending on the degree of affiliation, all of them would share, to a greater or lesser extent, a mystical identity of soul and personality.

2. Asatchaq may also have been named after his maternal great-grandmother (see fig. 1).

FIGURE I. Asatchaq's family

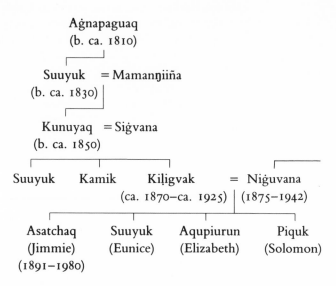

```
                    Aġnapaguaq
                    (b. ca. 1810)
                    ┌──────┐
              Suuyuk   = Mamanŋiiña
              (b. ca. 1830)│
                    ┌──┘
              Kunuyaq  = Siġvana
              (b. ca. 1850)
     ┌──────────┬──────────┬─────────────────────┐            ┌──────
  Suuyuk      Kamik      Kiḷigvak      = Niġuvana
                         (ca. 1870–ca. 1925) │ (1875–1942)
              ┌──────────┬──────────┬──────────┐
         Asatchaq     Suuyuk    Aqupiurun      Piquk
         (Jimmie)    (Eunice)   (Elizabeth)   (Solomon)
         (1891–1980)
```

almost as familiar with hardtack, calico, and firearms as with seal meat, caribou skin, and harpoons.

Rooted though his family was in the precontact tradition, Kiḷigvak, like many Tikiġaq men, established strong ties both with the Jabbertown whalers and the seasonal traders who plied the coast each summer. In the summer of 1913 Kiḷigvak imported enough lumber to build the first native-owned European-style house in the village. Asatchaq eventually inherited this house.

It was in July 1913 that Vilhjálmur Stefánsson passed Tikiġaq on the ill-fated *Karluk* en route to the Canadian Arctic. Asatchaq and another Tikiġaq man joined the expedition as hunters and dog handlers. Fortunately, Asatchaq was hunting caribou when the *Karluk* was destroyed by ice off the north Alaskan coast that January; by the time Stefánsson had regrouped, Asatchaq was back in Tikiġaq (according to Asatchaq's account, which diverges from Stefánsson's [1921]). This abortive journey was just the first of fifteen years' adventuring with traders, miners, and other white explorers up and down the coast. Nonetheless, Asatchaq always returned; he married twice, raised two families, and in 1925 took over his father's *umiaq* (skinboat) to become an *umialik* (whaleboat

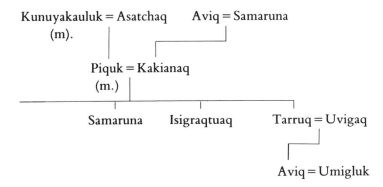

Kunuyakauluk = Asatchaq Aviq = Samaruna
  (m).

    Piquk = Kakianaq
     (m.)

   Samaruna Isigraqtuaq Tarruq = Uvigaq

            Aviq = Umigluk

owner).[3] Asatchaq continued as a year-round hunter and at a young age became central to the qalgi rituals that had survived. He absorbed an immense repertoire of ancient songs and added many of his own songs and dances to the common store. But as he reentered the village routine, Asatchaq was disturbed by the increasing displacement of his childhood experience: memories of shamans, the qalgis, and those elements of ritual life which had survived Christianization.

Tikiġaq in the 1920s remained, to the Western eye, an exotic society of monolingual, skin-clad eaters of raw meat, subsisting in sod houses and a few primitive cabins. But large areas of the intellectual and spiritual culture had eroded. Most Tikiġaġmiut knew how their grandparents had lived and thought before contact, but since the arrival of Dr. Driggs (*Taktailuk,* "big doctor") it had become increasingly difficult to believe in the spiritual theories which had been so fundamental to the

---

3. The bowhead herd, depleted as it was by the 1870s, had begun to recover when the bottom fell out of the baleen market in 1915. The Jabbertown community, however, started to dwindle around 1900 and by 1916 was gone (Vanstone 1962).

culture. Without the support of these beliefs, much traditional practice started to disintegrate.

The most dramatic expression of this disintegration was the collapse of the qalgis, where the whaling rituals and storytelling cycles had taken place each autumn. Demoralized and half-starved, Tikiġaq simply let its community houses cave in, and their ruins on the north shore were soon swept into the sea. In the absence of the qalgis, the iglus of various elders became meeting houses for storytelling, singing, and the general transmission of knowledge. One of the masters of this village lore was Asatchaq's uncle, Samaruna, and when the thirty-five-year-old Asatchaq settled back in Tikiġaq, he apprenticed himself to his uncle and systematically committed to memory the legends, histories, and songs he had known casually since childhood. Samaruna died in the 1930s, and well before his time Asatchaq inherited his uncle's place as a village savant.

The decades that followed, to the early 1960s, were perhaps Tikiġaq's most peaceful era. Life in the Arctic is never easy, but the genius of the Iñupiaqs has always been to maneuver skillfully through nearly impossible conditions. For the first half of the century Tikiġaq people survived culture contact in a similar fashion, attaching almost as little blame to the white man as they might to rough ice conditions. At the end of the 1960s the village entered a new period of Americanization, which climaxed in the midseventies with the construction of the trans-Alaska pipeline and the economic changes that followed the Land Claims Settlement. The oil boom brought development and a new range of ills, against which Tikiġaq was little better defended than it had been against measles.

In the summer of 1973 I visited Tikiġaq to record stories for an educational project run by the Alaska State Museum. Asatchaq was out of the village, but his reputation as a storyteller prompted me to look for him when I returned to Alaska the following year.

After three months in Tikiġaq I moved south, where I tracked Asatchaq down in a nursing home in Fairbanks. Marooned there with a bad chest and crippling arthritis, Asatchaq's fixed idea was to get back to the village. This move involved difficulties. By now Asatchaq was the oldest Tikiġaġmiu and so was related to virtually all four hundred people in the community. But just as he had traveled the Arctic in his twenties, his own children had long left Tikiġaq, and he had no immediate family to look after him. Since half the village had just moved two miles inland from its old site, there was also a chronic housing shortage in Tikiġaq.

Asatchaq's homecoming posed other problems as well. His status as patriarch and sage, well acknowledged as it was, elicited a certain avoidance. As I slowly came to know him, I began to see why. Asatchaq had outlived his own generation, and his worldview was quite different from that of his younger contemporaries. And while to modern Tikiġaġmiut the precontact era was an idealized, authentic good, its value depended partly on its inaccessibility. Most people under twenty-five spoke little or no Iñupiaq. The middle generation had been brought up as Christians and educated with the American future rather than the Iñupiaq past in view. The elders, now in their sixties and seventies, were deeply learned in songs, dances, history, and subsistence practice. There was, however, a gap between what these elders knew and the knowledge of Asatchaq's generation.

The crucial separating factor was shamanism, which was not only an area of great procedural and linguistic complexity but, subsequent to Dr. Driggs, a taboo subject, difficult of access, hard to understand out of context, and morally dangerous. Asatchaq's historical isolation was thus reinforced by a psychological barrier. To know the shamanistic order was partly to contain it. This knowledge was both frightening and impressive. Asatchaq made no attempt to dispel the effect, and his social isolation was compounded by a severe, didactic manner somewhat jarring to the modern temper. Such were the main factors. But Asatchaq's authority as a guardian of tradition lay partly in this refusal or inability to compromise. His grasp of history was matched by a fierce grip on life. Whether he sat on his tidy bed in Fairbanks or in the rank deprivation of his Arctic cabin, he created around him an orderly space of which he was master. I got on well with Asatchaq—indeed, we grew to love each other—partly because it was in my interest that he should maintain his preeminence, and whether it involved recording his memories or emptying his wastepot, I did what he told me. Given these terms and the few months we had together on the old, half-empty, village site, he found just enough energy to reclaim part of its history.

We started off alone in late December 1975, Tukummiq joined our project in the new year, and the three of us worked together for six months, recording stories each weekday evening, while my days were taken up with transcribing Tukummiq's translations and preparing questions to ask at the next storytelling session. By the end of the whaling festival in June, Asatchaq was exhausted. With a difficult winter behind him, the summer seemed equally uncertain. Our last session together was disrupted when the cabin started shaking violently: the village removal crew had come to drag the house to the new town site.

That day Asatchaq decided to return to Fairbanks. When I asked him for a statement on our work, he said:

> I told the stories. Tukummiq translated them. I did my best to tell them and the truth about them. I tried to please. These pages [of translation] are the proof of our work. What is in here, I did my best to tell it right. Work about our people gets back to us and we see it. The things you have written will give you the power to show what we've done. Three sticks [our three-person team, bound together] can't be broken.

I typed out Tukummiq's translation; Asatchaq signed it in his decorous copperplate and then flew south.

Asatchaq and I worked together intermittently in Fairbanks and again in Tikiġaq until shortly before his death in 1980. Throughout, Asatchaq saw our collaboration as a kind of "government work" designed to save old stories for the non-Iñupiaq-speaking new generation and thus to restore a semblance of the old dispensation. Asatchaq had worked with ethnographers and archaeologists since 1913 and had known the likes of Diamond Jenness, Knud Rasmussen, Froelich Rainey, and Helge Larsen. Assuming perhaps that Europeans shared some sort of communal power, Asatchaq seemed to hold an exaggerated notion of my place in the order of things. Once when I told him I was flying down to the state capital, he rapped out, "Go and tell the governor!" The idea was that once the authorities had heard his stories, they would somehow reinstitute the quasi-shamanistic structures they represented to him. I didn't make it to the governor, but we did organize a series of bilingual broadcasts from the local radio station. Asatchaq died before he heard the tapes aired.

This, more than twelve years later, is the book he encouraged me to put together. It is not difficult to imagine the old man weighing it up as he would have an artifact or a tool, his hand resting on the cover before absently reverting to those times and images so inevitably changed in these translations.

TIKIĠAQ

The main village of Tikiġaq lies at the tip of a low-lying peninsula which juts into the Chukchi Sea 130 miles above the Arctic Circle. Surrounded by sea on three sides, summer temperatures on the Point range from forty to sixty degrees Fahrenheit; the winter average of minus thirty degrees is intensified by brutal winds. The village of Tikiġaq

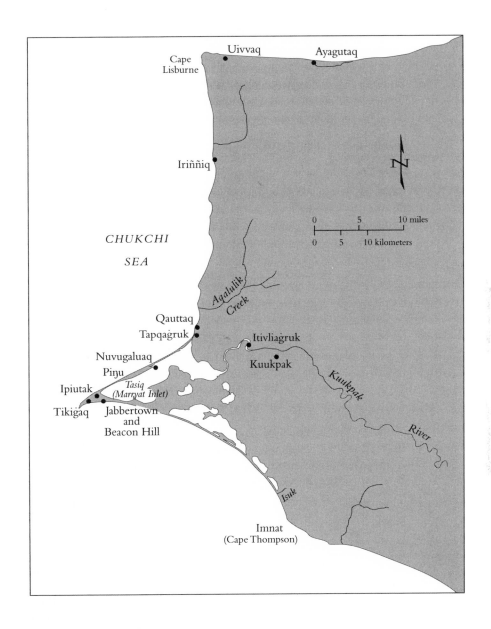

Principal Sites around the Tikiġaq Peninsula

("index finger") was itself only the principal settlement in a larger territory. Of the estimated thirteen hundred people of the precontact population, about six hundred inhabited the Point itself (Burch 1981), while others moved between smaller settlements up and down the coast and along rivers.

Tikiġaq society, as it existed before the nineteenth century, was the latest in a series of cultures going back more than two thousand years. The earliest site on the Point that has been accurately dated was Ipiutak (ca. A.D. 1–500), whose spectacular ivory relics were excavated by Larsen and Rainey in 1939–40. Then, over a period of a thousand years, the whale-hunting cultures developed, principally Birnirk; from Birnirk evolved the more elaborate Thule culture, which spread east across the Arctic from Alaska. Precontact Tikiġaq, with its large, part-whalebone houses and diversified economy, was the last expression of western Thule.

The whale hunt was always central to Tikiġaq life, and the origin myth that heads this collection lies at the heart of Tikiġaq identity by explaining how the Point itself was once a whalelike being. The Point does have a cyclic, living and dying quality. Storms push thousands of tons of gravel from the cliffs to the southeast up onto the south shore each summer; yards of turf on the north side are cut away annually by the same storms. Thus the Point keeps its shape in the sea by growing each year on one side while on the other it decays (Moore 1966). Into the beach ridges created by this continual movement Tikiġaq people built their semisubterranean houses. The Tikiġaq iglu was a chamber roughly ten feet square made of driftwood logs from the south beach. Entry was through the *qanitchaq,* a whalebone passage with access to the chamber through the *katak,* a round hole in the chamber floor. In addition to its function as a cold trap, the qanitchaq was a storage area, with cooking and sleeping alcoves set in its walls. The iglu was lit and partially ventilated by a skylight covered with seal gut and a small hole called "the nose." Beneath the skylight and set into the north wall was a sleeping bench for the household elders; under the bench and at the katak the women and girls tended seal-oil lamps. Insulated on the outside with thick layers of sod, most iglus were surmounted by storage racks to keep meat and equipment from dogs and foxes.

THE TIKIĠAQ YEAR

The whale hunt was Tikiġaq's prime seasonal activity. It traditionally began in April, when north winds and currents open a channel in the sea ice; through this the bowhead migrates to its summer feeding grounds. When the first bowhead or belukha dolphin were sighted, Tikiġaq men dragged their skinboats to the open water, where they silently waited with harpoons, drag-floats, spears, and butchering equipment. Each skinboat (*umiaq*) was owned by a married couple (*umialik*). While the husband hunted from the ice with his eight-man crew, the woman conducted much of the esoteric whaling ceremonial in the village. The female umialik's visit to the butchering site to give the whale a drink from her ritual waterpot, or *qattaq*, was one of the high points in the ceremonial year. The soul of the whale, which had been placated with a libation of fresh water and its head rolled back to the sea, returned to its "country" for reincarnation and to tell its fellows of the hunters' kindness. In the meantime, tons of meat, fat, bone, and baleen were carefully distributed and hauled back to the village, where the bounty was stored underground.

Whaling continued until late May and was followed by a three-day feast which honored successful umialiks and the souls of dead whales. This rite, like several other autumn and winter rites, was organized by the qalgis, in whose grounds umialik women distributed sliced-up whale fluke. Thousands of pounds of raw meat, gums, tripe, liver, heart, and *maktak* (whale skin and blubber) were shared within and between the qalgis, along with the duck, goose, murre, crane, belukha, and seal meat the new season had brought. On the final day of the feast there were dances and games, in particular the famous skin toss (*nalukataq*).

Spring in the Arctic can be bright, if not warm, and by whale-feast time the first tundra flowers have sprung up on the higher ground and on graves and old middens. The Point has been barren of animals all winter. Now the sun shines all night and the squirrels emerge; buntings and Lapland longspurs return to nest on hummocks and around iglus; ducks, geese, and murres in tens of thousands migrate across the Point. Closer to the earth there are flies and bees and other insects; later in the summer there are even butterflies.

In the precontact period, by June most Tikiġaġmiut had left their iglus and were living in tents along the south shore within reach of the seals, bearded seals (*ugruk*), and walrus that haul up on ice floes to bask. The ugruk was prized for its meat and fat, and its skin was vital for bootsoles, rope, and skinboat covers. It was at this time that umialiks acquired the six or eight ugruk hides they would need for the next whaling season.

When the ice dispersed and the seal hunt was over, everyone in Tikiġaq except the old and sick and those who planned to build new iglus began their summer travels. Some poorer families set out on foot, but most went by umiaq. Paddling along the shore, and with dogs line-hauling where possible, some families went south to the trade fair at Sisualik, while others traveled north to barter at the mouth of the Utuqqaq River. At Imnat (Cape Thompson) on the way south and around Uivvaq (Cape Lisburne) to the north, most families stopped to raid the cliff ledges for murres eggs. In July the second migration of belukhas was hunted with nets and harpoons from the beaches. Trout and salmon were taken later in the summer with nets extended from shore. Summer was also when Tikiġaġmiut hunted caribou and marmot for the skins they would need the following winter. While some of their parties camped on the beaches, hunters struck inland along river valleys to shoot and snare caribou. Some people stayed to hunt in Tikiġaq territory all summer, but others went on to barter sea-mammal goods in return for fish, caribou, and black bear meat as well as for the muskrat, marmot, wolverine, and fox furs they were offered by inland people.

Trading with strangers was risky and often dangerous, but most Tikiġaġmiut inherited or developed partnerships with people from the Kobuk and Noatak Rivers in the south and, in the north, with the residents of Utqiaġvik (Barrow) and the interior. The fair at Sisualik saw an extraordinary convergence of northwest Alaskan and occasionally Siberian peoples. There they traded, competed in athletics, exchanged news and stories, held shamanistic séances, hunted belukha, swapped spouses, and sometimes fought. During the rest of the year most of these societies lived in a state of mutual hostility—sometimes open warfare—so violence frequently erupted. The fairs nonetheless reinforced the individual ties that lay within these tensions.

Once they had filled their boats and before the autumn storms set in, Tikiġaġmiut started for home. Along the way they hunted, gathered berries, and retrieved the meat and eggs they had cached underground or in caves en route. Travelers from the south often stopped for salmon fishing in the Kivalina region, while others moved straight to Tikiġaq's Kuukpak River to hunt caribou, pick berries, trap, and, at fresh-water freeze-up, fish through the ice for grayling. People who wintered in the smaller coastal settlements continued to hunt on the land until the sea froze. But by late October, when the seal hunt was set to begin, Tikiġaġmiut were reestablished up and down the coast in their winter iglus.

Tikiġaq village now became the center of intense ceremonial activity. Other than some duck and geese in early fall and stranded tomcod which old people and children gathered on the beaches, there would be virtually no hunting from the Point until after freeze-up. While the women scoured their iglus, the men set about cleaning the qalgis. Far larger than the iglu, although structurally identical but for its whale jaws set in the ceiling and benches around the sides, the qalgi was where the men made their hunting gear and ritual equipment. The latter regalia included ancestor masks and figurines of men, umiaqs, and animals that were hung for the ceremonial period from the qalgi ceiling. A second group of hangings was made new each year to be ritually burned before seal hunting started.

An uninterrupted period of extraordinary and elaborate rituals in the qalgis ensued: day-and-night storytelling sessions, gift exchange, feasts, masked dances, shamanistic séances, interqalgi games, more feasting, dances, and gift exchange, and finally a long, solemn series of whaling rites in which the umialiks enjoined the spirits of the whales to visit Tikiġaq next spring. The ceremonies, which were largely but not exclusively the men's preserve, ended with a fabulous display of animal and human puppets.

Soon after the ceremonies, in the first weeks of November when the sea had frozen, seal hunting started. For the rest of the winter, the men, who had been eating and working almost entirely in the qalgis, moved into their iglus, and domestic life took over. There were few times in the year when the women were not tanning, cutting, and sewing caribou and seal skins, and by now they had their families' parkas, trousers, boots, and mittens ready for the winter. When the ice was firm, the men walked out each morning for the short hours of daylight, either alone or with a partner or a younger relative, and waited for seals at breathing holes and little ponds. The sea ice near Tikiġaq, with its high pressure ridges, ice rocks, and unpredictable shifts, was too dangerous to risk traveling with the four or five large dogs that most families used for coastal and inland sled travel. Some men did take their dogs when they went polar bear hunting. Others walked alone, miles south over the pack ice, speared a bear, skinned and butchered it on the spot, and hauled the meat home after dark, against the wind.

Skillful as hunters were, and encyclopedic as their knowledge of the ice had to be, they were often stranded when the ice moved. The fortunate ones survived until they could make their way to some recognizable landfall. Others perished at sea or drifted into hostile territory, where they were usually murdered. Strangers could expect the same fate in Tikiġaq territory.

The hunting routine continued from November to March with little variation. The diet of raw or boiled seal meat might be broken with dried or frozen game kept over from the summer. Caribou were sometimes taken in the river valleys; wolves, wolverines, and foxes were hunted for their fur to make parka ruffs and boot trimmings. The great change came, however, as the days drew out in March and whaling fever gripped the village.

The basic unit of Tikiġaq social life was the extended family. Within this unit, parents, their siblings, and grandparents shared responsibility for bringing up children. Put another way, the privilege of looking after their future providers was shared according to circumstance, and children, whether or not adopted, usually grew up moving between households and around the territory. This movement was not confined to the young. People came and went, casually and without having to explain their presence, and life in the iglu was crowded, hospitable, and diverse. Many families lived in clusters of houses with interconnecting passages, the whole group constituting a close-knit clan, which formed part of a qalgi. The male relatives at the head of this clan would likewise form whale-hunting crews.

There was no centralized political structure in Tikiġaq. Power lay with umialiks for as long as their skill brought them wealth and charisma. This power, however, extended scarcely further than the family and skinboat crew; only the shamans and old people exerted a more generalized authority outside their qalgis.

Though women weren't excluded from the qalgis, their lives centered on child rearing, skin sewing, and a host of other practicalities in the iglu. Marriage was generally by male choice, sometimes capture, but a woman could simply walk back to her own kin if she failed to establish herself in her husband's iglu or if she were abused. Physically as well as psychologically tough, Tikiġaq women were men's social equals; and though their roles were quite distinct, the female umialik, to give just one example, was her husband's equal as a whaleboat owner and was often his boss.

Tikiġaġmiut were an athletic, ebullient, and competitive people. The harshness of the land and weather was matched, especially during winter in the main village, by the intensity of a close-packed, quasi-urban social life. The warmth of the family and reverential loyalty to elders had its converse in strenuous, often agonizing competitive games and a brooding, generations-long proclivity for taking umbrage. Interfamily feuds could simmer for decades until the longed-for opportunity for retribution came. Shamans seemed to act faster when they took offense.

All-out war with other Iñupiaqs, and even Kutchin Indians, was common. More than once before contact Tikiġaq was decimated by invading warriors.

Transcending such enmities were the many types of nonkin partnership that Tikiġaġmiut created both within the village and outside it. Men and women bearing the same name automatically had affectionate *atiq* (name or namesake) partnerships. There was a special relationship (*uuma*, "nonsexual sweetheart") between a person and his or her namesake's spouse. Most people had joking partners, who could, up to a point, cheerfully insult them. Perennial good relations between namesakes and uumas were reinforced by dances and gift exchange during the autumn rituals. Although most large-scale goods exchange was done on an interregional basis, many people also had trade partners within the village. Married couples often established sexual copartnerships designed to create happy relations between all four participants. Spouse exchange outside the village was particularly important because it created networks of affiliation in otherwise hostile societies. All the children of spouse-sharing partners were regarded as siblings (*qataŋun*). Thus both Tikiġaq and immense regions controlled by other societies were crisscrossed with lines of mutual friendship. Some of the stories in this book explore the nature of partnerships: their obligations and advantages as well as the limits beyond which they could not be pushed. But crowning such alliances and transcending rivalries was the fervent, nationalistic devotion of the Tikiġaġmiut to home and its inhabitants—not least to the animals, whose presence, in equal measure to their usefulness, gave joy.

SPIRITUAL LIFE AND SHAMANISM

There was a mystical basis for the Tikiġaq people's attachment to the world. Everything, from humans through animals to the land and sea, was imbued with spirit. Humans were a complex of three main parts: two souls (*iñuusiq* and *iḷitqusiq:* perhaps "life force" and "personal spirit") and a name soul (*atiq*). After death, the iñuusiq departed for the east, but the other soul components could be reborn. The whole universe was filled with souls. Tikiġaq Point itself has once been a sea beast, and periodically its spirit stirred as a reminder of its presence. Lakes, hills, rivers, rocks, lagoons, old graves, and iglus held presiding spirits (*iñuas*). These ranged from monsters and ghouls to the helpful souls of old umialiks or the cannibal shades of murdered babies. Disaffiliated spirits (*tuuṅ̇aqs*), generated in the earth or air or transformed from iḷitqusiqs, filled shamanic séances with gibberish and screaming. Families of grotesque spirit people lived inside the Point. Under the sea were "couples," part whale, vaguely human. Then there were supernatural, quasi–flesh-and-blood beings scattered through the territory: giants at the cliffs, nine-legged polar bears, whale-fishing eagles, massively strong nomadic dwarves, and the man with ivory eyes who punished disobedient children.

Not least were the animals. Tikiġaq's relationship to its game was a complex of worship and brutality, and into this ambivalence were meshed countless rituals. Since animals were killed and their bodies eaten, animal souls had to be placated; otherwise, they would look for worthier hunters. But providing they were honored, animals would gladly "lend people their meat and skins." The animals' spirits were helpful, too. All Tikiġaġmiut owned at least one animal amulet, from bears, seals, loons, and eagles to crustacea and fossils. Shamans went further and could metamorphose into the shape of their animal protector.

Presiding over all these beings was the spirit of the moon (*tatqim iñua*). Originally a Tikiġaq man and his sister's lover, the moon spirit was keeper of the game and the object of umialik women's supplication. Like the animals in his care, tatqim iñua—the prime criminal of myth (see "Aliŋnaq")—could always smell out infractions of taboo. His anger would then lead him to withhold game from Tikiġaq hunters.

Everyone was touched by the unseen world, and many types of practitioner specialized in its manipulation, at many levels of prowess: diviners, casters of spells, healers, clairvoyants, composers of magic invulnerable warriors, children born with the potent souls of animals, craftsmen who made magical equipment. Umialik women held quasi-shamanic converse with the moon. Old people kept power (*qiḷa*) in reserve should society fail in its obligations to them.

But none of these was a shaman (*aŋatkuq*) unless he or she had entered the spirit world. Initiation took many forms. Some apprenticed themselves to older aŋatkuqs, who put them through ascetic ordeals where they waited for spirits to appear with songs and arcane instruction. Other candidates were dismembered and eaten by animal spirits or abducted by tuuṅ̇aqs and held prisoner until they had absorbed the power to return to themselves whole. Some aŋatkuqs, waylaid by a talking caribou or seal, caught a glimpse of its iñua (the animal's part-human spirit, visible as a human face beneath the skin) or learned to speak animal languages.

Having once dwelled or wrestled with the unseen forces, shamans then commanded certain spirits. This control gave aŋatkuqs the power to cure or kill, to change the weather, to lure animals to them or drive them away, to revive the dead, to mutilate themselves, to die only to emerge whole and alive, and to perform other feats that defied nature.

Although the content of the first ordeal was at least partly involuntary, initiated aŋatkuqs entered trance at will, and trips to nonhuman worlds became part of their repertoire. Narcotics and intoxicants were unknown to Iñupiaqs; the two-beat rhythm of the drum (qiḷaun, from qiḷa, "power"), repetitive songs, and exhausting dances sent the shaman into trance. As the body lay asleep, the free soul (the iḷitqusiq) traveled to the moon, the seabed, or other spirit realms. There the shaman bargained for animals or for human souls that the spirits held captive.

Once an aŋatkuq's initiation was acknowledged, he entered the public sphere and built up a clientele of the most influential people he could attach to himself. It was a dangerous and exhausting practice, and perhaps this was why some of the female aŋatkuq minority chose to work secretly. Tikiġaq was famous for its powerful shamans, and many of the shaman's needs might be met by handsome payments, but psychic stress and the rivalry of competitors made for a life fraught with crises and danger.

It was this dark aspect of the practice that many Tikiġaġmiut were glad to see die in the missionary era. Many old men and women refused to talk about this frightening—and, so they were taught, shameful—aspect of Tikiġaq's past. Others regretted the disappearance of the aŋatkuqs. The practice was in innumerable ways creative and altruistic, but these positive aspects unfortunately do not survive in many stories. More important, it was the shamans who maintained the intricate weave of beliefs and ceremonial that linked Tikiġaġmiut with the nonhuman world and who made poetic sense of the cosmos of myths in which they participated.

STORIES AND STORYTELLING

Just as a name held the spirit of its past owner, so stories, which brought past lives into the present, were vehicles of souls. There were two categories of narrative. First were unipkaaqs: myths, legends, and folktales which took place "back then" in the indefinite past (taimmani). Then there were ancestor stories, uqaluktuaqs, which recorded family histories of feuds, journeys, hunting accidents, and shamanic events as far back as five generations. Beyond that a history would usually merge with others of its kind, slip into unipkaaq, or be forgotten. All stories were nonetheless said to be true, and the lives of the present generation were given context, justified, and guided by the heroes and ancestors whose coexistence they thus honored. Some stories, such as "Niġliq and Suuyuk" and "Sea-Ice Strandings," were told partly to chastise antisocial behavior and preempt the disintegration of order that they describe.

Storytelling was the prerogative of the older men and women at any gathering: ceremoniously in the qalgi and iglu, and with less formality wherever the opportunity arose on the tundra, sea ice, and beaches. Few places in Tikiġaq territory did not have some narrative association, and people seldom traveled anywhere without recalling what had happened to others before them in the same places. The following account (recorded in spring 1976) of Asatchaq's first childhood journey to the rockfall at Iriññiq (Cape Lewis) beautifully combines an evocation of the storytelling process and the story of Iriññiq:

> While the men [in this unipkaaq] were on the cliffs, the women were in their tents sewing.
> And when *we* went there, I was in my uncle Isigraqtuaq's skinboat. This was the first time I traveled north. Natchiġun and his wife were with us . . . And Natchiġun told us the story of Iriññiq. We left Tikiġaq while there was still sea ice. As we traveled, Natchiġun told us how the rocks had fallen. We came ashore near Iriññiq, and the men went up the cliffs for eggs. I was scared of climbing. I was never a climber. So I made my aunt Tarruq hold my hand as we went up. And I seemed to be slipping, even though I'm hanging on to someone . . . *Irrigi!* [Exclamation of fear.] And while the men went up the cliffs, Natchiġun and Tikiq told the women how the rocks had fallen.
> The men had told those women not to sew while they were climbing. But the women and children were buried alive when the cliffs fell down on them. When they returned, the men could hear their cries under the rocks. But they couldn't help them.
> So when the men [in our party] began to climb, Natchiġun and Tikiq told us what had happened to those earlier people. They warned the women not to do what made the cliffs fall down on those earlier people [i.e., break the taboo against sewing].

This narrative describes storytelling at its most informal and spontaneous. At the other extreme were long recitations each autumn at which stories formed the first part of qalgi ceremonials. The ceremonies began soon after people returned from their summer travels and continued while the men in their qalgis prepared the equipment they would need for the winter (Rainey 1947). When the sun began to set in line with the Point, the men in each qalgi stopped work, and sitting in the bench places they had inherited from their elder relatives, they listened to the old men telling stories. First came the histories. These included the didactic alġaġuuns ("warnings"), which described how to cope with dangerous ice and weather. Two examples of alġaġuuns appear in "Sea-Ice Strandings."

When the old men had finished telling uqaluktuaqs, they turned to the older stories, starting with the origin of Tikiġaq and continuing through the night and next day until the qalgi members were satisfied. Since any qalgi's repertoire could have filled several weeks of recitation, it is hard to know how stories were selected. But since storytelling was often a semicommunal process, with two or more old men encouraging the central voice with rhythmic concurrence ("*Ii!* Yes! That's where it happened"), repetition of the story's phrases, extra detail, questions, emendation, and refinement, each year the event presumably took on the shape its leading participants gave it. But by the time the storytellers had fallen silent and the whaling rituals had started, the men who had been absent from the Point in small groups all summer were reintegrated with their land, myths, and history.

Though women were excluded from these qalgi events, the same autumn period was taken up with storytelling in the iglu. And after the qalgis were closed for the winter, the nights were filled with cycles of fantastic tales, such as "Ukuŋniq" and its many analogues. People so delighted in listening to stories as they went to sleep that, as Asatchaq described to me, the tales mingled with their dreams and were thus transformed and made doubly familiar. In the context of this imaginative surround, children naturally became storytellers themselves and entertained each other, especially with brief, elegantly pointless fables that accompanied their games. Many of these tales—often shared by Inuit across the Arctic—were dialogues between animals, whose gestures and voices the children mimed or conjured in the movements of string figures (*ayaġhaaq*). Often the animals broke into song, but the boundary in this realm between story and song was indistinct, as this favorite story illustrates:

Aviŋŋauraq
igalaam siñaani

kiavalukkatauraqsiruq;
kiavalukatauraliami,
kataktuq igalaamiñ,
qiagaqsiruq:
"Suŋŋaŋ-aŋaa!
Suŋŋaŋ-aŋaa!
Tulimaata navipalukkikka!"

A little lemming
around the iglu skylight
starts circling;
goes around,
falls from the skylight,
starts crying:
"Suŋŋaŋ-aŋaa!
Suŋŋaŋ-aŋaa!
I think I've broken my ribs!"

Styles of adult recitation differed, but behind the variations there was a rough vocal paradigm, softly enunciated and matter-of-fact, impossible to convey in written English. Asatchaq's gravelly, unemphatic voice, with its unspoken suggestion that he simply told things as they were, exemplified this type of delivery. Using the language and rhythms of daily speech, the storyteller retired to a nondaily condition. He was in the present, but also in the story time; he spoke from a distance which removed him from the audience but which also obliterated the distance between audience and story. Sometimes in midstory Asatchaq addressed me or Tukummiq without altering the tone of his exposition. Or he laughed, belched, made asides, responded to our questions, drank tea, or scolded himself for forgetting some name or incident. These extras and interruptions made no difference to the formality of the occasion. Each story was prepared beforehand and delivered with a ritualized and courteous solemnity.

Asatchaq's voice, like the voices of many of his younger colleagues, was severe, restrained, didactic. Now and then he would modulate his hypnotic monotone with a menacing rise, at the moment of a killing or on some labyrinthine polymorpheme, while the vocal descent conveyed a harpoon strike, the blow of a knife, or arrows flying. The death of Niġliq is conveyed within this frightening syllabic contour. Likewise, the rush of caribou in "Iqiasuaq" is enacted in a stream of jostling, rhythmic phrases, end-stopped abruptly as the herd meets the cliff edge.

In a softer mode, the fool in "Kinnaq" calls up to women on high riverbanks and hilltops. Asatchaq voices their responses in a ghostly falsetto, disembodied from the grain of the surrounding narrative. This sense of a voice projected upward or downward occurs in many stories. When someone stands at the iglu skylight to summon the child shaman in "Aniŋatchaq," we hear his voice from both above and outside. Likewise, when Suuyuk calls up Uivvaq beach to his wife in her tent (in "Niġliq and Suuyuk"), his words are half-lost, extended through vocally implied distance.

Some storytellers accompanied their recitations with broad, theatrical movements. One ninety-year-old woman in Kotzebue who told me a version of "Iqiasuaq" crouched on the floor to enact a caribou scraping back its "mask" to reveal the human face beneath it. Crippled by arthritic knees and half-paralyzed by a stroke during our first month together, Asatchaq's gestures were confined to his arms and hands. These he used in slow, arcing movements to suggest paddling a kayak or harpooning a whale. Sitting with his back to the north beach, Asatchaq also oriented himself precisely to the movements and journeys in each narrative he told. "It happened over there," he'd say, jabbing toward the school incinerator, which stood on the site of Qaġmaqtuuq qalgi. Many of his gestures were sharp and abrupt; others conveyed violence or its aftermath with a sudden, sculptural halt in midair. His hands then fell peacefully, and the voice rolled on, as though following some line in the wind around his cabin.

But the authority and self-confidence of Asatchaq's performances were always subordinate to tradition. The grave tone of his delivery and his (often quite misplaced) contempt for less knowledgeable younger people was matched by his total obedience to the forebears' word, which he strove to reproduce exactly. This effort, with its idealized notion of ancestral reality, also falls within Iñupiaq convention. Comparing himself to the real old-timers, Asatchaq believed that he "knew nothing," that he "had a very bad memory." The old stories, the shamans, the ancestors—these held the real power; he was simply the vehicle through which they spoke. If in the service of Samaruna's stories he had cultivated his memory—that most prized Iñupiaq intellectual function—this was as nothing to the capacity of his mentors, even though he had witnessed them correcting each others' performances. This submission to precedent was a precondition for his right to speak, as it had been his uncle's and grandfather's, and so on back. But comparatively inadequate as the forebears may have felt, at least they had deferred to their own past in the confidence that they were only the latest in a connected cycle which it was inconceivable to break. They had, furthermore, the means to hand on what they knew intact.

Asatchaq, by contrast, was conscious of being alienated in a new and agonizing way. The twentieth century had inexorably intervened. At the far end, it lay between him and his parents' generation; and now, toward the close of his life, between himself and the future. The illusion of a historical falling-off, so far as the continuity of tradition was concerned, had thus become real. "When I'm dead," he used to say, "and someone comes and asks a question, Asatchaq will be gone. There'll be no more questions." This was true; we wouldn't even know what to ask. That he should nonetheless, in age and sickness, tell these stories for the last time to a non-Iñupiaq was heroically to penetrate the future and, albeit as a stranger, connect himself with it.

The texts collected here derive from both classes of narrative, *unipkaaq* (old stories) and *uqaluktuaq* (ancestor histories), in approximately equal number. Since all Asatchaq's stories were recited in the same conversational measure, I have tried to suggest a difference of spirit and atmosphere by breaking the unipkaaq into lines which roughly follow units of meaning and rhythm, while the uqaluktuaq are paragraphed. Though the unipkaaqs therefore look like poetry, they are poems only in the sense that their originals belong to the world of shamanistic imagination. "Niġliq and Suuyuk," an uqaluktuaq whose drama forced itself into lines, is the exception to this rule.

Most of the texts here were recorded during my first period of fieldwork in Tikiġaq, from 1975 to 1977. Following Tukummiq's literal translations and with constant recourse to Asatchaq's tapes, I have tried, as far as possible, to maintain the style and pace of each performance. Each text therefore represents a specific, formal recitation without additions or deletions. Extra detail and discussion arising from conversations with Asatchaq, other Tikiġaq elders, and secondary sources appear in the commentaries to the texts. Asatchaq's comments to Tukummiq and myself are given in parentheses; editorial interpolations appear in brackets. The title of the book was Tukummiq's spontaneous translation of the term *uqaluktuaq*.

Asatchaq opened his recording sequence with Tikiġaq's origin myth, but apart from the chronological and thematic groupings mentioned in the commentaries, he told the rest in more or less random order. I have therefore arranged my selections according to theme, in two sections each of unipkaaqs and uqaluktuaqs. Thus Part 1 is devoted to stories of creation and other ancient, protoshamanistic tales, while Part 2 contains legends about Tikiġaq's most celebrated shamans; Part 3 consists of ancestor histories from the early and mid-nineteenth century, and Part 4 of late nineteenth- and early twentieth-century histories. This pattern echoes the Iñupiaq preference for telling stories in symmetrical groups of two. "If the first story is left standing alone," they say, "it will fall over."

All of the stories presented here were recorded in Tikiġaq (Point Hope), during the following months:

1.	Tuluŋigraq	January 1976
2.	Aliŋnaq	March 1976
3.	Women's Moon Rites	April 1976
4.	Ukuŋniq	May 1976
5.	Iqiasuaq	March 1976
6.	Kinnaq	May 1976
7.	Qipuġaluatchiaq	March 1976
8.	Aniŋatchaq	March 1976
9.	Qaunnaiḷaq	March 1976
10.	Tigguasiña	March 1976
11.	Siġvana and the Old Shaman	May 1976
12.	Aquppak	March 1976
13.	Unipkaluktuaq	May 1976
14.	Niġliq and Suuyuk	March 1976
15.	Paniunayuk and Aqsaqauraq	March 1976
16.	Utuaġaaluk	March 1976
17.	Taŋnaaluk	March 1976
18.	Sea-Ice Strandings	March 1976
19.	Asatchaq	? 1940
20.	Suuyuk the Elder	March 1976
21.	Suuyuk the Younger	May 1976
22.	Jabbertown and Ataŋauraq	April 1976
23.	Ayagiiyaq and Pisiktaġaaq	July 1977
24.	Pisiktaġaaq	July 1977

All except the first part of story 1 and stories 19, 23, and 24 were collected from Asatchaq. I reconstructed the first part of story 1 ("The Creation of Tuluŋigraq") from fragments supplied by three story-tellers: Aġviqsiiña (whose partial account is preserved in Rainey's 1940 field notes), Asatchaq (1976), and Umigluk (1977). Story 19 was re-counted to Froelich Rainey in 1940 by Aġviqsiiña; the story was probably told in Iñupiaq and translated in session by Aġviqsiiña's son, David Frankson, who also told us story 23, in English. (Aġviqsiiña's English name was Frank. His son Umigluk, born in 1900, was named after Aġviqsiiña's father, the shaman mentioned in the commentary to story 19. Dr. Driggs christened the younger Umigluk "David Frankson.") Story 24 was told, again in English, by David Frankson's wife, Aviq (Dinah Frankson, born 1908). Aviq was the daughter of Asatchaq's mother's younger sister, Tarruq, and Uvigaq, a Kivalina man who set-tled in Tikiġaq in 1893 (see fig. 1, pp. xxii–xxiii).

Copies of the cassettes of the stories recorded in Iñupiaq are in the possession of the author; in the Alaska State Library, Juneau; and at the Alaska Native Language Center, University of Alaska, Fairbanks. The unedited typescript of story 19 is included in Froelich Rainey's field notes, Rainey Collection, Archives of the University of Alaska. The cassettes of the two stories told in English (23 and 24) are in the author's possession.

THE THINGS THAT WERE SAID OF THEM

I. SHAMAN TRICKSTER STORIES

TULUŊIGRAQ: THE ORIGINS OF TIKIĠAQ

Behind this origin myth of the Tikiġaq peninsula lies the figure of a primal **1**
shamanic grandmother who creates the trickster Raven Man, Tuluŋigraq: part
man, part raven. (The name means "something like a raven.") The story's
focus quickly moves to Tuluŋigraq himself as he pursues three tasks. First
is his conquest of the shamanic uiḷuaqtaq *("the woman who won't marry");*
the second is to harpoon the sea beast or whale whose dead body will
become Tikiġaq. In his third adventure, and in raven's guise, Tuluŋigraq
steals daylight, thus ensuring that light and darkness are balanced in the newly
made world. Tuluŋigraq's pursuit of creative power and erotic control is first
thwarted then extended by the figure of the uiḷuaqtaq, an archaic female
presence who, like Tuluŋigraq, haunts Tikiġaq legend.

THE CREATION OF TULUŊIGRAQ

In the beginning there was an old woman.
The old woman was an *aana,* a grandmother.
The aana lived with her grandson in an iglu at the edge of a village.
They were *aanagiik,* grandmother and another.
No one knows where they lived.
South of Tikiġaq, maybe, on high ground.
Perhaps farther south, near Qikiqtaġruk.
It was dark in those days.
The sun didn't shine.
At night there was no moon.
And things were opposite to how they are today.
People walked on their hands.
Snow was seal oil, seal oil was caribou fat.

5

Now this aana spent her days on the iglu sleeping bench.
She kept her lamp there.
In those days people chewed their lamp-oil sediment.
They chewed it with down from their murre-skin parkas.*
It turned into gum. The aana did this too.
She chewed *puiya,* burnt lamp oil,
and made gum from it with murres' down.
This lamp oil was black.
It turned white when she chewed it.
Then one day the aana made the figure of a man with lamp-oil gum.
She put a bird's bill on the forehead, the bill of a *tulugaq,* a raven.
Then she stood it on the bench and went to sleep.
When the aana woke up, the figure was gone.
She looked around her.
There on the floor a young man sat.
He had a raven's bill on his forehead.
"Where have you come from?" the old woman asked him.
She named all the villages she knew.
But he didn't come from any of them.
Then she remembered what she'd made before she slept.
She said, "You must by my puiya."
"Yes," said the man. And this was Tuluŋigraq.

TULUŊIGRAQ AND THE ORIGINS OF TIKIĠAQ

At that time Tuluŋigraq lived north of Qikiqtaġruk.
There was no daylight.
When men went to hunt, they waited for the moon.
They went hunting in kayaks.
When they went home, the men gathered in the qalgi.
And there was a woman in the village that they used to talk about.
This woman didn't want a husband.
She was a *uiḷuaqtaq:* a woman who won't marry.
This uiḷuaqtaq wouldn't take a husband, though men asked her.
When Tuluŋigraq heard them talk about this woman,
he decided to go and ask her himself.
He left the qalgi and approached her iglu.

"murre-skin": The common murre or guillemot (*Uria aalge*), a bird that summers in the northwest Arctic.

(A woman who won't take a husband is called uiḷuaqtaq.)
Tuluŋigraq went to the uiḷuaqtaq's iglu.
But before he entered, he climbed on the iglu roof,
and lifting a corner of the skylight, looked inside.
Tuluŋigraq looked in. He saw the uiḷuaqtaq there; she was sewing.
Then Tuluŋigraq started to sing. He sang a sleep song,
he sang to make the uiḷuaqtaq sleep. (I don't know the song.)
When Tuluŋigraq stopped singing, the woman began nodding.
She was getting sleepy. The song had got her.
The uiḷuaqtaq laid her head where she'd been sewing.
Now she was asleep, Tuluŋigraq entered the iglu.
(She'd gone to the passage to fetch a skin to sleep on.)
Tuluŋigraq went in. He came up through the *katak* [entrance hole].
But the noise did not wake her.
Now before he'd sung the sleep song,
Tuluŋigraq had gone around looking for a piece of woman's
    anaq [excrement].
(There are two kinds of anaq, a man's and a woman's;
a woman's is thicker than a man's.)
Tuluŋigraq had found a frozen piece of woman's anaq,
and thawed it while he stood in the entrance passage.
Then he entered the iglu.
Tuluŋigraq undressed and lay down by the woman;
    he pushed the anaq under her buttocks.
The woman didn't wake.
He started to feel the woman's *utchuk* [vagina].
The uiḷuaqtaq went on sleeping. But soon he woke her.
"Who is this in bed with me?" she cried,
and she started to push Tuluŋigraq away,
she tried to push him out through the katak.
They fought together. As they were fighting, Tuluŋigraq said,
"What if I go and tell the men about you?
What if I tell the men in the qalgi that you shat in your sleeping skin?"
"No! don't tell them that!" said the woman.
But still she didn't want a husband.
So Tuluŋigraq said he'd go and tell the men what he'd seen,
how she shat in her sleeping skin.
The uiḷuaqtaq told him not to; then she changed her mind:
she decided she would take Tuluŋigraq.
They became husband and wife. The uiḷuaqtaq slept with him.

When they woke in the morning,
Tuluŋigraq went to the qalgi and told the men he'd married
    the uiḷuaqtaq.
Now while Tuluŋigraq was in the qalgi, the men were telling stories.
They talked about an animal that no one could capture.
No one could do anything; no one could catch it.
When Tuluŋigraq woke the next day, he took his kayak, his harpoon,
    and hunting gear.
He traveled by kayak. One day he stopped.
Tuluŋigraq heard something rise to breathe.
It was some kind of animal.
He paddled close in his kayak. There was something on the surface.
Tuluŋigraq paddled to the place where it had risen and waited.
When it rose again to breathe, Tuluŋigraq harpooned it.
He harpooned the animal. It dived with the drag-float.
When he saw the animal had dived, Tuluŋigraq sang a song
    to make it rise.
(I don't know the song. I know songs for other animals, but I never
    learned Tuluŋigraq's song.)
The animal surfaced. Tuluŋigraq's harpoon was stuck fast.
The animal came up dry. It rose in the water.
It was dry land. It was Tikiġaq.
When Tuluŋigraq had done this, he took his kayak
and went back to the uiḷuaqtaq. He told the people he'd harpooned
    Tikiġaq.
(You can still see the place where Tuluŋigraq harpooned Tikiġaq.)

And while he was at home, Tuluŋigraq listened to the people talking.
They used to talk about a place where daylight could be found.
It was being hoarded. No one could get it.
Tuluŋigraq heard about the man who kept the daylight.
He lived with his wife and daughter,
and they kept two balls hanging from the ceiling of their iglu.
One ball was bright, the other was dull.
The bright one gave out light in the iglu.
But no one could take the daylight from this iglu.
Tuluŋigraq decided he would find the place where they kept daylight.
When he woke the next day, he took his kayak,
and traveled toward the place where they kept daylight.
When he reached the place, he went to the daylight owner's iglu.
He hid in the entrance passage.
Inside the iglu, the man's daughter was asking her father for something.

She was asking for one of the caribou-skin balls that were hanging
   on the ceiling.
When her father gave in, Tuluŋigraq used his thought.
He made the girl choose the darker ball to play with.
She started playing with the ball,
and her father covered the katak with a tent skin.
He covered the hole with a skin while she played.
Tuluŋigraq used his thought again.
He made the girl want to take the skin off the katak.
She begged her father to open the katak,
and at last he did what she asked him.
The girl went on playing, and the ball escaped through the katak.
The ball fell into the passage where Tuluŋigraq was waiting.
Tuluŋigraq grabbed the ball. He ran out of the passage.
As he ran, Tuluŋigraq tried tearing the ball open.
But someone was chasing him. He looked back.
A peregrine was chasing him. Peregrine ran behind him shouting,
"Trickster! Thief! I'll kill you when I catch you!"
Tuluŋigraq ran. He was trying to tear the ball open.
Tuluŋigraq noticed some willow bushes.
"Tuluŋigraq! Thief!" shouted Peregrine,
"When I catch you, I'll kill you!"
Tuluŋigraq was still tearing at the ball with his beak.
Finally the skin tore.
It opened. Daylight flew up. Daylight!
Now that there was light, Peregrine cried, "Darkness!"
"Light!" shouted Raven.
"Darkness!" cried Peregrine.
And so they went on, shouting "Darkness!" "Daylight!" at each
   other.
Tuluŋigraq brought daylight. There was light in the sky.
(That's why we have day and night now, and they follow one another.)
Tuluŋigraq shouted, "Daylight! Light for earth now!"

When daylight appeared, and Peregrine had gone away,
Tuluŋigraq came out from the bushes.
He went to his kayak and left for his home by the hills.
There was day now.
When Tuluŋigraq got home, there was day and night there too.
So Tuluŋigraq made two things: Tikiġaq and daylight.
(I know the place where Tikiġaq was harpooned.
It's over there, just west of where we're sitting.)

. . .

The character of Tikiġaq's creator is twofold in two ways. First, he is both a member of an aanagiik family ("grandmother and another" or "grandmother plus one") and the traveling aspect of the sedentary and supernatural aana, who creates the Raven Man with lamp oil and saliva. Saliva was always shamanistically powerful: until recently it was used in Tikiġaq in healing rites and for the transmission of power songs. Burnt lamp oil and soot recur frequently in pan-Inuit legend, especially in moon lore, in women's lunar rites (stories 2 and 3), in soul recovery (story 21), and not least in acts of primordial creativity, as in the raven and loon story quoted at the end of these comments.

Second, although Tuluŋigraq is predominantly human (he is an iḷiappaq, "orphan," like the grandson he replaces in the narrative), his raven-bill forehead proclaims his supernatural identity. He is both man and raven: the name Tuluŋigraq means "something like a raven" *(tulugaq)*. The human face with its bird's bill (a device most commonly associated with the animal-and-human soul masks of the Yup'ik) introduces the notion of *iñua*, which has two main meanings in this story. First, iñua is the "human soul" within the composite spiritual structure of an animal or mythic part-animal. In Tuluŋigraq's case, the iñua is the human face surmounted by the "mask" of his raven bill.

The second type of iñua is a "resident spirit" or "spirit of place," which could have human or mythic animal form. Among the iñuas inhabiting the half-finished earth were helpful and dangerous "spirit human" presences. The aana and the uiḷuaqtaq are creative and destructive earth iñuas of this sort. Once Tuluŋigraq has abandoned the grandmother, he fights, marries, and thus neutralizes this negative but nubile aspect of the aana. Joined by the uiḷuaqtaq's magical power, he then harpoons the sea beast, which belongs to the class of monster iñuas inherent in primal earth and water and which questing heroes wandered the newly created world to exterminate. Most important to the inhabitants of the Point, the body of the beast becomes Tikiġaq *nuna* ("land"). Tikiġaq's iñua was thus the primal whalelike animal.

Though parts of this text—as if scavenged from Pacific rim templates by Tikiġaq's Raven—are of a diffused mythic nature (Swanton 1909; Boas 1910; Kleivan 1971), the story of Tuluŋigraq is perfectly matched to the land whose origin it explains. In that the Point is built of gravel and mud from the cliffs to the south and the Kuukpak River, Tikiġaq *did* rise from the sea. The story was likewise appropriate to a society that used its village as a base for the whale hunt, and a whaling element predating the historical whale hunt is introduced when the storyteller, alluding to a "drag-float song" *(avataqsiun),* transforms the death of the sea beast into a successful whale hunt. Parallel texts (see story 13) show the iñua of the Point coming to life as a whale in the iglu entrance hole; similarly, Tikiġaq's nickname was *niġrun,* "the animal."

One visible reminder of the myth lay in Tikiġaq nuna. This reminder was Tuluŋigraq's harpoon-wound scar, a grassy hollow visible after the spring thaw at the northwest end of the spit. Though Asatchaq says here that you could still see the wound, this place, as he and others later affirmed, was cut away by the sea in the 1940s. Until recently Tuluŋigraq's story nonetheless continued to be talismanically recited by boat owners as the men waited on the ice for the bowhead whale's arrival. The birth of Tikiġaq land to a conspicuously married harpooner has its pertinent analogue in the organization of the Tikiġaq whale hunt, which is conducted by male and female umialiks.

In *Ancient Land: Sacred Whale* (Lowenstein 1993), I outline how Tikiġaq umialiks enacted the roles of Tuluŋigraq and the uiļuaqtaq in the course of the whale hunt. Here it is worth pointing out how Tikiġaq's story relates to the widespread sea deity myth, which has otherwise not been recorded in the western Arctic.

The most celebrated uiļuaqtaq in Inuit myth is the Mother of the Sea Beasts from Canadian and Greenlandic lore. This Mother is Nulia-yuk or "Sedna," who, like the women of the Tikiġaq stories, refuses to get married. After she has been punished with marriage to an animal, Nuliayuk repents and her father fetches her from exile, but a storm provokes him into throwing her into the sea. As she clings to the skinboat, the father chops off her fingers; the joints metamorphose into the sea mammals, and Nuliayuk descends to become their deity and keeper. For part of the time Nuliayuk is generous, but sometimes she is retentive. Thus when animals are scarce, a shaman must make a spirit journey to her seabed iglu to persuade her to release them. First the shaman wrestles with the deity to get near her; then he combs out the vermin that, on account of human taboo infractions, swarm in her hair. Once Nuliayuk is clean and has agreed to the shaman's demand, the animals reappear (Boas 1888; Rasmussen 1930). The shamanic rites that attend this myth inform Tuluŋigraq's story. Here the shamaness sits sewing or combing (the versions in Tikiġaq are interchangeable) until a man of power arrives. Then, just as the vanquished Nuliayuk releases whales and seals, so Raven Man's conflict and union with the uiḻuaqtaq is followed by the harpooning of the sea beast.

The first two episodes of Tuluŋigraq's story take place in darkness. The hero's final task is to release daylight, which coexists with primal darkness but, like the uiḻuaqtaq's sexuality, has been uselessly hoarded. The grandmother-and-boy motif is inverted here, for the keeper of light is a single man living in isolation with a daughter. To complete his conversion of upside-down time into life as we know it, Tuluŋigraq must trick the father and daughter, as he did the uiḻuaqtaq. The struggle between Raven Man and the keeper of light is suddenly transformed into a beast fable when the name Tuluŋigraq becomes *tulugaq* (Raven), and his opponent becomes the speckled Peregrine falcon (Kleivan 1971). Like the birds in pan-Inuit creation stories who quarrelsomely paint each other with lamp soot, Raven and Peregrine hurl "Light!" and "Darkness!" at each other.

> In times gone by the raven and the loon (or snowy owl or peregrine in other versions) lived in human form. One day they agreed to tattoo each other. The loon was to be tattooed first, and all the fine little patterns of its plumage (*kukual arniquit,* actually, the little fire sparks) are the tattooings that the raven gave it. But then the raven became impatient and took a handful of ashes and threw them over the loon. That is why its back is grey. At this the loon became furious and gathered soot from its cooking-pot and threw it all at the raven, with the result that its whole body became black. Before that time, it is said, all ravens were white. (Rasmussen 1931: 399)

As in the struggle with the uiḻuaqtaq, the contest ends in peace and balance. "It would be no good if we had daylight or darkness all the time. Tuluŋigraq saw to it that they follow each other," the storyteller concludes.

ALIŊNAQ: THE SPIRITS OF THE SUN AND MOON

This story of incest expresses a paradox of Inuit thought. Aliŋnaq, a young **2**
Tikiġaq hunter, rapes his sister; but when she confronts him with his crime, he
simultaneously escapes from shame on earth and achieves celestial apotheosis.
Like Raven Man in "Tuluŋigraq," Aliŋnaq is a trickster whose power flows
from contact with a woman. On the one hand, an Inuit audience repudiates
the violation of taboo; on the other hand, at the level of archaic symbol, sibling
incest represents the closest union of male and female. But this absolute
oneness is impermissible. Aliŋnaq's experiment with unity nonetheless
translates him to the moon and ironically elevates him to guardian against
further earthly taboo infractions. This story of maximum union and
eternal separation thus mirrors the story of Raven Man and the uiḷuaqtaq:
Earth's creation myth has its "sibling" in the sky myth of the sibling spirits.

I'm going to tell the story of Aliŋnaq,
the man who became Spirit of the Moon.
(Aniqsuayaaq wanted to hear this one.)*
Aliŋnaq was a man, and he lived in Tikiġaq.
He had no wife; but he had a younger sister.
And this sister didn't have a husband. The man's name was Aliŋnaq.
And when Aliŋnaq came home from hunting, he would go to his
    qalgi.

But sometimes when Aliŋnaq's sister was alone in their iglu,
she saw the seal-oil lamps go out.
She didn't know why this was happening.
Aliŋnaq's sister didn't have a husband.

"Aniqsuayaaq": Aniqsuayaaq is the Iñupiaq name that was given to Tom Lowenstein.
Storytellers often "called" someone in their audience by name to focus their recitation.

Now when the lamps went out, she found a man had come
    into the iglu.
This man would make love to her in the darkness.
When the lamps went out, a man entered and made love to her.
When she knew this man was coming in the evenings,
when she knew what was happening,
Aliŋnaq's sister made preparations for his visit.
She went to the *qulliq* [oil lamp],
and she dipped her finger in the bottom of the qulliq:
there's always soot or burnt oil at the bottom of the qulliq.
Now she was ready: when this man lay on top of her,
she could brush her finger with the soot on his forehead,
and this is what she did when he came to make love to her.
So when he next came to visit,
she brushed his forehead with soot on her finger.
And the next evening, when Aliŋnaq was at his qalgi,
Aliŋnaq's sister left the iglu
in search of the man whose forehead had the soot mark on it.
She went looking for that man in all the qalgis.
Now Aliŋnaq spent his evenings in his qalgi.
(I don't know which qalgi he belonged to.
There were six qalgis in Tikiġaq: Qalgiiraq, Saugvik, Qaŋiḷiqpak,
    Qaġmaqtuuq, and Uŋasiksikaaq.
I can't remember the sixth qalgi.)
Aliŋnaq always spent his evenings in the qalgi.
And Aliŋnaq's sister went round all the qalgis.
She silently went to the qalgi skylight and lifted the corner of the
    membrane window.
She looked down through the skylight.
She was looking for the man with the mark on his forehead.
And when she lifted the edge of the qalgi skylight,
she saw the men sitting there, the men sitting in their qalgi.
When she looked inside the qalgi, she saw Aliŋnaq, her brother.
It was her brother who had lamp soot on his forehead.
It was her brother who had come to make love to her.
Her older brother had done this and had shamed her.
She went back to her iglu.
She now knew it was Aliŋnaq.
She went home and defecated,
and she urinated in her *quġvik* [waste pot].
And she took her knife and cut her breasts off.

When she'd cut her breasts off, she chopped them in pieces;
then she dropped the pieces in her quġvik,
and stirred them up with her blood and excrement.
When she'd done this, she picked up the quġvik,
returned to the qalgi where her brother was sitting, and went in.
She went in.
Aliŋnaq was there, sitting with the qalgi men.
She came in through the katak
and approached her brother, carrying the quġvik.
And she offered him the quġvik.
She put the pot on the floor where Aliŋnaq was sitting.
And she said to her brother,
"Since you love me so much,
here, take my breasts, my blood, my excrement and urine. Eat them!"
Aliŋnaq was silent. He said nothing.
Silently he gathered his tools. Then he stood up.
When he'd stood up, he started walking round the oil lamp, in the
  sun's direction.
He walked in the direction that the sun moves.
And his sister picked up her quġvik, and she followed him.
And she said to him,
"Since you love me so much,
here, take my breasts, my blood, my excrement and urine. Eat them!"
Aliŋnaq continued to walk, avoiding his sister and her quġvik.
She followed as he circled round the oil lamp.
And as Aliŋnaq circled, when Aliŋnaq was underneath the skylight,
he started to rise from the floor, through the skylight.
And his sister followed. She rose after him.
She was carrying her quġvik and repeating what she'd said to him.
He wouldn't eat them.
She followed him and left the qalgi through the skylight.
And when they reached the sky, Aliŋnaq called out to her,
"Listen! I'm a man and you're a woman. You don't go hunting.
You don't go hunting in the winter. You go to the sun.
I am a hunter. I'll go to the moon.
You go to the sun. I'll go to the moon."
So Aliŋnaq's sister went to the sun, and Aliŋnaq went to the moon.
That's why the sun's red in the morning, why it's red in the evening.
It's the blood from her breasts, from Aliŋnaq's sister,
when she cut off her breasts and took them to her brother in the qalgi.

. . .

"Aliŋnaq" is the most widely distributed Inuit myth, and people tell it, with local variations, throughout the Arctic. But whereas in Canada and Greenland the sea goddess is supreme, in Tikiġaq, as in most Alaskan Iñupiaq groups, the moon spirit is the highest deity, for the spirit of the moon controlled the game on which Tikiġaq relied so heavily.

After his ascent to the sky, Aliŋnaq became *tatqim iñua,* "the moon's person, spirit, owner." Outside his iglu on the moon Aliŋnaq kept a vast tub of whales and seals, while caribou raced round the inner walls of the house. Most important, the moon spirit controlled the game which people on earth spent their whole lives tracking. The moon's erratic course, they said—for Aliŋnaq continued hunting in the sky— is like a man's on the sea ice and tundra. Aliŋnaq's incestuous love burned on: he continued to chase his sister around the sky, and when he occasionally caught up with her, there was an eclipse, followed by an earthquake on the Point. Tikiġaq men and women responded to these disturbances by going into trance-sleep, as male and female shamans did, for four and five days each.

Tikiġaq shamans confronted Aliŋnaq in person when they took spirit trips in times of scarcity to persuade him to release game. Between fall and spring umialik women observed a monthly new-moon ritual (*manilaaq*) in which they, too, claimed what they needed from the moon. These rites reached a climax in the spring, when Aliŋnaq's help was enlisted for the whale hunt. Standing on their iglus as the moon rose, the women shouted to the moon and raised pots of consecrated water to the "sky hole," which connected the earth to the moon. If their water reached Aliŋnaq, he would drop whale effigies made of lamp tar into their pots. In a vivid account of this ritual ("Women's Moon Rites: A Dream"), Asatchaq tells how these effigies appeared in his own mother's ritual pot.

The sun sister haunted Tikiġaq each January. After three weeks of twilight, the first glimmer of the sun since its disappearance around the solstice emerges over the southern sea ice. Umialik couples awaited this event on the tops of their iglus and greeted the sun's brief emergence with a barking joy-shout (*qatchalaaq*). As the sun struggles higher each day, its disk, deformed and smoldering, streaked orange and crimson, leans exhausted on Imnat cliffs southeast of the village (*siqiñiq ayapaqtuq,* "the sun is leaning"). During this period Tikiġaq people are reminded of the sun sister's rape and mutilation. The fiery orb, so uncomfortably close to the village, is the macerated flesh of Aliŋnaq's sister.

A number of rites, half-remembered by the elders of the 1940s, were directed to the sun. In addition to the sun greeting, these included a ritual in which women raised boys to the newborn sun to make them strong and athletic. The feet of the dead were also aligned toward the sunrise, and the onset of the whale hunt was calendrically measured by the movement of sunrise along the eastern hills.

If the pot-raising rite is a transformation of the sister's blood offering to Aliŋnaq, the relationship between the companion myths of "Aliŋnaq" and "Tuluŋigraq" is equally evocative. Both men are without parents and thus have the archetypal orphan's shamanic potential. Like Tuluŋigraq's bride, the sun sister is a uiḷuaqtaq; both women are raped by a "brother" in power. While the Raven steals daylight, Aliŋnaq and his sister become deities of daylight and night. The first uiḷuaqtaq is tricked with soiling excrement; the sun sister smears lampblack on her brother's forehead. Lampblack streaks the brother's brow, just as Raven and Peregrine are variously marked in the fable that parallels the daylight episode in "Tuluŋigraq." Similarly, the streaked sun in January echoes Peregrine's speckles, and Aliŋnaq's whales, made of lamp residue, repeat the lamp origin of the primal Raven whaler. "First daylight" is greeted by umialiks, who enact in the whale hunt the roles of the Raven harpooner and his shaman consort. (See Lowenstein 1993.)

These symmetries weaving through story and ritual are embraced by two sets of sometimes hostile but productive, mutually dependent couples. Tikiġaq people say that stories also complement each other. "You must always tell two. Stories lean against each other. Otherwise the first one is alone and will fall over." And so it is with these myths at the source of the tradition, echoing the mutually reflective spheres of cosmos and gender.

WOMEN'S MOON RITES: A DREAM

While oral traditions were preserved by recitation, they were also extended   **3**
through both conscious and unconscious participation. In this story, which dates
back to about 1900, Iḷaŋiaqpak, a friend of the storyteller's mother,
Niġuvana, dreams about Niġuvana's ritual supplication of the spirit of the
moon. The prophetic dream reinforces the urgency of whaling ritual at a time
when Tikiġaq faced both famine and cultural erosion. Asatchaq's reminiscence
also provides a beautiful and poignant example of the way new stories were
generated by a people deeply identified with received metaphysical truths. Born
around 1875, Niġuvana, herself a visionary, was soon to become a
Christian. The story's image of the young umialik still wholly engaged in
Tikiġaq myth stands starkly on the threshold of the changing order.

Iḷaŋiaqpak dreamed about my mother. In his dream, he was visiting the
moon. (*To Tukummiq:* That Iḷaŋiaqpak . . . Did you know him? Before
you reached consciousness, perhaps. I called him father.)

He had a dream. He was on the moon. He looked down from the
moon and saw the women holding up their qattaqs [ritual water pots]
to be filled by Tatqim iñua [the moon spirit].

In those days all the umialik women raised their qattaqs to the moon.
All the umialiks had a qattaq that they raised to be filled. That was how
the women asked the moon spirit for whales.

And in this dream Iḷaŋiaqpak watched Tatqim iñua drop little whales
toward the women. But not all the whales went into their qattaqs. Tatqim
iñua has a large qattaq on the moon, and it's filled with little whales.
Iḷaŋiaqpak heard them splashing.

And not all the little whales are caught in the women's upraised qattaqs.
Some fall to one side, for it's a long way from the moon to earth. Not

all the little whales fall into their qattaqs. One of the women he saw was Mamanŋiiña, who was the shaman Anaqulutuq's wife.*

And Iḷaŋiaqpak saw that only two of the women's qattaqs were directly under the sky hole. My mother's qattaq was in line. It reached all the way to the moon to be filled. The moon spirit put two whales in my mother's qattaq. And that same day, they caught two whales: my mother and my father caught two whales. They were big ones. They were caught the same day.

.   .   .

During the 1893 famine that struck much of northwest Alaska, a number of Kivalina River people walked north to Tikiġaq, where hunting was marginally better. Many were taken in by Tikiġaġmiut with whom they already had trading or spouse-exchange partnerships. Asatchaq's parents, Niġuvana and Kiḷigvak, had strong ties with a number of Kivalina people, and Iḷaŋiaqpak, among others, settled in Tikiġaq for good. Though Kivalina people did not regularly hunt whale, they shared Tikiġaq's moon myth, and their shamans practiced lunar spirit flight. Iḷaŋiaqpak worked as a skinboat crewman for Kiḷigvak and Niġuvana, and his whaling dream occurred at that time.

The *qattaq* (or *qattauraq*, "little qattaq," or *imiun*, "waterpot") was a woman umialik's most important ritual object. The water she raised to the moon spirit (and later offered the whale her husband caught) came from Umigraaġvik, about one mile northeast of the village. This is the freshwater pond where a whale had once been magically created from the blood-stained parka hem of a uiḷuaqtaq who had been raped. The water was gathered as ice during the autumn ceremonies and divided between the men, who used it for qalgi window panes, and the women, who melted it for libations. The qattaq was made from bentwood and baleen by a craftsman in the pay of the umialiks, and in late traditional times it often held small ivory carvings of whales. The correspondence between this water vessel and the waste pot (*quġvik*) which the sun sister offered to Aliŋnaq is reinforced by the motif of the uiḷuaqtaq blood in the legend of the freshwater pond. Aliŋnaq, too, has a qattaq on the moon where he keeps whales. The transfer is thus from one large qattaq to its small, sublunary woman's version.

"Anaqulutuq": Anaqulutuq was a shaman associated with Kiḷigvak and Niġuvana's whaling crew.

Further, Aliŋnaq will respond to a woman's demands only if she is spiritually powerful enough to get her water through to him and even splash his face with it.

The little whales that landed in the successful umialik's pot were fashioned of lamp-oil tar, and women kept these effigies in their iglus until after whaling. The symbolism of oil-lamp products may be traced to Tikiġaq's origin stories and their cognates. The ancient aana made Tuluŋigraq from lamp tar; raven and loon decorated each other with lamp soot (see p. 12); the sun sister smeared Aliŋnaq with lamp soot. In harmony with these symbols, Tikiġaq girls were tattooed with soot at puberty, thus implying kinship both with the lamp and with the sun and moon spirits. As mentioned in the commentary to "Tuluŋigraq," burnt lamp oil was also used in soul-restoration rituals.

Since the umialik woman's pot carried water from a pond where a uiḷuaqtaq's vaginal blood had helped create a whale, the convergence of this water with a lunar lamp-tar whale represented a powerful synthesis of female generative elements. The lamp-oil whale then "gestated" in its pot by the lamp in the umialik's iglu until the husband could harpoon its biological simulacrum at the spring whale hunt.

UKUᴎNIQ: A WANDERING SHAMAN

The two primal creative tricksters of "Tuluᵑigraq" and "Aliᵑnaq" belong largely to the world of spirit. While Tuluᵑigraq had a supernatural origin and combined the identities of bird and human, Aliᵑnaq's initial humanity is translated into a purely spiritual realm on the moon. Ukuᵑniq's story presents us with a trickster who is a man; but although the narrator gives Tikiġaq as his place of origin, the story belongs to a legendary sphere which predates village organization. Like the grandmother, Raven Man, and uiḻuaqtaq of "Tuluᵑigraq," Ukuᵑniq is an agent of shamanic power before shamanism has become a social institution. Like Tuluᵑigraq and Aliᵑnaq, Ukuᵑniq is kinless, an orphan boy (iḷiappaq) roaming the world in search of spiritual challenges. As he proceeds south on his solitary walk, Ukuᵑniq accumulates amulets; on the basis of their power, he overwhelms a dangerous uiḻuaqtaq. The child of their partnership is Qayaqtuġuᵑnaqtuaq, the hero of a vast new questing saga.

4

Ukuᵑniq was a Tikiġaq man.
He was walking on the south shore by himself.
He'd heard that men who walked the beach in that direction
    never returned home.
He walked the south shore toward the cliffs.
And when he was almost at the cliffs, he saw a driftwood tree trunk.
Scattered round it were the bones of humans.
And stuck in the tree trunk was a wedge, made from whale's jaw,
    used for splitting driftwood.
It was stuck in the tree trunk.
When he reached it, Ukuᵑniq looked around him.
There was an axe and the whale's-jaw wedge.
The wedge had two holes in it.
Ukuᵑniq picked up the bone and was going to strike it;

but before doing this, he smeared it with some excrement.
Then he hammered the whale jaw into the tree trunk.
Aanaugaa! He hit it! Once.
The bone flew up at his head and just missed him.

As Ukuŋniq stood there, two men appeared.
They approached Ukuŋniq.
When they reached him, they kept their eyes on his feet, those people.
Ukuŋniq's boots had holes in the toes.
And Ukuŋniq moved his toes up and down as the two men looked at
    them.
When Ukuŋniq did this, one of the men asked,
"What do your toes eat?" And they asked a second time,
"Ukuŋniq, what do your toes eat?"
Ukuŋniq shifted his toes up and down and answered:
"People. They eat people."
That's what the two men asked, and that's what Ukuŋniq answered.
Then they said to Ukuŋniq, "Grab your toes before they get us."
And Ukuŋniq held his feet while the two men ran away.
Ukuŋniq shouted after them,
"Quick! Run faster! I'm going to start! My toes!"
The men ran off quickly, and Ukuŋniq let his feet go.

It was the tree trunk that had killed those people.
They'd been trying to split the tree trunk,
but the wedge had flown up and knocked them on the head
    and killed them.
The same thing almost happened to Ukuŋniq.
Ukuŋniq left and continued going south.
On he walked along the shore, and saw nothing strange.
At last, the first snow came. Ukuŋniq continued walking.
He traveled a long way, but nothing else happened.
And when the snow had settled,
Ukuŋniq saw some other people who were traveling.
Ukuŋniq joined them.
And almost at once he took a woman from among them:
he became a brother to the travelers.
Ukuŋniq lay down with the woman.
He slept. But after he had slept a while, the cold woke him.
Ukuŋniq found himself without a sleeping skin. He looked around.
There was nothing. All he saw was a ptarmigan's wing.

It was lying on top of him.
He and his wife were covered by a ptarmigan wing.
It was ptarmigans he'd met.
He'd taken a woman from among the ptarmigans.
The ptarmigans left him,
and Ukuŋniq went on walking.

Now it was midwinter, and Ukuŋniq came to another group of
   people.
These people had nothing. They were hungry.
Ukuŋniq could see a lot of rabbits,
but the strangers didn't know how to hunt them.
Ukuŋniq snared some rabbits;
these people's food didn't satisfy his hunger.
Ukuŋniq snared a lot of rabbits and brought them home with him.
And when he started throwing rabbits into their iglus through the
   entrance passage,
Ukuŋniq heard a voice inside one iglu saying,
"*Anniqtinasi, anniqtinasi!* Don't get hurt, don't get hurt!"
And while he was throwing the rabbits in their iglus,
one rabbit hit a man and killed him.
That's what these people were like—whatever they were—they were
   killed so easily.
Simply by touching one, Ukuŋniq killed him.
Ukuŋniq left these people, and went on. He traveled alone.

And while he was walking he met another being.
This one pulled a sled and wore snowshoes.
And the snowshoes made this sound: it was "*Ipuputima, ipuputima.*"
Ukuŋniq listened: "*Ipuputima, ipuputima.*"
This was the sound the snowshoes made.
The sled was made of copper. The man carried nothing on it.
A voice came from the snowshoes.
And the man started following Ukuŋniq and said to him,
"I want to eat you."
When he knew what was happening,
Ukuŋniq took off his outer parka
and filled it with branches.
Then the man took out his snare,
and Ukuŋniq held his parka full of sticks in front of him
and let the snare fall on the parka.

Then the man said to the parka, thinking it was Ukuŋniq,
"Try to escape. Now do you think you're clever?"
Ukuŋniq climbed a small hill while the man built a fire.
Ukuŋniq climbed a little hill and watched him.
And Ukuŋniq called down, "You! *Kinnaq ilvin!* You're crazy!
Take down your pants and jump in your fire!"
Then the man took his head off, and fell into his fire.
(I don't know who he was. I don't think he was human.
My uncle Samaruna didn't say what kind of man this was.)
But he had snowshoes made of copper which made that sound, and
    Ukuŋniq took them.

Ukuŋniq put on the snowshoes and traveled further.
He came to the river.
He went upstream, following the river.
This time he came to some genuine people: Iñupiaq people.
And Ukuŋniq heard these people talk about a family living upriver.
This was a man and woman with a uiḷuaqtaq daughter, who refused a
    husband.
Now, men would visit her iglu, but she refused every one of them.
When a man came in, the uiḷuaqtaq combed her hair.
As she combed, the uiḷuaqtaq turned her head sideways,
and the man sitting in the iglu vanished.
No one could find out what had happened to him.
The uiḷuaqtaq's hair killed men when she combed it.
That's what those people told Ukuŋniq when he left to walk upriver.
And when they asked why he traveled alone, Ukuŋniq answered,
"I'm just visiting people . . .
I'll go and find that uiḷuaqtaq too," said Ukuŋniq.

So when he woke next day, he left, and went on, following the river.
He reached the place where the man and woman lived with their
    daughter.
Ukuŋniq entered their iglu.
The parents told their daughter to give meat to Ukuŋniq.
They knew why he'd come.
But after he had eaten, the uiḷuaqtaq asked Ukuŋniq what he wanted.
Ukuŋniq answered, "I heard about a uiḷuaqtaq around here, and
    I came to see her."
That's what he answered.
"*Ii . . . Iii . . .* Yes! Let's fight," said the uiḷuaqtaq.

And they got on the floor and fought there, man and woman.
Now while they were fighting, suddenly the uiḷuaqtaq lost him.
She lost touch with him.*
She was fighting the floor.
The uiḷuaqtaq lost Ukuŋniq. He was nowhere.
And when the uiḷuaqtaq couldn't find him, she began braiding her
    hair.
She took her braids and started to unravel them.
She knew why Ukuŋniq had come.
When men visited, she just picked up her comb and made them
    disappear.
She threw them somewhere.
This was how she rid herself of the men who came to visit her.
The uiḷuaqtaq started combing.
She started to pull the comb through her hair.
Ukuŋniq didn't know what was happening.
He lost consciousness. When his mind came back to him,
the first thing Ukuŋniq heard was *"Ipuputima, ipuputima."*
It was the snowshoes.
Ukuŋniq moved toward the snowshoes: *ipuputima, ipuputima.*
It was coming from the uiḷuaqtaq's iglu.
The sound was coming from the iglu: *ipuputima, ipuputima.*
He got to the iglu. There was his sled, the sled made of copper.
He entered the iglu.
When he went in, the uiḷuaqtaq greeted him.
"Well, you got back," said the uiḷuaqtaq.
"Others before you didn't make it."
"*Ii, airuŋa.* Yes, I've come back.
I'm here to take you as my wife," said Ukuŋniq.
"You can take me," said the uiḷuaqtaq.

Next, Ukuŋniq scraped some dirt from between the floorboards
    of the iglu,
and started to roll it in his fingers.

"She lost touch with him": The confusion suggested in the fight between Ukuŋniq and
the uiḷuaqtaq is internal to the story, for neither party seems to know what is happening.
Though the uiḷuaqtaq made all her previous suitors "vanish," Ukuŋniq's display of power
in the struggle makes his own disappearance (and supposed death) very puzzling. But
even though Ukuŋniq is almost overcome by the uiḷuaqtaq's power, suffering the equiv-
alent of a shamanic death-trance, he will emerge all the stronger. He is recalled to
consciousness by the magic syllables of his snowshoes; and when he returns to the iglu,
it is clear to the uiḷuaqtaq that she has met her equal.

He watched the uiḷuaqtaq get ready for the night.

He held the dirt in his fingers, rolling it.

When the dirt was hard, he flicked it with his thumb toward the uiḷuaqtaq.

It landed inside her. When it landed, Ukuŋniq did nothing.

After it landed, the uiḷuaqtaq grew full-bellied.

She got pregnant quickly.

When she was fully pregnant, the uiḷuaqtaq told her parents she was ready to give birth.

She cried out in pain, "*Arri!*"

And her parents helped deliver the baby.

She gave birth to a son.

The child she'd given birth to said,

"My mother, the first thing that I want in my mouth

and for my amulet is your comb."

The uiḷuaqtaq gave this to Ukuŋniq, and Ukuŋniq did as he was asked.

When he'd given his son the comb—it was Ukuŋniq's son by flicking— the boy ate it.

He was Ukuŋniq's son by flicking dirt.

The child ate the comb, and said to Ukuŋniq,

"Father, give me your boots, the ones with the holes, as my amulet:

I want to eat them."

Ukuŋniq took off his boots, and his son ate them.

His son asked for many things.

He asked for the snowshoes, and Ukuŋniq quickly gave him the snowshoes.

He asked for the whalebone wedge. Ukuŋniq took it to him.

The child asked for everything they owned, and soon they had no more to give him.

He had eaten everything.

He had eaten all his mother's shaman things,

the shaman things she had used against people.

And when the child had finished eating, he was bigger, though not full grown yet.

He was Qayaqtuġuŋnaqtuaq's beginning.

His parents lived on the Kuuvak River.

But people who live south of here, in Kivaliñiq and in Qikiqtaġruk, never say Ukuŋniq came from Tikiġaq.

And the child's name was Tutuk: because the dirt he came from is called *tutuk*.

And later Tutuk had children of his own, when he'd taken a woman.

Their descendants were many because they were protected by the whalebone amulet.

That's all I know about Qayaqtuġuŋnaqtuaq's beginning.

.   .   .

"He was Qayaqtuġuŋnaqtuaq's beginning," says the storyteller at the end of "Ukuŋniq." Qayaqtuġuŋnaqtuaq, the hero of an immense quest saga, travels the early world "fixing things up" by destroying the monsters and spirits that plague it. While the Qayaqtuġuŋnaqtuaq story belongs to the river communities of Kobuk and Noatak and the Seward peninsula, Tikiġaq people believed the hero's father to have been an *iḷiappaq*—an orphan, poor boy, legendary protoshaman— from their own territory.

The first of the half-shod Ukuŋniq's ordeals takes place on the beach at Imnat cliffs, about thirty miles southeast of the village. With its piles of driftwood tree trunks and the tundra rolling inland from the cape, the landscape is unchanged today. Walking Tikiġaq's south beach can be a hypnotic experience, and other supernatural stories, some likewise involving magical driftwood, are set here. The two men who appear to Ukuŋniq are in fact spirits who "own the trap" before Ukuŋniq turns their game against them. In these early sagas, such reversals are the shaman's tactic. The shaman in another legend is accosted at the same cliffs by a giant and challenged to a game of whale carrying. Like Ukuŋniq, who carries off the whalebone wedge, the victorious hero extracts an amulet from the confrontation.

The beach event is the first in a series of trials through which Ukuŋniq accumulates both amulets and vision power. But the audience has already recognized Ukuŋniq as a protoshaman since all "poor boys" of legend have supernatural careers. In "Ukuŋniq," this shamanic future is expressed in the symbol of the tattered boots through which toes so menacingly waggle. As in "Tuluŋigraq," "Aniŋatchaq," and "Tigguasiña," Ukuŋniq progresses from poverty through vision and ordeal to shamanistic authority and social integration. While Ukuŋniq's boots are a sign of shamanic potential, his principal asset in the first ordeal lies in his anus. Both excrement and flatus had shamanistic application, and the excrement here foreshadows the "floorboard dirt" which impregnates the uiḷuaqtaq in the final episode.* This detail

---

*For the power of excrement, see Tuluŋigraq's trick and "Paniunayuk and Aqsaqauraq" (story 15). Other stories, not in this collection, have farts that heal and farts that kill.

links Ukuŋniq with both Tuluŋigraq, who tricks the uiḷuaqtaq with "woman's excrement," and the trickster Raven of Northwest coast myth, whose mother is impregnated with dirt (Swanton 1909).

The hero's next two encounters are with inland species, and these episodes reemphasize the orphan's marginality. By now Ukuŋniq has left Tikiġaq's sea-mammal hunting grounds and consorts with small, weak animals and "people who can't feed themselves." Phantasmagoric isolation and dreamlike species interfusion weave together in the ptarmigan episode. But this is just one stage of Ukuŋniq's voyage through the realm of spirit. Beneath the apparently random surface of his journey lies the uiḷuaqtaq, drawing him south. Ukuŋniq's voyage is thus symmetrical. Just as the sun, which is born from the south in winter, held a female spirit, Tikiġaq identified south with the female; north, like the errant moon and the wandering hunter, was male. Animal migrants likewise came from southern "countries." Ukuŋniq's movement toward his wife and shamanic counterpart takes place within this web of symbols.

After the encounters with the ptarmigan and rabbits, Ukuŋniq's adventures become violent, and he emerges armed for his marriage battle. Copper, which was sometimes obtained from Canadian and Siberian metalworking people, almost always connotes magic in Iñupiaq myth. One Tikiġaq story has a little girl with copper teeth in her vagina, while her brother has a (scratched) copper penis. The same tale has a shaman's animal wife call for "water that tastes of copper." Here the amulet magic of the copper is expressed in the beautifully rhythmic nonsense of Ukuŋniq's snowshoes. Against these shoes the uiḷuaqtaq's hair and comb amulets are, in the end, impotent. When her child—conceived, much like Tuluŋigraq, with oily dirt— eats boots, snowshoes, and comb, he assimilates the dual power that has converged in his parents' marriage. With the uiḷuaqtaq tamed and the wanderer socialized, the story ends with the promise of more powerful heroes.

IQIASUAQ: THE LAZY MAN

The story of Iqiasuaq comes from the nunamiut (inland Inuit), but its themes and **5**
details were familiar to Tikiġaq people through parallel stories. The narrative
centers on a lazy man, Iqiasuaq, who metamorphoses, of his own volition, into a
caribou. Unlike the tricksters Tuluŋigraq and Ukuŋniq, who seek progressively
more challenging ordeals, Iqiasuaq, also a visionary "poor boy" in the shaman
trickster tradition, gives up. Though the story starts with the breakdown of proper
relations among a man, his community, and the caribou he should be hunting, it
ends in peaceful reconciliation between animals and humans.

The people were many.
And among them was a man who had a wife and a boy child.
People called this man Iqiasuaq because he was lazy.
He had a wife and child.
And because Iqiasuaq was lazy,
his wife took care of him, begging meat from the families
    of other hunters.
Iqiasuaq never went out and hunted. He stayed home sleeping.
And one morning Iqiasuaq's child woke up and started crying.
He wouldn't stop crying because he was hungry.
At last the child's father pulled his boots on.
He got ready. His woman saw he'd decided to go hunting.
And when he'd pulled his boots on and was ready, he left the iglu.
The child was crying.
Iqiasuaq went down into the entrance passage, picked up his snowshoes
    and his snare, and left the iglu.
He took his bow and arrows and left the village.

He walked inland . . . This was Iqiasuaq . . . the lazy one:
so people called him, because he stayed at home and did nothing.

Iqiasuaq walked. And while he was still walking on the tundra he saw
    caribou ahead of him.
He started to go toward them. But when he was close they ran away
    from him.
Iqiasuaq followed their tracks; he followed them.
(*Laughing:* He's lazy, but he's able to follow their tracks, apparently!)
The caribou stopped to graze;
Iqiasuaq approached them, and they ran away again.
Iqiasuaq continued following.
He got nearer the caribou, but they fled from him again.
Now when they stopped, Iqiasuaq went toward them,
and when he was close, he sat down by them, at the edge of the herd.
A caribou approached him. A caribou approached him, eating.
And when it reached him, the caribou pushed back its hood.
Aŋun una: it was a "man," this one. The "man" asked,
"Why are you following us caribou?
You have weapons, but you aren't hunting!
You haven't tried to kill a single one of us.
Why are you following? You're not even trying to get something to
    eat for yourself.
Drop your hunting gear, your snowshoes, your bow, your arrows,
    and your snare:
then if you want to follow us, follow!"
So the man dropped his hunting gear and followed the caribou.
He started living with them, and they didn't run away from him.
They weren't frightened. Iqiasuaq traveled with them.
And when they stopped again, another caribou approached him.
"Why are you following?" it asked. "Do you want to be like us?
If you want to be like us,
you'll have to drop those things you have we're frightened of."
The caribou told him to stand up.
"Now you'll have to drop the things we caribou are frightened of."
When Iqiasuaq stood up, the caribou pushed him.
When it pushed him, his bed of willow branches fell.
The caribou said to Iqiasuaq, "You sleep too long in the morning!
You always sleep too long in the morning!
Stand up," said the caribou, "I'm going to push you."
Iqiasuaq stood up, and the caribou pushed him to the ground again.

His waterpot fell. It had his cup inside it.

The caribou said, "*Ki!* Listen! You always pick up the pot and drink
from it with the cup inside.

That is another thing we caribou are frightened of.

Stand up," said the caribou, "I'm going to push you."

Iqiasuaq stood up, and the caribou pushed him to the ground.

His elbow rest fell. "Listen," said the caribou,

"you're always leaning on that piece of wood when you eat in your
iglu.

That's another thing we're frightened of.

But that's all you have that we fear. Now you may follow.

And if you want to eat, you'll have to eat like this."

They taught him to dig in the snow.

The caribou said, "Look, here's cooked caribou and whale meat."

When he dug in the ground, he found the meat there.

Iqiasuaq felt nothing on his back. He was rid of his burden.

He followed the caribou. He followed them, and dug for his meat.

He found caribou and whale meat. Sometimes he ate berries.

He traveled with the caribou. Iqiasuaq had joined them.

Now one day, suddenly, he saw the caribou take flight.

Iqiasuaq ran with them. Some men were chasing them.

The men didn't get him.

But next time this happened, all the caribou began to run
toward the hunter.

The herd followed the lead caribou that ran toward the hunter.

The man was singing, and they heard him singing.

The song was a charm to make animals on land approach you.

The caribou had no choice but to go to him.

There was no space to go sideways.

Cliffs were there suddenly.

The song had made cliffs appear.

There was no space to go sideways.

And so they came toward the hunter.

He had a bow and arrow, and he started shooting.

Iqiasuaq was one that fell. By now he was a large bull caribou.

But when the hunter killed him, he did nothing.

Some of the caribou he'd killed got up and left that place.

Iqiasuaq lay where he had fallen; his spirit couldn't move.

The man skinned Iqiasuaq and cut the meat up.

But he left Iqiasuaq's top neck joint attached to the head.

Iqiasuaq lay where he had fallen.
The spirits of the other caribou had left already.
But Iqiasuaq's spirit was trapped on account of the top vertebra.
He couldn't escape.
And as he lay there he saw the other caribou spirits run off at a gallop.
But *he* couldn't move.
He lay on the earth, and time passed.
As he lay there, another hunter came toward him.
He approached Iqiasuaq and picked his head up, by the antlers.
The rack was not a small one.
When the man took hold of the caribou antlers,
Iqiasuaq felt something loosened:
the vertebra stuck to his head fell off.
As time had passed, the vertebra had sunk in the tundra.
The man said,
"*Ki,* go! *Tuttu!* Caribou! Perhaps I'll catch you one day, *tuttu.*"
Iqiasuaq stood up and left. *Tavra isua:* the story ends here.

·   ·   ·

Asatchaq learned this story from Pete Suvalliq, a *nunamiu,* on a visit to
Barrow in 1908. The action centers on Iqiasuaq ("lazy one"), a man
so burdened by the responsibilities of being human that he seeks the
trouble-free life of the warmly clad caribou.

The story oscillates between two time spheres: a dreamtime of
interspecies fluidity, when humans and animals shared certain aspects
of identity, and the human period, when caribou and men were
separate. Iqiasuaq inhabits the first sphere as a man and the second as a
caribou. Before Iqiasuaq is transformed, however, he must rid himself of physical and moral grime, for his slovenly ways and dirty
equipment frighten and disgust the animals. The episode of purifica-
tion, in which Iqiasuaq symbolically sheds his burden of human filth
in the caribou's presence, is particularly moving.

But while Iqiasuaq's humanity is defiled, the caribou themselves
have partial human identity as a component of their spiritual com-
pleteness. This human identity is manifested in the *iñua* ("its person"),
an element of the animal's composite soul under the "mask" of its
face. Like humans (see the Introduction), animals had a complex soul
structure. The iñua, like Tuluŋigraq's human face beneath his raven's
bill, was the part which animals revealed to visionaries seeking to

ally themselves to an animal's soul power. In this sense, the lazy man enjoys the privilege of vision before he is himself somewhat clumsily assimilated by it.

At first Iqiasuaq is successful in his simplified condition. Ironically, though, he encounters an *iqiasuk* ("lazy") hunter who kills him and pays no attention to the fate of his spirit. Among the observances that bound hunters to their game was that of ritual butchering. The animal's head had to be removed at the atlas vertebra to allow its soul to escape for reincarnation. On returning to its *nuna* (the "country" where each species had its rebirth), an animal soul reported any disrespect it had encountered so that guilty hunters could be identified and avoided. When Iqiasuaq is lazily butchered, his soul lies trapped until a second man lifts his skull from the vertebra, which has sunk into the tundra. With this graceful gesture and the hunter's blessing, the story ends in harmony between the species.

These five stories about Kinnaq (his name means "crazy") mock a blunderer's
attempt to hunt animals and find a woman. The Kinnaq stories parody the world
of the questing trickster shamans. However, whereas the shamans mastered the
spirits and women they battled, the "upside-down" Kinnaq lives in a world
of failure and hallucination. The classic American Indian trickster was a
semisupernatural being who both tricked and suffered trickery. Iñupiaq stories
split this archetype. Trickster shamans like Tuluŋigraq and Ukuŋniq are figures
of supernatural power; but the fool Kinnaq is no shaman.

6

KINNAQ AND THE NIVIAQSIAQ

A man was traveling downstream in his kayak.
It was Kinnaq traveling downriver.
And as he went downriver, Kinnaq saw some people,
he saw four girls [*niviaqsiaq*] on the riverbank.
And when the girls saw him, they called out,
"Kinnaq, Kinnaq, take us across!"
Kinnaq paddled toward them.
The oldest girl climbed into the kayak, and he took her across.
Kinnaq went back for the second.
He went back for the third. He took them both across.
And the last he went back for was the youngest and prettiest.
When the youngest climbed into the kayak,
Kinnaq said, "My kayak doesn't feel like moving."
Instead of going across river, Kinnaq let the kayak drift downstream.
He just let the current take them.
"We're going the wrong way," said the niviaqsiaq.
"The current's too strong, I can't turn," said Kinnaq.

He was taking her downstream with him.
So the girl took the sinew that she tied her braids with,
and she tied the end of Kinnaq's parka to the kayak, to his own kayak.
Then she said, "Kinnaq, I want to shit, I need somewhere to shit!"
Kinnaq paddled for the bank.
When they arrived, the girl got out and started climbing the bluff.
Kinnaq wanted to fuck her.
He called out, "Don't go all the way up there, do it here!
Don't go that far," he shouted, "just do it here!"
"I have to get higher," said the niviaqsiaq.
"I need a place where there's something to wipe myself with."
The girl was retreating. Kinnaq started to get angry.
He started to climb out of his kayak,
but his parka was tied to it, and he couldn't pull himself loose.
So dragging his kayak along with him,
he chased the girl through the willows.
But he couldn't keep up, and he ruined his kayak.
He couldn't keep up with the niviaqsiaq, he got tangled in the willows.
So she went her way without him.
Kinnaq sat there, and looked around him.
He saw a lemming hole, so he took out his penis and fucked the
    burrow.
Kinnaq called the burrow *niviaqsiaq*.

KINNAQ'S NOSEBLEED

Here is Kinnaq again. I'll tell a Kinnaq story.
Kinnaq had a kayak, yes a kayak . . .
And Kinnaq saw a girl. And that girl was dancing.
She was dancing in the middle of a lake, on the surface of the water.
When he saw the girl, Kinnaq started to undress.
Then he changed his mind, and didn't undress.
He kept his clothes on and dived into the water:
he'd seen the girl dancing and he went in to get her.
Kinnaq looked everywhere under the water,
but he couldn't find the girl.
And when he could hold his breath no longer, he came to the surface.
There she was again, dancing on the water.
Kinnaq climbed out. He was soaked to the skin.
He started to shiver. His parka was soaking!

Kinnaq left that place and went on. He came to a creek.
He looked into the water. He saw fish there, swimming downstream.
Kinnaq's outer parka was already soaking, so he took it off.
He cut a hole in the ice, and dipped his parka into the water,
    trying to catch fish with it.
But Kinnaq could catch nothing with his parka. Nothing.
He didn't catch a single fish . . . (That Kinnaq . . . !)
But he had to try, he had to try to feed himself. He had nothing to eat.
And though at first he hadn't caught any fish,
he dipped his parka into the creek again.
But when he pulled it up, he'd again caught nothing.
Kinnaq was getting cold.
He lay down, and dug himself a little into the ground:
he tried to warm himself, because his clothes were soaking.
Now as Kinnaq lay there, somebody came up: it was someone who
    knew him.
And this man gave him a little kick, and said,
"Kinnaq, it's time to get up! It's time to get up!"
But Kinnaq didn't wake up, though the man was kicking him.
Kinnaq couldn't wake up: Kinnaq was frozen.
When Kinnaq didn't wake, the man shat next to Kinnaq's nose.
Then he urinated on him.
Now Kinnaq woke up; he was woken by the urine falling;
"It must be raining!" exclaimed Kinnaq.
And he put his tongue on the shit by his nose,
and he said, "My nose must be bleeding."
He kept licking the shit, and repeating,
"My nose is bleeding! My nose is bleeding!"

KINNAQ'S BIG CATCH

Here's another one, another Kinnaq story.
Kinnaq was traveling by kayak,
and as he traveled along, he caught sight of an iglu.
So he paddled to the riverbank,
and when he'd landed, climbed up to the iglu.
Kinnaq walked to the iglu skylight
and he pulled back the edge of the skylight and looked inside.
There were two old women in there.

They sat opposite each other, sewing.
When Kinnaq had seen them, and he knew who they were,
he went to the iglu ventilation hole
and he took his penis out and hung it through the hole.
When he had hung it through into the iglu, one of the old women
  said,
"I smell something that smells like an *usuk* [penis]! I can smell it.
I'll have that man for myself: I smelled it first."
The two old women ran out of the iglu.
Both of them wanted to get that usuk.
Kinnaq started to run down the bank to his kayak.
He got to his kayak just as the old women reached him,
and before they could lay a hand on him he pushed off downriver.
And the two old women said, "Kinnaq's been a fool!"
They called out to Kinnaq, telling him to come ashore so he could be
  their husband.
But Kinnaq wouldn't and continued downstream.
And those two old women cursed his usuk,
twice they cursed his usuk, wished bad luck to it.
And as Kinnaq went downstream, he felt his usuk growing.
He pushed the end of it into his boot:
but the usuk went on growing, and he had to take it out again.
The usuk grew longer:
Kinnaq dragged it in the water behind his kayak.
And when he came to where the people were, the children saw him
  and shouted,
"Kinnaq's caught something! Kinnaq's caught something!"
When he heard them saying this, Kinnaq shouted,
"It's my usuk, it's my usuk!"
But though he'd told them it was his usuk, the children started chopping
  at it.
They chopped it up, and started chewing pieces of it.
All this happened to Kinnaq.

KINNAQ AND THE SEAL BONE

Here is another Kinnaq story. (I will sing in this one.)
Kinnaq was in his kayak, and he saw an iglu.
When he saw the iglu he paddled to the riverbank and went ashore.

Up on land someone in the iglu started singing.
The singer was a girl. This was her song:

> *Kinnaq urruma-a-a-a,*
> *Kinnaq urruma-a-a-a,*
> *Qailutit kuyagluk,*
> *Qailutit kuyagluk.*

> Kinnaq down there,
> Kinnaq down there,
> Come up here and fuck a little,
> Come up here and fuck a little.

That was her song.
As soon as Kinnaq heard the word *kuyak* ["fuck"],
he ran to the iglu.
The singer wanted to make love with him.
But when Kinnaq got to the iglu, there was no one inside it.
Kinnaq looked everywhere.
There was no one inside it.
So Kinnaq came out again, and went back to his kayak.
He got into his kayak and was leaving
when the girl came out again, and started singing:

> Kinnaq down there,
> Kinnaq down there,
> Come up here and fuck a little,
> Come up here and fuck a little.

When he heard the word *kuyak,* Kinnaq jumped from his kayak,
and ran toward the girl; this time he was going to catch her.
When he reached the iglu, Kinnaq went in.
But no one was in there.
Kinnaq looked round: he saw a tiny seal's bone:
(It was the size of this little finger joint:
it was the smallest joint of the flipper.)
And the joint was on the drying rack.
And Kinnaq also found the stick they trimmed the lamp with.
(This piece of wood is a thin one.)
And since he had nothing else to do,

Kinnaq took his penis out and rubbed it on the seal's joint.
Then he went out and got into his kayak.
He heard no more singing.
That seal's joint had turned into a woman, and had sung to Kinnaq.
It was she who'd asked him to make love with her.

KINNAQ AND THE OWL

Here is this Kinnaq again, in his kayak.
And from his kayak, he caught sight of someone standing
on a small rise in the ground.
And the figure was dancing, just dancing by itself.
It was a woman up there. Kinnaq saw her.
She was dancing as she sang to Kinnaq.
The girl was singing to him:

> *Kinnaq urruma-a-a-a,*
> *Kinnaq urruma-a-a-a,*
> *Qailutit kuyagluk,*
> *Qailutit kuyagluk.*

> You Kinnaq down there,
> You Kinnaq down there,
> Come up here and fuck a little,
> Come up here and fuck a little.

The girl sang to Kinnaq, "Come and kuyak.
Let's go to bed," she called.
"Let's go to bed," she called to him.
Kinnaq was excited.
As soon as he heard the word *kuyak*, he went after her.
The girl was on top of a little rise in the ground.
Kinnaq ran. He reached the hilltop.
There was the girl.
Kinnaq put his hand out to her.
But the girl flew off in the air.
It was an owl who'd turned into a woman and sung to Kinnaq.*
The owl flew away. Kinnaq had nothing. He was left with nothing.

"It was an owl": Asatchaq uses the term *nipaiḷuktuq,* "short-eared owl" (literally, "makes no noise").

Though their own shallow rivers could be navigated by kayak when the water was high, Tikiġaq people were, on the whole, sea kayakers. Kinnaq ("crazy," "fool") is therefore to be identified less with Tikiġaq than with the Kobuk or Noatak Rivers, where stories of his adventures were a routine part of entertainment. Kinnaq's regional affinities are likewise with the folk hero of the southern Iñupiaq rivers, Qayaqtuġuŋnaqtuaq, "the one who always traveled by kayak." Many incidents from the saga of Qayaqtuġuŋnaqtuaq crop up in the Kinnaq genre, and the fool has comparable thematic relationships with Tuluŋigraq and Ukuŋniq. Note, for example, the coincidence of Ukuŋniq's ptarmigan with Kinnaq's owl; however, while Ukuŋniq sleeps with the ptarmigan woman, Kinnaq's chase never gets off the ground. And while Tuluŋigraq and Ukuŋniq eventually conquer the uiḷuaqtaq, the fool is condemned to wander alone. Defeated by the simplest challenge, victim and dupe of a world whose coherence eludes him, the Fool—and anti-ideal of Iñupiaq hunters—can't even catch fish, the puniest of prey. Initially the storyteller said, "Kinnaq isn't funny!" One of Kinnaq's functions, in a society that demanded the most finely tuned perceptions, was to be scolded as scapegoat for its potential blunderers. But the harshness of the Kinnaq idiom is sometimes magically softened by beautiful songs and the poetic evocation of what the fool can't reach. And people did laugh, as the storyteller later demonstrated, at these punishing and ribald comedies.

II.   THE GREAT TIKIĠAQ SHAMANS

QIPUĠALUATCHIAQ:
CARIBOU WOMAN AND POLAR BEAR MAN

With the story of Qipuġaluatchiaq, we emerge from the mythic stratum of unipkaaq into a recognizably socialized world. This story is unipkaaq (legend), but unlike the texts in part 1, its supernaturalism is rooted in human affairs. Qipuġaluatchiaq's initiation removes him from secular experience into a spirit world which was the reality of archaic unipkaaq. The shaman's marriage to a caribou and his trips into the sea, and through the earth and winter ice were all journeys of the kind that Tikiġaq people expected of their spiritual adepts.

7

Here is Qipuġaluatchiaq, a hunter, a whale hunter.
And a young girl lived here in the village with her *aana* [grandmother]:
in Tikiġaq, where Qipuġaluatchiaq came from.
And the girl was really quite young.
It was the time of whaling.
And the girl went down to the sea ice when the hunters caught a whale
and hauled back meat and blubber.
When Qipuġaluatchiaq caught a whale she went down to his camp
and hauled back meat and blubber for her aana.

So now this Qipuġaluatchiaq has caught a whale,
he walks around while his crew is butchering it.
And the girl has come down to the ice,
and when she reaches Qipuġaluatchiaq,
she brushes him with her shoulder, she brushes against him on purpose.
Qipuġaluatchiaq didn't have a woman.
When she brushed her shoulder, she said out loud for everyone to
    hear,
'How come Qipuġaluatchiaq brushes his shoulder against me.
He doesn't have a woman!'' Qipuġaluatchiaq didn't have a woman.

She used to say this to him even when the other skinboats caught a
   whale.
First she brushed him with her shoulder, then she said,
"How come you brush against my shoulder? I'm not your woman."

And one day after she had said this and tried to embarrass him—
because the men had heard her speak to him like this—
Qipuġaluatchiaq followed her when she left for home with her dogsled.
She left the ice for Tikiġaq.
The men who'd heard her speak to Qipuġaluatchiaq told him to go
   home with her.
And when she reached her iglu, Qipuġaluatchiaq followed.
It didn't seem a big place to him, the aana's iglu.
That night he took her as his wife, and they stayed there.
They stayed for a while, but then they quarreled.
Qipuġaluatchiaq took the woman to his own iglu. They still quarreled.
One day she vanished. Qipuġaluatchiaq couldn't find her.
He went to all the iglus in the village, but he couldn't find her.
"Where did you get your daughter?" Qipuġaluatchiaq asked the aana.
"From the Katchiq people," the aana told him, "from those
   Katchiġmiut."*
Qipuġaluatchiaq left the aana's iglu and traveled the river a long way
   inland.
When he was approaching Katchiq, where the Katchiġmiut lived,
Qipuġaluatchiaq saw an iglu;
and a woman stood with a child on her back outside the front of it.
It was his woman, unexpectedly to Qipuġaluatchiaq, the one standing.
She had a child on her back. She was carrying a child inside her parka.
She must have given birth after she'd left Tikiġaq.
When Qipuġaluatchiaq reached her she went inside;
when Qipuġaluatchiaq reached her he went in after her.
He said, "I'm going to take you back to Tikiġaq."
So they went back together. They had a son. It was a caribou calf.
They traveled to Tikiġaq. Their son was a little caribou.
She put it on her back and carried it.
But they went no farther than Ipiutak.
She insisted on putting their tent up there, and staying out of Tikiġaq.
They camped at Ipiutak; she insisted.
So when the calf grew, it started to run around.

"Katchiġmiut": The Katchiġmiut were a legendary inland people.

And these Tikiġaġmiut heard Qipuġaluatchiaq had a caribou.
They constantly teased him about it. They asked him,
"Qipuġaluatchiaq, how's our caribou nephew?"
And the caribou calf knew who was saying this about him.

Now Qipuġaluatchiaq and his woman went to Tikiġaq,
and the caribou went with them, with full knowledge of who'd asked
    about him as the caribou nephew.
And as he went ahead, he saw a man approaching.
He recognized a man who'd teased his father,
one who'd asked him how "our caribou nephew" was doing.
They reached each other. The caribou knew him, and struck him with
    his antlers.
He threw him up on his antlers and let him land there.
The caribou killed two men that way, because they'd taunted
    Qipuġaluatchiaq.
Then and there he became a man.

And Qipuġaluatchiaq and his wife were skinboat owners.
(Samaruna didn't tell me about Qipuġaluatchiaq's parents.)
And whenever the man-caribou was hungry, Qipuġaluatchiaq's wife
    cut his meat for him.
She had to cut his meat before he'd eat it.
And when Qipuġaluatchiaq and his woman caught a whale,
she'd put this cut-up meat beside the oil lamp in the iglu.
She had a son who wasn't human in some ways:
Qipuġaluatchiaq's woman had to cut up his food for him.
He wasn't human in some ways, the caribou.
He grew up. And they had visitors from Kivaliñiq and from Kuuvak,
    among them a young woman.
And the one who was a caribou and not human asked his mother,
"What should I do? Should I go and get that girl and bring her home
    with me?"
"Yes," she nodded. He wanted her for his wife.
So he went to fetch her, and made her his wife although she was from
    another place,
and that young woman got herself a man who was a caribou.

Now once when Qipuġaluatchiaq caught a whale,
the caribou's wife cut some meat for him.
He couldn't cut his meat. So she cut his meat, and put it by the oil
    lamp.

And now it's his wife and not the mother who cuts meat for him.
And one time, when some people caught a whale,
the young woman cut up meat,
and left it for him and walked down to the ice to haul back whale
meat.
When she went down she left the caribou behind.
And he got his antlers caught on the drying rack;
it was next to the oil lamp, and he drowned in the seal oil.
It must have been his meat he was trying to get to.
When his wife came back, she did nothing. His mother did nothing
either.
She left the body where she found it . . . caribou.
Later, she smelled it, for it was in the iglu.
And when the woman slept with her husband's body, caribou hair
came off on her side.
When she lay next to the body, hair came off on her. The caribou that
drowned in the oil lamp.
And when it was near whale-feast time a little later,
she took her caribou's body to the *pisiktaġvik:* the place men practiced
shooting arrows.
Qipuġaluatchiaq and his woman helped her.
When they reached the pisiktaġvik, the mother and wife began building
a fire.
The pisiktaġvik's on the north side, near Tikiġaq point.
(Long ago, the men made caribou of snow and practiced shooting at
them.
Later, they moved the pisiktaġvik to near Qaġmaqtuuq [a qalgi] and
shot south.
But before they moved it, the pisiktaġvik was in line with an iglu:
it belonged to an old woman and her grandchild.
It was a small iglu, but the archers had to aim directly at it.
The old woman lived at the edge of the village.
And one day the archers found their bowstrings came undone.
They were aiming in line with the old woman's iglu.
But she'd done something to their bowstrings,
for fear her grandchild would be wounded by an arrow.
After this, they moved the pisiktaġvik.)

Now after they had passed out the whale flippers,
and done the skin jump at whaling feast,
the mother of the caribou built a fire by her son's body.

They piled on wood till the fire was hot,
and when the fire was burning hot, the mother jumped in:
she also was a caribou.
She had been human while she built the fire.
Qipuġaluatchiaq put his son's body in the fire.
And when the fire burned down, when it was dead,
Qipuġaluatchiaq saw the antlers of a female caribou appear from the ashes.
It was Qipuġaluatchiaq's wife; and then came his son.
And the two of them left for the place where they'd come from.
A female caribou and calf. They started running inland.
The mother took the calf with her. They left Tikiġaq.

After his wife left him, Qipuġaluatchiaq found another woman.
This time his wife was a human being—Iñupiaq.
And they left Tikiġaq together and went north to near Nuvugaluaq, not far from Tikiġaq.
They put up a tent by the sea, and camped there.
Then Qipuġaluatchiaq said to his wife,
"My mind is thinking of going farther."
They were camped north of Piŋu.
"I want to go farther north, to Qauttaq," said Qipuġaluatchiaq.
He took his kayak and went north toward Qauttaq.
When he crossed the inlet, he went toward Qauttaq where the cliffs start.
Then he left his kayak and began walking.
He stopped and said aloud (there was no one to listen),
"My mind wants me to leap into the water. My mind wants me to jump."
When he'd spoken, he ran toward the waves.
He started running to the sea.
He jumped toward the water.
He landed on the water, but was flung back somehow.
He was not successful. Qipuġaluatchiaq went back to shore.
He walked round the beach in search of an amulet.
Eventually he found the body of a lemming; he picked this up and went back to the water.
He took the lemming with him. And he said to himself, "I still want to jump."
This time, when he jumped, he sank straight into the water.

He was carrying the lemming.

When he reached the bottom, he saw a trail that went out to the middle of the sea.

He started following the trail.

Alongside the trail old ivory had drifted.

Old ivory was heaped along the trail.

He went on walking till he saw an iglu.

It was right in front of him.

Qipuġaluatchiaq was getting closer to it.

When he reached it, while he stood outside it, a woman came out of the iglu.

She said to him, "*Qamma pigaatiñ!* You are wanted!" He went in.

When he entered, he saw a man there.

The man said to him, "It was I who wanted you.

It was I who made you come. I want you to take a piece of my parka. That is what I made you come for."

The woman brought a piece of *maktak* [whale skin].

The man turned out to be a whale:

and the part of his own body the whale was giving him has white markings on the skin [under the jaw].

Then the whale said, "Don't let the piece of skin I have given you shrink before you get home."

That man who'd dived into the sea was a shaman.

Qipuġaluatchiaq was a shaman.

"If you get that home before it shrinks to nothing,
     the rest of the whale will follow.

If you manage to take a small piece back to where you came from,
     the rest will follow.

If the weather is good, the whale will drift in to where your family is staying."

(That was at Nuvugaluaq, where they used to hunt belukhas, long ago.)

Qipuġaluatchiaq ate a piece of maktak and wrapped the rest
     in his gut-skin raincoat.

He went back. And the whale had told him, "Have your children watch the horizon of the sea tomorrow.

The rest of the whale will come if it wants to."

Qipuġaluatchiaq was told by the man who had invited him
     to keep that maktak from becoming smaller.

But when he reached camp, the maktak started shrinking.

That maktak kept him busy.

But when he reached his place, he still had a small piece with him.
So he told his children to watch the sea's horizon the next morning.
The next morning they woke up, and the day was clear.
The children watched the sea.
And when they saw a shape approaching, they shouted,
"Something's coming! Something black on the sea there!"
And it was a whale, a dead whale. It was floating toward them.
The whale drifted in to where they were camping, and came to rest on
     the beach there.
They started butchering the whale.
Qipuġaluatchiaq and his family got a whale, without any great effort.
And when they'd taken everything they wanted from it, they stopped
     working.
It had been a whole whale.
And Qipuġaluatchiaq took the jawbones . . . It was hardly a small
     whale.
They brought the jawbones up from the water at Nuvugaluaq.
And people traveled from Tikiġaq to Nuvugaluaq, to find out
     what had happened.
Now some people started quarreling with Qipuġaluatchiaq
     over the jawbones.
They wanted to take home one of the jaws for themselves.
They wanted the jawbone from one side.

Next winter, when Qipuġaluatchiaq was in Qaŋiliqpak, his qalgi,
while he was sitting in Qaŋiḷiqpak,
he told some young men, "Go fetch the jawbones of my whale,
     from Qauttaq."*
So they took an open sled, and went north for the jawbones.
They didn't have to pull hard. They brought the bones in easily.
The jawbones weren't heavy.
The young men ran with them, over the young sea ice.
But when they reached a place where there were footprints, the sled
     stuck and the load got heavy.
And they brought in the bones and arranged them,
each across the ceiling of the qalgi at either end of the qalgi.
These were the bones the people had quarreled over.
That same winter when someone from that qalgi was dying,

"Quattaq": "Qauttaq" is a narrative slip for Nuvugaluaq.

the jawbone that was quarreled over cracked.
This was a sign: if a whale's jawbone cracked, the qalgi owning it
would suffer.
The jawbone that they quarreled over cracked.

That same winter Qipuġaluatchiaq spent the night out on the ice,
netting seals.
Then the wind came up from the south.
Bad weather set in, and he went back to Tikiġaq.
While he sat at home, someone called in through the skylight.
"Qipuġaluatchiaq, your nephew has drifted out. Your nephew's drifted
from the south side, to the north!"
Qipuġaluatchiaq didn't keep his silence for too long. He said,
"Maġuan isn't quick enough. That is why he's drifted out."
And Qipuġaluatchiaq started to go out.
But he didn't lower his feet through the katak. He went head first.
He went out, looking for his nephew.
He saw the tracks of a polar bear, and followed them.
And he found Maġuan,
facing the wind
and weeping all alone.
When Qipuġaluatchiaq reached him, he said,
"Stop crying, nephew, and get on. Put your gear on your back."
And what Maġuan saw was a polar bear.
It was Qipuġaluatchiaq afloat in the water.
He climbed on the bear, and put his arms around the bear's head.
The wind was from the south.

And as they neared shore,
and the land was opening and shutting,
Qipuġaluatchiaq said to his nephew:
"You must use all your strength to reach the other side,
and land while you are able.
If you don't make it, you'll go under,
you won't reach home if you don't make it.
It's up to you to use your strength to get there."
Qipuġaluatchiaq's nephew watched the land swing toward him, and
then jumped.
He made it. Maġuan got home safely.
Qipuġaluatchiaq turned himself into a bear
because he had that in him, truly.

. . .

Part 1 of this story follows the course of a marriage between a Tikiġaq man and his half-caribou wife. Qipuġaluatchiaq is presented as a Tikiġaq whale hunter, and although the storyteller suggests he is a boat owner, his status as a single man makes this unlikely. We are, however, in the realm of folklore here: Qipuġaluatchiaq's future wife is an orphan, living at the edge of the village with her grandmother (*aana*), and thus we know, as in all child-aana stories, that the girl has a supernatural character. Above this folkloric substrate, the comic naturalism of the girl's behavior on the sea ice—ludicrously inappropriate to the discipline of the whale hunt—immediately foreshadows a disastrous mismatch.

The woman's boldness in the first episode is echoed, after the birth of her son, by the ridicule both father and son attract from the Tikiġaq men. These encounters express the often jovial antagonism between economically interdependent caribou-hunting and sea-mammal–hunting societies.

The climax of the caribou section shows Qipuġaluatchiaq disengaging from his initial supranormal connections by releasing his son's soul by fire; nevertheless, his status as shaman derives in part from the other-worldly initiation that his marriage represents.

After Qipuġaluatchiaq marries an Iñupiaq ("real person"), the story focuses on a self-generated spiritual career. The shaman's peaceful summer is broken by the involuntary impulse to take a spirit trip. Significantly, Qipuġaluatchiaq's leap is empowered by a land-animal spirit whose body lies on the seashore, thus echoing the land/sea contrast of the first half. But Qipuġaluatchiaq's identification with the sea is reinforced by the fact that it was a whale spirit that summoned him to the seabed. The image of the magic path offshore at Qauttaq adds topographic interest to the depth of symbol: Qauttaq is the one point on the coast where surf regularly throws up walrus and mastodon ivory.

Qipuġaluatchiaq's apotheosis comes when he is shown as a qalgi elder and polar bear amulet shaman with the envied power of transforming into his amulet animal. The story's final nightmarish image of land that opens and shuts is obscure; it may describe the movement of inshore ice on the south side of Tikiġaq.

ANIŊATCHAQ: A CHILD'S INITIATION
BY THE WHALING SPIRITS

*Tikiġaq children often played at being shamans, so it is not surprising that some
were initiated in childhood. According to legend, childhood initiation happened
most often to orphans, and Aniŋatchaq, the hero of this tale, is presented as a
solitary child. Identified by spirits as a shamanic candidate, Aniŋatchaq's soul is
drawn to the Itivyaaq spirit iglu. There he learns that the adult shamans are
too weak to risk the same dangerous journey, and he returns to the village
as a powerful shaman himself. In the story's second part, the adult Aniŋatchaq
goes on trading journeys from Tikiġaq. He provokes conflicts with other shamans
and is eventually killed by rivals from the Kobuk River.*

8

THE CHILD SHAMAN

This is a story about a shaman, a young shaman.
His name was Aniŋatchaq. He was raised by an uncle.
Aniŋatchaq . . . He became a shaman while he was still a boy.

And Aniŋatchaq went down to the south shore one morning;
a north wind was blowing.
(We call the south shore *nali*, the north shore we call *aki*.)

He went down to the south shore in a north wind, looking for tomcod.
And when he got there, it wasn't long before he found a tomcod.
He put the fish in a bag he was carrying.
He went on a little, found another, and put that in his bag.
The bag was soon full, so he climbed the beach,
and emptied the bag where the waves couldn't reach them.

Then he went back and gathered more tomcod.
When the bag was full again, he emptied it as he'd done previously.

Aniŋatchaq walked on down the beach finding more and more tomcod:
these he put in his bag and continued to walk and pick up fish.

Not far from where he'd found the last fish, Aniŋatchaq smelled
    cooking.
Where was the smoke coming from? he wondered.
He knew of no iglus here.
But it was smoke all right, and he was drawn toward it.
Someone was cooking. He walked farther.
Then he saw it: there was an iglu,
with smoke rising from the cooking area.
Aniŋatchaq stood looking, wondering if he should enter.
As he stood there, out came a woman from the entrance tunnel
    of the iglu,
and called to Aniŋatchaq. "*Qamma pigaatiñ!* You are wanted!"
This is what she called to him, so Aniŋatchaq entered.

Now when he entered, Aniŋatchaq saw two people on the sleeping
    bench.
One had long ears. The other had a tail.
The one with a tail was Pamiuġuksaaq.
Pamiuġuksaaq was the one with a tail.
And the other had big ears.
Including the woman, there were three of them living there.
But under the sleeping bench Aniŋatchaq saw a crowd of beings piled
    on top of one another.
And right at the bottom, Aniŋatchaq saw someone he recognized.

And Pamiuġuksaaq said to the boy, "It was I who brought you.
Those [shamans] who used to visit us no longer come here.
In the future we expect your visits."
Aniŋatchaq stayed. He stayed in that iglu.
(I don't know how long he stayed there.)
He stayed with Pamiuġuksaaq and his wife,
and the one with big ears that moved by themselves, as they listened
    to Tikiġaq.
That was Siutitaq, or Siutituyualuk.

(I have listened to the shamans myself when they returned from
    Itivyaaq.
When the shamans came back to Tikiġaq, I listened.
But I was a child. I didn't understand what they were saying.)

And when Aniŋatchaq had been there for a while, he was told
  to go home.
His four-day sleep was over.*
Pamiuġuksaaq told him to go home.
(A man has four trance days, a woman six; a man has four, a
  woman six.)

So Aniŋatchaq went out and walked back to the seashore.
He picked up his tomcod and started to go home with them.
He carried the fish to his uncle's iglu, and stored them in the entrance
  passage.

So Aniŋatchaq came home, and he told them that he'd brought fish
  back with him.
He said also that he'd visited some people,
and that he'd stayed there longer than he'd meant to.
"But when they told me to go home, I came home.
Otherwise, I'd not return. I'd die, they said. So I came back to Tikiġaq."

(That's how it used to be. A man had four days to return.
My uncle Suuyuk came home on the fourth day. That story ["Suuyuk
  the Younger"] is a good one too.)

Now when it was March and still winter,
the Tikiġaq umialiks started visiting Itivyaaq.
And Aniŋatchaq's uncle paid a shaman to visit the Itivyaaq spirits
  for him.
When they were all ready, the umialik man and woman walked over
  to the south shore with their shaman.
Then they walked east.
The shaman went first, and the umialiks followed.
A shaman always took his drum with him.
So they walked along the shore,
and when they were past Kuugaq, they went inland, the shaman still
  leading.*
When they came to a place where squirrels had burrowed,*

"His four-day sleep was over": Men had a four-day limit in shamanic trance. After that,
the journeying soul was incapable of return.

"Kuugaq": "Little river," a ditch in the middle of the Point.

"where squirrels had burrowed": Northeast of the village is an area where the burrowing
of squirrels has contoured the tundra to resemble iglu mounds.

the shaman stopped where the squirrels had burrowed,
and there he sat down, and the man and woman sat down
    one to each side of him,
the man on his left side, the woman on his right.
The shaman began drumming.
Alvaqtuq: he went into a trance, only part of him was there.
(But when he comes back from his trance, the shaman will speak to
    them.
He's been paid by the umialik. Aniŋatchaq's uncle is the shaman's
    umialik.)
Now when the shaman returned he started talking:
"The Itivyaaq people have gone out already!"
When the shaman returned he told them they'd gone out already.
"The Itivyaaq people are at their ice camp. They've gone whaling
    already.
The Itivyaaq spirits are not in their iglu,
we'll have to go out on the sea to find them, where there is open
    water."
It was not a big, open lead they had to look for,
but a crack in the ice, a narrow lead of water.
Now the shaman stopped at a crack in the ice and sat down by it.
The woman sat down on his right, the man on his left.
The shaman began drumming.
After he had drummed for a while and had gone into a trance,
he came back to consciousness, and started telling them
    what he had seen.
"They've gone out whaling, those Itivyaaq spirits, they've gone out
    whaling!"
He went into a trance again. And when he returned he told them,
"The Itivyaaq spirits have caught a whale already!
I almost slipped on the flipper."
The shaman had been there with them. This is what he told the man
    and woman.
"Now we must return to Tikiġaq." So they started for home.
When they were opposite the umialiks' iglu,
they went up the beach and into the village.
As they approached, the people gathered at their iglu to hear what
    they'd say.
(I too used to listen to them when I was a boy.
I listened to the shamans who came back from Itivyaaq.
That was long ago I listened to them.)

And the shaman announced there'd be a north wind next day.
"There'll be a north wind tomorrow," said the shaman.
When he'd told the people this, he entered the umialik's iglu.
The shaman was now given a small *qattaq* by the umialik woman.*
The pot contained water, and he drank the water.
Now all the people went into the iglu; the umialik and his wife
    went in too.
When they were in, the shaman began drumming.
They were all in the iglu.
(Before a shaman started to drum, they would cover the skylight
    to make it dark in the iglu.)
Aniŋatchaq was listening and watching as the shaman got ready.
The shaman began describing what he'd seen.
It wasn't true. He was lying to them; none of it was true.
And when the shaman left the iglu, Aniŋatchaq said,
"He has not mentioned what he should have mentioned."*
He didn't know that an old man by the sleeping bench was listening.
And when the old man left the iglu, he told the people
    what Aniŋatchaq had said.

Now there was another old man who owned a skinboat.
He used it every spring, but he'd never caught a whale.
This umialik began to pay Aniŋatchaq to be his shaman
because Aniŋatchaq had shown the other shaman was lying.
And late that evening, someone called down through the iglu skylight,
and the voice said, "*Qamma!* You are wanted!"
Aniŋatchaq's uncle and his wife exchanged glances:
because that person at the skylight had said Aniŋatchaq was wanted.
They couldn't understand why someone should call that through their
    skylight.*
They were told to send Aniŋatchaq to Itivyaaq.
When they got up next morning, Aniŋatchaq went out to Itivyaaq
    with the old umialik and his wife.

"a small *qattaq*": The *qattaq* was a bentwood pot used for offering water to the moon spirit before whaling and to dead sea mammals.

"He has not mentioned . . .": Aniŋatchaq says this under his breath but intends to be overheard, thus revealing his initiation.

"They couldn't understand": Aniŋatchaq had told his uncle that he'd been "visiting some people." The ambiguity is clarified later when he says he would have died if he hadn't returned quickly. The storyteller leads us to assume that the boy had secretly confessed his initiation to his uncle. The family's surprise may be a narrative lapse.

The boy, Aniŋatchaq, went with them.

When they'd left the beach, and reached the place where the squirrels burrowed,

Aniŋatchaq took his drum, and started drumming.

After he had drummed a while, he said, "The spirits are not at home, we'll have to go out on the ice to find them." It was as before.

So they went down to the same crack that was narrow, but had open water in it.

Aniŋatchaq sat down at the crack and started drumming.

He went into trance.

And when he returned Aniŋatchaq said,

"The Itivyaaq spirits have got a whale already."

(They always bore a hole in the flipper, those spirits.*

My great-grandfather Suuyuk found an auger out there. I never saw it though.

If I had seen it, I would have saved it. It belonged to the spirits.)

When Aniŋatchaq got home, he told the people:

"Pamiuġuksaaq says there will be a north wind in the morning."

(Pamiuġuksaaq goes into the air to watch the weather.

And the Itivyaaq woman goes down in the sea to test it.

That is what they say about that man and woman.)

Aniŋatchaq decided he'd do everything right.

He returned to the umialik's iglu. It was dirty; they hadn't cleaned up properly.*

There were also the qattaqs to attend to.

When Aniŋatchaq entered, the umialik woman took her qattaq and went out and filled it.

Then they all went out. The woman offered water from the qattaq to Aniŋatchaq.

(These pots always stood to the right of the katak.)

And when Aniŋatchaq took the qattaq, he drank all the water and then ate the container.

He ate the qattaq. Then they all entered the iglu.

And when Aniŋatchaq went into the iglu,

he saw the qattaq he had eaten in its usual place:

it was the qattaq he had already eaten.

"They always bore a hole": The hole in the flipper is to secure a towline.

"the umialik's iglu. It was dirty": All the iglus in the village had to be scoured before whaling. The whales hated filth, particularly in the entrance passage, and would avoid the Tikiġaq hunters if the village was dirty.

And the man for whom Aniŋatchaq had drummed went whaling.
All the people who had skinboats went whaling.
Aniŋatchaq had said to his umialik,
"When the sun has risen in the morning,
 and has traveled over the hills, you will catch a whale."
He said this to the man who'd never caught a whale.
"And my uncle, too, will catch a whale, toward sundown,"
 said Aniŋatchaq.
So while they fished for crabs at whale camp,* they watched the sun's
 motion.
And what Aniŋatchaq said came true: they caught two whales.
They caught one in the morning, and one they caught toward sundown.
(Those things were so. I'll stop now for a while.)

THE SHAMAN'S TRADING JOURNEYS

Now I'll continue Aniŋatchaq's story.
Aniŋatchaq took a wife; and together they owned a skinboat.
They traveled north one summer.
They went by boat to Utqiaġvik.
They expected to come home with fine caribou skins.
Tikiġaq people traded seal oil and whale oil
in exchange for skins from the north-coast people.
And Aniŋatchaq heard about a man called Anaugraq.
Anaugraq was from Utqiaġvik.
The two men became trading partners.
And Aniŋatchaq heard that his partner owned a wolverine skin.
It was a very fine skin. Anaugraq owned it.
Aniŋatchaq wanted to trade him for the skin,
and later he asked his partner to give it to him.
But Anaugraq wouldn't part with the wolverine.
He wouldn't give it to Aniŋatchaq.
So Aniŋatchaq told his partner he'd return to Tikiġaq,
and he started home with his wife in their skinboat.
But they went no farther than the end of the lagoon,
and they made camp for the night there.
(I've seen that place. They camped for the night there.)

"they fished for crabs": When the whales weren't running, men fished for crabs with grids
lowered to the seabed.

Aniŋatchaq and his family made camp for the night there.
And when evening came and it was dark,
Aniŋatchaq returned to Utqiaġvik in his kayak.
He found Anaugraq's skinboat and began searching it:
he went through all the storage bags his partner kept there.
And at last he found the skin he wanted. (It was very good wolverine.)
He took the skin and headed for camp again.
When he reached their place at the end of the lagoon,
they took the skinboat out on the ocean and headed for Tikiġaq.
Aniŋatchaq carried the wolverine skin with him.

Now in early autumn, Aniŋatchaq had visitors from Utqiaġvik.*
Some Utqiaġvik shamans came to fetch him:
their spirits traveled south to Tikiġaq,
but Aniŋatchaq refused to go with them.
Finally the shamans made him listen:
he went north with their spirits.
When he arrived he went into the entrance passage of an iglu.
His partner, Anaugraq, was inside the iglu.
Anaugraq was also a shaman.
Then they started to lower a wolverine skin through the katak,
and they called out, "Look, Aniŋatchaq! Here's your wolverine!"
They wanted to trap him, and the skin was the bait they used.
They pushed Aniŋatchaq toward the katak and dangled the skin through.
But every time Aniŋatchaq grabbed at the skin, it moved, and he
    couldn't get hold of it.
And inside the iglu were two men with a whaling spear.
They were waiting for Aniŋatchaq to put his arms through the katak.
And he almost had the wolverine when they speared him.
Then they tested the line attached to the harpoon, and said,
"Aniŋatchaq, you always boasted of the great things you could do:
what's happened to you now?" They harpooned Aniŋatchaq.
But when Aniŋatchaq returned to consciousness, he left the iglu.
And by mistake, they'd harpooned Anaugraq, one of their own people.
Anaugraq was also a shaman.
When they tugged on the line they felt something at the end of it.
But it wasn't Aniŋatchaq.
And when Aniŋatchaq went out, he made himself into an eider duck.

"Aniŋatchaq had visitors": The visitors are spirits of Anaugraq's shaman colleagues sent
to fetch Aniŋatchaq.

Then he turned into a peregrine falcon, a bird which flies fast.
And he flew toward Tikiġaq. He took Anaugraq with him.
But he found he was slow. He felt heavy.
He tried wolf-form, he tried fox and weasel.
But at a place where the fish swam upriver
where the water was swift, Aniŋatchaq grew faster.
He reached Amaaqtusuk. (I traveled there when I was younger.)*
And on the seaward side of Amaaqtusuk
he found a man and a woman living: they lived under water.
And Aniŋatchaq left Anaugraq with them. They were glad of a visitor.
But they left him to himself all winter.
And Aniŋatchaq returned to Tikiġaq.

Next spring, travelers arrived at Tikiġaq.
And they told Aniŋatchaq his partner had died at Utqiaġvik.
They had tried many ways to get rid of Aniŋatchaq.
But the whale he had killed always saved him.*

Now in the summer Aniŋatchaq still had the wolverine.
And he decided to go south to Qikiqtaġruk.
He took the wolverine to trade there.
They reached Qikiqtaġruk.
And when they'd settled, he asked another man to take the skin and
    trade it at Kannuni.
The skin was excellent.
Now there were two brothers: Qaagraq and his brother.
They were also shamans. (I forget the name of the second brother.)
And when the wolverine was brought to them, they took possession
    of it.
They were shamans from the Kobuk River.
They took the skin and kept it.
They gave nothing in exchange. They simply kept it.

Now Aniŋatchaq went to Qaagraq and his brother and said to them:

"He reached Amaaqtusuk": The journey to Amaaqtusuk (Cape Beaufort) takes place by
spirit flight; the man and woman living there are unidentified spirits.
"But the whale he had killed": Aniŋatchaq carries an amulet associated with the soul of the
whale he'd killed.

"Take a long look at the hills,
This may be the last time you'll see them!"
He knew Qaagraq wouldn't return the wolverine.
And Qaagraq replied:
"Ii! Yes! . . . Take a long look at the hills yourself.
You're going to die!"*

Aniŋatchaq decided to return to Tikiġaq.
He launched the skinboat and started to go north.
But when they reached Sisualik, they went ashore.
Aniŋatchaq started walking on the beach.
And after some time, he found a salmon carcass.
Just the bones with the skin attached. A fish from the ocean.
Aniŋatchaq picked up the bones and made flesh grow round them.
The flesh grew round the skeleton, and the fish came alive again.
Aniŋatchaq took the fish and threw it in the water;
he threw it toward the Kobuk River, saying,

> *Allamun pisaanak,*
> *Allamun pisaanak!*

> *Tatqamma*
> *Qaagratkuk*
> *kuvrunaknun:*
> *napitchiallakniarumuatin,*
> *allasirnak!*

> Don't go to other people,
> Don't go to other people!

> Go upriver
> to Qaagraq and his brother:
> be caught in their net,
> not by others!

(He told the fish that Qaagraq and his brother had a fishnet.
He told the fish to let itself be caught by Qaagraq.)

"Take a long look at the hills . . .": This exchange probably occurred within view of the
hills east of Sisualik and Cape Krusenstern.

So the fish he'd brought to life went leaping away.
Aniŋatchaq went home.
In the meantime Qaagraq and his brother put a net out,
wanting fish the next morning.
And when they'd put a net out, they went back to their camp place.
When they woke in the morning, and everyone else was still sleeping,
Qaagraq and his brother checked their fish net.
They'd caught one salmon. Just one fish:
there were no other fish apart from the salmon.
Qaagraq and his brother returned to their camp place; they woke their
    wives up.
The women cooked the salmon. The four of them ate it.
After they'd eaten, the men went to the qalgi.
Nobody else had eaten the salmon.
Now earlier, Qaagraq had hung the wolverine skin
    from the top of the tent poles.
And while he sat in the qalgi Qaagraq heard a wolverine growling.
It came from his tent.
He walked to the tent, and when he got inside he found the skin fallen.
So he cut the head off, and went back to the qalgi.
And while he sat in the qalgi he heard a wolverine growling.
He went back to his tent and dealt with the skin again.
But as soon as he was in the qalgi he again heard the wolverine.
So Qaagraq hacked the skin to pieces.
And after he'd cut the skin up, he returned to the qalgi.
And later, in his tent, he burned the skin. He destroyed it completely.

Now after he had burned the skin, Qaagraq grew sick.
He was sick all day, groaning and staggering.
"For sure, Aniŋatchaq told me to look at the hills," he said,
"a last look at the hills." And Qaagraq died.

And when Aniŋatchaq woke, he went to check his net.
He too wanted to eat fish. So he pulled his net in.
And caught in the net, there were fish bones:
a salmon's skeleton, no flesh on it; and nothing in the net beside it.
Now if there'd been flesh on the bones,
it would have been the other way:
Aniŋatchaq, not Qaagraq, would have died like that.

Early that winter, Aniŋatchaq was back in Tikiġaq,
and the shamans from the Kobuk River started to attack him
    with their medicine.
They tried to do this in many ways, but none was successful.
One thing they tried was to get him in a fish trap.
But when Aniŋatchaq was caught in it,
his whale charm saved him. He swam loose from the center.

Then two people came to fetch him: they had a new sled
    and a dog team.
Aniŋatchaq was far from frightened. He knew what was happening.
So he traveled [south] with them.
And they came to an iglu. They went into the iglu.
There was a girl inside. A very beautiful girl:
Aniŋatchaq saw her and he liked her.
But he knew the girl had been put there by shamans:
they'd turned a dog into a woman to entice him.
Aniŋatchaq knew they'd set a trap for him.
At first he wouldn't go into the iglu.
Finally he entered, and he slept with the woman.
When they woke in the morning, Aniŋatchaq decided to go hunting.
But as he left the iglu, the trap got him: he couldn't get out of it.
He tried all his shaman powers, his whale charm and his amulets;
he tried to free himself, but there was no way to do it.
Aniŋatchaq was trapped. The dog had trapped him.
And the trap in the iglu was a human scapula,
with a rib bone and a human tibia supporting it.
When the shoulder fell on him, Aniŋatchaq was trapped there.
This was the weapon they used on Aniŋatchaq.
He was caught there by the shoulder blade. The shoulder trapped him.
The story ends here.

[The storyteller Tiŋuk added: "On the Kobuk River, above Kiana, to
the north, there's a rocky bluff a giant used to juggle with. It was next
to this rock Aniŋatchaq was trapped. I saw the place when I was a boy;
and they used to tell me this was where Aniŋatchaq died. I saw the
place. Aniŋatchaq was killed there."]

·   ·   ·

The first part of this tale, "The Child Shaman," contains a precise account of one of Tikiġaq's most important whaling ceremonials, the Itivyaaq spirit-house visit. Here, we follow Aniŋatchaq's initiation during a period when the power of the shamans was in decline. The Itivyaaq spirits lived in an iglu about two miles northeast of the village. Three "people" lived there: Pamiuġuksaaq, his wife, and Siutitaq. Pamiuġuksaaq (from *pamiuq*, "tail") had a wolf's or dog's tail, and Siutitaq (from *siutik*, "two ears") had long ears, with which he "listened to Tikiġaq," monitoring infractions against taboo.

In late April, every skinboat-owning couple was taken by a shaman to visit the spirit iglu to find out who would catch a whale. Froelich Rainey offers the following description of this ritual and the beliefs surrounding it:

> Each *aŋatkuq*, carrying his drum and accompanied by the wife of his patron *umialik* bearing her special pot, went to [the iglu mound] of the Itivyaaq. There, near a vertebral plate of a whale protruding from the mound, he "got his power spirit" while beating his drum, and "sent it down." Later the men and women proceeded to the shore and repeated this performance at the shore crack in the ice. Before returning to the home of the *umialik*, the *aŋatkuqs* and the *umialik's* wife also "visited" the *nuvuŋmiut*, "underground people," living at Nuvuk, the very tip of the bar.
>
> At the house of the patron *umialik* people were gathered to hear the *aŋatkuq's* story of his visit to the Itivyaaq spirits and the *nuvuŋmiut*. According to his tale his spirit found in the underground house of the Itivyaaqs a creature like a man, but with very long ears who heard everything said in Tikiġaq ("a kind of radio operator," according to the interpreter). The *aŋatkuq* sought the spirit of someone then living in Tikiġaq, but because of the crowds of spirits moving about in the Itivyaaq *iglu*, that particular spirit could not be found. When he went down through the shore crack near the *iglu* of the Itivyaaq spirits, the *aŋatkuq* found the undersea whaling camp of these same people and saw that they had already killed a whale. At this camp below the ice there was a man, with a tail like a dog, and the man's wife. The man told the *aŋatkuq* that he was going up into the air, the source of the weather, so that he could change the wind to the north (needed for the whale hunt). His wife, he said, was going down into the sea to the house of the *niġġivik* (a woman who feeds people), and she would make the sea calm.
>
> When the *aŋatkuq* went to the underground house of the Nuvuk people, he found them so lazy that they sat in shavings and scraps of seals up to their chests. The *aŋatkuq* cleaned up this place before returning to tell his tale.

The Tikiġaġmiut believed that the Itivyaaq spirits and Nuvuk people really lived below the surface at these two places. The story is told how Nuiraq, a great whale hunter who lived during the last century, actually saw the navel of a whale killed by the Itivyaaqs at their undersea whaling camp. (Rainey 1947, 257–58)

Asatchaq recorded the second part of the story, "The Shaman's Trading Journeys," the next evening. Here local legend gives way to a chronicle of interregional trade and shamanic conflict. Aniŋatchaq has become a successful shaman and umialik and like most Tikiġaq people spends the summer traveling north or south along the coast to barter with other Iñupiaqs. His first trip takes him to the annual fair at the mouth of the Utuqqaq River; the next year he travels south to the fair at Sisualik and along the Kobuk River with his almost preternaturally fine wolverine skin. The rest of the story focuses on the consequences of Aniŋatchaq's greedy violation of his trading partnership. One explanation for the shaman's behavior is simple arrogance and dishonesty. Like several other shamans and umialiks in Tikiġaq history—for example, Qaunnaiḷaq, Aquppak, and Niġliq—Aniŋatchaq may be swept along by a sense of his own power and importance, but his character is harder to read than those of these other shamans.

There is, however, an uncanny resemblance between the shaman's character and the nature of the skin he so prizes. The dark, thick fur of the wolverine was relatively hard to get and was thus a valuable trade item. It was prized for its virtue of being frost repellent. While the breath freezes and tangles the hairs on other furs, frost can be lightly brushed off wolverine fur. Because of this quality, wolverine was used for parka ruffs and to trim mittens and boot tops, and was especially in demand for ceremonial dress. The carnivorous wolverine is a formidable fighter whose only rival is the brown bear, which leaves it well alone. All these attributes correspond to elements in Aniŋatchaq's character and status: rich, powerful, and combative. One is therefore tempted to think that Aniŋatchaq is somehow talismanically magnetized by the skin and that along with his whale amulet, he perhaps carries the skin and other parts of a wolverine as charms. If so, Aniŋatchaq may have had a wolverine spirit empower the skin in Qaagraq's tent and help kill his foe when he began to cut up the skin. But this incident is puzzling, and my explanation conjectural.

Aniŋatchaq's business with the salmon is less obscure. Shamans who reassembled bones and sent the resulting animal creation on missions were practicing *tupitkaq*. The supernatural energy they brought to these familiars came from special power songs. Once the reanimated creature reached the shaman's enemy, it either poisoned him or burrowed into his flesh and "ate his heart."

Aniŋatchaq's own death is hard to interpret. Possibly he belonged to the birth-amulet class (see the Introduction) and was therefore fatally allergic to the touch of grave goods. Aniŋatchaq has also just slept with the dog girl. However dangerous this might otherwise have been, the whale—the shaman's guardian spirit—was spiritually compatible with dogs (see p. 182 and Lowenstein 1993), and there is no suggestion that the dog's role here goes further than enticement and seduction. But individual shamans often created their own instruments of power, and Aniŋatchaq perhaps fell victim to a device which had no general usage.

QAUNNAILAQ: MARMOT SPIRIT BROTHERS

The tale of Qaunnaiḷaq lies on the borders of legend (unipkaaq) and ancestor history   **9**
(uqaluktuaq), and Asatchaq was inconsistent in his designation, describing it as
either one or the other on a number of occasions. The story is a legend because of its
supernaturalism and because the hero is both human and a marmot spirit; it is a
history in that Qaunnaiḷaq was also remembered as an ancestor families today still
claim connection with this early nineteenth-century trickster shaman. Despite a
substrate of spirit lore woven into the telling, most of the action is fast-paced
and naturalistic. And as a tale of revenge, the story is a subtle and complex
exposition of both village and interregional affiliations and the conflicts that could
arise when joking partnerships and marriage connections were put under stress.

Here is Qaunnaiḷaq: this is an ancestor story.
Before he was born as a human, his spirit went around looking
    for a mother,
the right mother, who could bear him.
There were two of them, Pauluaġana and Qaunnaiḷaq: they were
    marmot spirits:*
marmot spirits, and they wanted to be born as humans.
Qaunnaiḷaq was born in Tikiġaq, a man, and he became a shaman.
And he used to travel to the cliffs to the north.

And Qaunnaiḷaq's partner was visiting Tikiġaq from Utqiaġvik:
his name was Qilugiuq. Qilugiuq had his wife with him.

"There were two of them": Qaunnaiḷaq originally had nine marmot siblings, two of whom
were born in Tikiġaq. See "The Real Tuunġaq" in the commentary to "Tigguasiña"
(story 10).

And while Qilugiuq was north at the cliffs with his wife,
Qaunnaiḷaq heard the Tikiġaq people planned to kill Qilugiuq.

When Qaunnaiḷaq heard they were saying this,
he decided he would kill the man himself, so the others
   wouldn't have to.
He wouldn't feel bad if he killed the man himself:
he wouldn't have to take revenge on his partner's murderer.
So Qaunnaiḷaq killed Qilugiuq, the man who'd come from Utqiaġvik
   and who had a woman.
And Qaunnaiḷaq took the woman for his wife.

Now some time later, Qaunnaiḷaq and some Tikiġaq men were sitting
   in the qalgi.
And Qaunnaiḷaq had joking partners:
they used to joke together in the qalgi, trying to outdo each other.
And Qaunnaiḷaq challenged them to an exchange of banter:
but he went too far and said things that he didn't mean.
And his partners did the same. They said things that they regretted.
Qaunnaiḷaq left the qalgi.
And as he went out through the katak, his partners said,
"Why did he have to speak to us like that?
We're not like him. He is the one who killed Qilugiuq.
We don't have blood on our hands.
If we had killed the man, we would have gone to his place at Utqiaġvik
   and put oil on his body."
That's what they said to each other.
Qaunnaiḷaq heard them. He went back and put his head through the
   katak and said,
"Ii. Yes . . . When summer comes, I'll go and put oil on my victim,
   on Qilugiuq."
His two partners tried to talk him out of it, persuade him not to make
   the journey.
But Qaunnaiḷaq had decided.
When summer came, he would go to Utqiaġvik.

And next summer, Qaunnaiḷaq and his wife went by skinboat to
   Utqiaġvik.
Qaunnaiḷaq had taken Qilugiuq's woman, and now they traveled.
But first, for a while, they stopped at Utuqqaq.
(Utuqqaq is north of here; it's where the rivers meet the sea.

Little rivers meet there at the sea. It's north of Kali [Point Lay].
Tikiġaq people always used to pass it on their way north.
That was their route when they took goods up to exchange for caribou
    skins.)
Qaunnaiḷaq went on toward Utqiaġvik,
and he told the man with him to take his skinboat back to Tikiġaq
    when they reached Utqiaġvik.
They went on toward Utqiaġvik.
They didn't travel fast, but they kept moving.
Qaunnaiḷaq took his time.
He wanted the Utqiaġvik men to be home from caribou hunting
    when he got there
so that those who had a grudge against him would be there to meet
    him.
He didn't want them to regret missing him.
They wouldn't have forgotten what had happened to their kinsman:
they'd want Qaunnaiḷaq to stay in Utqiaġvik.

And the evening of the day when they were close to Utqiaġvik,
Qaunnaiḷaq told the man who was with him,
"I am the one who killed Qilugiuq.
Those with a grudge against me will meet us."
Qaunnaiḷaq had come to offer himself to them.
When they'd almost reached the village,
Qaunnaiḷaq took his place at the bow of the skinboat, prepared to
    jump ashore to the Utqiaġvik people.
He held a knife in his hand.
But the people of the village wouldn't let him land.
They tried to grab the people in the skinboat.
They knew it was Qaunnaiḷaq's party.
And after they had struggled to get ashore for a time, they finally
    succeeded.
Qaunnaiḷaq's woman put her arms around him, to protect his genitals.
Qaunnaiḷaq did not leave the skinboat.
And all that day and night, and the next day,
Qaunnaiḷaq and his woman were closely followed.
Finally they made toward a lake that he knew:
and the next evening, when they arrived there,
Qaunnaiḷaq went down to the lake.
People were trying to get him to go to the iglu of his *sakiġaq* [wife's
    brother].

The men followed him to the water, but they fell over.
Qaunnaiḷaq was a fighter, and a good one.
Turning back toward the shore,
Qaunnaiḷaq used those men as stepping-stones, and so he got to shore.
Finally his wife let go of him.
When he turned back, she finally released him.
Now on land, the men who had been watching grabbed him again.
Qaunnaiḷaq had a hard time pulling himself free; it was because of his arm.
His parka was made of *payniq*: thick, winter caribou skin that won't tear easily;
his wife had made it for him for this journey.
Finally Qaunnaiḷaq got the sleeve off and his arm was free.
His arm was free and he could fight more easily.
But his wife had left his side, and now he was in difficulty.
They'd got him a second time, when he came from the water.
He'd used those men as stepping-stones to get out of the ice and water.
(And it's said that Qaunnaiḷaq had a hard time when they grabbed him again.
His sleeve would not come off. But he finally got rid of it.
He wore a parka made of *payniq*. He'd had it made especially for that journey. That skin is not a soft one.)
When at last Qaunnaiḷaq landed safely, it was inside an iglu entrance passage; it was in the passage he landed.

He went into the iglu. And his sakiġaq was there: his wife's older brother.
When he went in, all the others went in too: Qaunnaiḷaq's enemies.
The iglu was crowded, there was no space to move.
They wanted Qaunnaiḷaq to start singing and dance.
So he sang a song although he owned no song.
And when he finished dancing, he raised one foot to show he'd finished.
Finally the people rose and left the iglu.
Qaunnaiḷaq and his wife passed the night there.
And in the morning someone called in through the skylight and said,
"Qilugiuq's younger brothers want you!"
His younger brothers wanted to see Qaunnaiḷaq.
And his wife's brother went with him.

He took his bow and arrow to protect them.
He had a knife as well. He entered the house first.
He looked inside the passage before they entered.
Then he went back to Qaunnaiḷaq and said, smiling,
"There's no one in the passage. There's no danger there."
Qaunnaiḷaq went in.
When he went in, he found the brothers were all standing: Qilugiuq's
    brothers.
Qaunnaiḷaq looked round and saw a board, a single sitting board.
He was told to sit down on it. He had his knife with him.
Qaunnaiḷaq sat down and crossed his ankles.
He crossed his feet and put his knife between them. He kept his knife
    ready.
And an old man sat at the end of the sleeping bench,
so placed that his feet could touch the board Qaunnaiḷaq
    was sitting on.
Qaunnaiḷaq saw him, but he still sat down on that board.
He put his knife between his feet. The brothers surrounded him.
And the old man on the sleeping bench kicked the board.
Qaunnaiḷaq lost balance. He heard something hit the ceiling.
But before he lost balance, he grabbed his knife.
The noise he heard was his knife on the ceiling.
He'd got his knife.
The brothers too had taken out their knives.
They jumped to where Qaunnaiḷaq should have landed.
But he didn't fall over: he landed on his feet,
though the board was kicked from under him.
The only noise that was heard in the iglu was the knife on the ceiling.
The brothers did nothing.

Now they heard someone at the skylight.
It was Qaunnaiḷaq's woman's brother.
He had taken off the skylight, and called down,
"*Isuuva surusi?* You are doing something, are you?"
This is what he called inside. He held his bow, with an arrow ready.

The brothers did nothing. Qaunnaiḷaq sat down.
The brothers had their knives out.
They did nothing, though they had their knives out,
because Qaunnaiḷaq was alive still.

Now Qaunnaiḷaq, still sitting, slid toward the katak.
He moved slowly to the katak.
When he reached it, he lowered his legs and left the iglu.
And as he left, he heard the brothers start to cry out.
He went back with his woman's brother and got home unharmed.
They had done nothing to him.

And when they woke next morning, the brothers sent for him again.
Qaunnaiḷaq was told he was to eat with them.
So he went a second time.
When he entered now, he saw the iglu was filled with people who had
    not been there before: children, women.
And Qaunnaiḷaq sat down on the sleeping bench.
An old woman sat next to him.
Now the old woman started rummaging for something and produced
    some meat.
And the old woman gave the meat to Qaunnaiḷaq
    and told him to eat it.
She made sure he ate it and said, "Eat that!" So Qaunnaiḷaq ate it.
The meat looked unclean to Qaunnaiḷaq; it was repulsive to him.
And when he'd finished eating, Qaunnaiḷaq rubbed his hands together.
He had nothing to wipe his hands with. So he wiped them
    on his belly.
And the meat was from the grave of someone who'd died recently.
The old woman thought that the meat would kill Qaunnaiḷaq.
But the meat didn't harm him.

And the old woman sitting next to him put her hands on Qaunnaiḷaq's
    chest.
Her hands were sticky.
And the woman said, "Your body reminds me of a son of mine I lost.
His name was Qilugiuq." She felt him with her hands.

Then Qaunnaiḷaq rubbed his belly and this killed the woman.
They woke up the next morning and she was dead.
When they saw that she was dead, they feared Qaunnaiḷaq.
Now nobody visits Qaunnaiḷaq and his wife except his wife's brother.
And they plugged the katak in the woman's brother's iglu with a
    large piece of whale meat.
This is what they used to close the katak. The meat was frozen.
It was so hard you couldn't cut it. It was frozen solid.

After this meat had been here for some time, Qaunnaiḷaq and his
  woman decided it was time to leave Utqiaġvik.
They would go home to Tikiġaq. It was midwinter.

Now when they were about to leave, when he was ready to go,
  Qaunnaiḷaq couldn't find his woman.
He looked for her among the people, in their iglus. But he couldn't
  find her.
He was leaving Utqiaġvik, but he couldn't find his woman.
So he took his daughter, and they traveled a short way, and then built
  a snow house.
The daughter's name was Ipiilik.
And he left his daughter in the snow house
and returned on foot to Utqiaġvik. He went back for his woman.
He left his daughter meat, and turned back to Utqiaġvik.

And he went to his woman's brother's iglu.
When he was in there he heard steps outside.
Qaunnaiḷaq waited in the entrance passage.
He recognized his woman's feet and legs when they appeared.
And when she came in, he stabbed her with his knife.
Qaunnaiḷaq killed his woman. When he'd killed her in the passage
he pushed her against the wall,
and pushed a sealskin storage bag against her, to hide the body.
He went into the iglu.
His wife's brother was disturbed to see him, but he said:
"I wanted you to return unharmed to Tikiġaq.
From now on I cannot protect you. You must defend yourself."

Now people started coming back into the iglu when they heard
  Qaunnaiḷaq had returned.
And when it seemed there were no more to enter, someone else came
  in.
It was Qaunnaiḷaq's woman.
She sat down next to him, presenting her wound to him.
She sat down by Qaunnaiḷaq.
With her wounded side against him, she sat down next to him.
After she recovered he led her out, and took her to their daughter.
Tavra isua: the story ends here.

·   ·   ·

"Qaunnaiḷaq" opens with an elliptical reference to animal souls that want human birth and "go around looking for a [human] mother" (*aakagriuqsiuq*). Qaunnaiḷaq, the story's hero, was a being of this nature, one of ten marmot spirits from somewhere east of Barrow. As one of Froelich Rainey's informants explained: "Their father got tired of feeding them. So the marmots left him and travelled south. Some died on the way, others, like Qaunnaiḷaq, ran inside 'clean bright women' [women who were ritually pure] when they went out to shit" (Rainey 1940–41).

The information about the marmots was given to Rainey by Aġviqsiiña (born circa 1875), the narrator of "Asatchaq" (story 19). Both Aġviqsiiña and the shaman Asatchaq were descendants of Qaunnaiḷaq, as was the strongman Ataŋauraq (see stories 21 and 22). Another famous member of this clan, which was known as the *iñugailiŋmiut* ("the people who live together"), was an unusual and distinguished woman seal hunter who covered her parka from the hem upward with the snout of every seal she harpooned. The legendary Qaunnaiḷaq and the woman hunter probably lived in the early nineteenth century, and they seem to have represented the earliest ancestors recognized by the last precontact generation.

The action in the text starts when Qaunnaiḷaq's cohusband and wife from Utqiaġvik visit him for spouse exchange. They hunt at the cliffs of Uivvaq until a group of Tikiġaq men, excited by the Utqiaġvik woman's beauty, conspire to kill Qilugiuq, Qaunnaiḷaq's male partner. Had the murder plan succeeded, Qaunnaiḷaq would have had to avenge his partner's death by killing his covillagers. Qaunnaiḷaq thus takes the murder on himself, in this way averting a feud within Tikiġaq. Qaunnaiḷaq is rewarded with a fine new wife, but his joking partners use the license implicit in their relationship to taunt him, for the crime of murder is compounded by the enormity of his having killed the very man he was responsible for protecting in alien territory.

In the next sequence, Qaunnaiḷaq travels 350 miles north by skinboat to brazen out the consequences of the murder with his victim's kin. Metaphorically, he will "put oil on his victim's grave"; in fact, he will atone for the murder by offering himself as a victim. If Qilugiuq's people can kill him, honor will be satisfied and balance between the two villages reestablished. But if Qaunnaiḷaq can outwit his pursuers with a display of power, they will let him go and he will return to Tikiġaq vindicated.

In the series of quasi-ritualistic challenges that follows, Qaunnaiḷaq outfaces his hunters by guile, acrobatics, and sheer nerve. The lake-ice sequence demonstrates Qaunnaiḷaq's almost magical athletic prowess, while the dance scene, with the male dancer's concluding one-foot balance, expresses his poise at the moment of greatest vulnerability. The pressure of the game intensifies when Qaunnaiḷaq is invited to an iglu which has been sprung like a trap. With his brother-in-law's backing, he survives this trap but must then continue unprotected—another expression of partnerships under intolerable strain.

The following scene is shamanic. Qaunnaiḷaq enters the iglu as a guest and routinely takes off his parka. When the blind woman explores his chest, she feels a patch of marmot hair. This patch identifies Qaunnaiḷaq as a marmot spirit in human incarnation and thus "brother" to her own dead marmot-spirit son. Only at this point does the audience realize that Qaunnaiḷaq's former partner and victim was also the Tikiġaq man's spiritual brother, born in Utqiaġvik. The old woman is, of course, the human mother of Qilugiuq, but not of Qaunnaiḷaq. As prearranged with the iglu owners—who presumably suspected what the old woman is invited to confirm—the woman tries to poison Qaunnaiḷaq with meat which is either rotten or dangerous because of his amulet affiliation. Since the meat had been on a grave, we are led to assume that a supernatural murder rather than a biological poisoning is intended. If this is the case, Qaunnaiḷaq's enemies must have known that he belonged to Tikiġaq's birth-amulet class (iġñiruaqtuqtuq) and was therefore allergic to grave goods. However, Qaunnaiḷaq transfers the poison to the woman with the shamanic, circular gesture of rubbing his belly.

Qaunnaiḷaq's final act of defiance is to "kill," or, rather, wound, his Utqiaġvik wife, thus completing his display of power, invulnerability, and fearlessness in the face of potential redress from her kin. Marriage, compared with the maintenance of balance within Tikiġaq society and between Tikiġaq and Utqiaġvik, is relatively unimportant. The central issue lies in Qaunnaiḷaq's violation of his joking and spouse-exchange partnerships. Paradoxically, despite having violated the latter, Qaunnaiḷaq averts both intravillage and interregional feuds by volunteering as victim. The issue is further and mysteriously complicated by the fact that, knowingly or not, Qaunnaiḷaq had murdered his spirit brother. At the end, the joking partnership that projected Qaunnaiḷaq into his ordeal is apparently the only one to survive. As in "Aliŋnaq" and other stories of violations of contract or taboo, the audience maintains a double attitude. The protagonist is admired for his power, but he is not to be emulated.

TIGGUASIÑA: A BOY SHAMAN AND A FRAUD

This deceptively lighthearted story traces the rise of another orphan to the status of **10**
shaman. But for all its humor, the story emerges from a mass of harsh realities:
the marginalized life of Tikiġaq's poor, from which shamanic initiation provided
one risky avenue of escape; the exploitation of lay people by unscrupulous
practitioners; and, not least of all, the often lethal competition between shamans
themselves, which here leads the young initiate to shame his rival in a public
contest. Despite this grim backdrop, though, the story of Tigguasiña beautifully
evokes one small corner of traditional Tikiġaq in winter.

I'll tell the story of a Tikiġaq boy
who spent all his time in the qalgi.
His home was the qalgi.
And whenever he heard there'd been a death in Tikiġaq
he'd take a strip of baleen that was lying in the qalgi
    and go to the katak.
And with his legs astride the katak
he'd lower the baleen into the entrance passage.
He also worked on the baleen, and sliced it into strips.
What he did was lower the strips of baleen and then raise them.
He did this when he heard there'd been a death in Tikiġaq.

Now one night he took an owl's-wing brush
and a lamp stick he had dipped in seal oil.
These are two things that spirits are scared of.
He placed these two things by the katak.
And while he sat in the qalgi, cold air started rising through the katak.
He kept the stick and the wing beside him. This was his habit.
And as he sat by the katak, the stick and the wing started bouncing:

they jumped up and down on their own, beside him at the katak.
(People used to talk a lot about spirits in those days.)
The stick and the wing chased a spirit away.
And in its flight, the spirit left some things belonging to it.
One thing a spirit sometimes leaves is its grave wrap.
The next man to enter the qalgi was heard saying,
"Some children have left a caribou skin in the passage."
This was what the spirit left: a grave wrap.

Now in the course of all this
Tigguasiña, the boy from the qalgi, confronted another boy involved
    in shamanizing.
And when they met, the second boy told him,
"They're going to shamanize in Qaġmaqtuuq qalgi!"
(There were six qalgis in those days.
Today there are only two in Tikiġaq: Uŋasiksikaaq and Qaġmaqtuuq.)
And when [Tigguasiña] heard they were going to shamanize in
    Qaġmaqtuuq,
he went to that qalgi: but they'd put a sled across the entrance.
They'd blocked the entrance.
But he moved the sled aside and lowered himself into the entrance
    passage.
He hid between two whalebones in the passage.
He stood between the jawbones of a whale and listened.
And he heard them starting to talk in the qalgi.
The name of the shaman was Utkusik ["Bowl"].
Utkusik had three people with him for instruction:
a man, a woman, and a small boy.
And while Tigguasiña hid in the passage, he heard them starting.
Utkusik said, "Take a light and search the passage."
He thought there might be someone hiding there.
Someone lit a stick and went to the passage. He saw nothing.
He didn't see Tigguasiña, who was hiding.
When he returned to the qalgi, he said,
"There's no one in the passage."
"*Ii*. Yes, all right," said Utkusik.
Some time later, Tigguasiña noticed the sled against the entrance
    moving.
A man came down into the passage, and then closed the entrance.
The man's face was invisible: he was masked in a wolf's head.
The teeth were still in it.

The man sat down in the middle of the floor with his face toward the
    katak.
Tigguasiña watched him from between the whale jaws.
Now a man's legs came down through the katak,
    but the wolf man snapped at them,
    and the man in the katak retreated into the qalgi.
He said he couldn't go down to the passage.
There was a spirit down there and he dare not approach it.
Now Utkusik told the boy to go down to the passage.
It was the boy's turn:
so he lowered his body through the katak and stopped.
The wolf jaws snapped at him and he too retreated.
He didn't dare approach the spirit. Utkusik said,
"Whoever approaches the thing in the passage will be a shaman."
That was what the shaman told them.
Now it was the woman's turn.
She lowered her legs through the katak and descended.
And the man who sat facing the katak with the wolf head took his
    mask off.
He beckoned the woman and she approached him.
Tigguasiña watched from where he was hiding.
And when the woman was beside him,
    the man pulled a deerskin from under his parka,
    and laid it on the floor of the passage.
And he told the woman to get on the skin, and lay down on her.
When they woke, the woman returned to the qalgi.
(I don't know which qalgi.)
Then they went back to their iglus. It was night time.

When Tigguasiña woke in the morning
    he looked for the boy who had been in the qalgi training to be
    shaman.
When he found him, he asked,
"Did you meet a *tuuṅaq* [spirit] yesterday?"
"Yes," said the boy.
"A *real* tuuṅaq?"
"A real one," said the boy.
    Tigguasiña pointed to an iglu. Its skylight was lit.
"You see that skylight? That's where your spirit lives."
    He told the boy about the man who had acted the spirit.
"The man in that iglu was your spirit."

And the boy said he'd get back from the shaman what he'd given for
   instruction.
Now he knew it wasn't a real spirit.
He said he'd get back what he'd paid the shaman.

And the Tikiġaq people were told that night to visit the qalgi.
Tigguasiña went too, and sat down by the wall bench.
(Some qalgis had a narrow bench around the walls for the men
   to sit on.)
And Utkusik began his performance.
He was carrying a piece of skin and a harpoon.
Utkusik started to walk round the qalgi,
and he aimed the harpoon at everyone seated there.
Eventually he came to Tigguasiña.
And Tigguasiña took some plaque from his teeth,
and he spat it on the harpoon when the shaman pointed at him.
The harpoon point fell off.
Again and again the shaman thrust at him:
but the harpoon point kept falling.
Now that Utkusik saw he was beaten, he took aim at himself.
He harpooned his own breast. Utkusik killed himself.
He'd been shamed by Tigguasiña. The story ends here.

.   .   .

Despite the widespread practice of adoption, Tikiġaq society had its
child outcasts (iḷiappaq, "orphans") who lived rough lives, sometimes
with the dogs, and were dependent on what they could beg and
scavenge. "Tigguasiña" sketches the life of a semidestitute child shaman
who lives by "fishing for spirits" in one of the qalgis. Tigguasiña is
already an aŋatkuq when we meet him, and his status may explain
why the elders connive at his occupation of Tikiġaq's central sacred
space.
   The story's initial focus is Tigguasiña's lonely authenticity; its
conclusion, his shamanic emergence. Just as the Itivyaaq spirits chose
the child Aniŋatchaq (story 8) to revitalize a tired shamanic tradition,
here Tigguasiña's initiation is set in the context of an old professional's
hocus-pocus. Children in other Inuit societies used to entertain their
families with skits of shamans in ecstatic seizure. On the one hand,
such parodies acted as windows onto a fraudulence that only children

had the immunity to proclaim. On the other hand, they provided a means of deintensifying for lay people behavior that was both frightening and necessary. In a similar way, gently mocking stories such as this one helped monitor or demystify the practice by satirizing self-indulgent and corrupt shamans.

As in many stories, the entrance passage is a locus of sex and shamanic vision. Here these events converge in the image of the seeing child among a mass of entrance-passage whale jaws, watching while the wolf man has intercourse with the woman initiate. Tigguasiña is already a shaman, but his place in village practice is secure only when he sees through what the old man's students fail to understand.

The question of shamanic authenticity which this story raises is cleverly pointed in the conversation between Tigguasiña and his friend the day after the entrance-passage fiasco. "A *real* tuuṅġaq?" the child asks, wonder mixed with incredulity in the storyteller's quasi-satirical falsetto. Intentionally or not, Asatchaq's phrase (*tuuṅġapiaq*, "real spirit") matches the following story, a parallel to "Tigguasiña" that Aġviqsiiña told Froelich Rainey in 1940.

THE REAL TUUṄĠAQ (SPIRIT)

Once there were two boys of about the same age and size. They used to play outside together. It was fall at the beginning of the qalgi ceremonies when the skinboat owners invited their crews to their iglus for the division of meat. This would be taken to the qalgi next day; but before that happened, they cut up bits of whale or other meat if they had not been successful the previous spring, and the children of the village would come to the iglu skylight and be given these pieces. The children all carried pointed sticks, and on these they spitted each piece of meat until the stick was full.

The two boys went around with all the other children, and when their sticks were full they took them down to Qaṇiḷiqpak qalgi at the northwest end of the village and went inside. The qalgis had already been opened for the fall, but everyone had gone that day to their iglus and the ceremonial house was empty.

When they got inside, however, the lamps were burning and there was a man sitting there making something. He asked the boys for their meat, and in return he would make them shamans. They didn't hesitate: they gave him all their meat and he ate it, and then he went and lay down on the wall-bench behind the katak. The boys sat on the bench at the opposite end. The man said they would now play a game, and they should roll up their mittens and throw them at him.

They did this and the man made some motions over the entrance hole and closed it so there was no way in or out of the qalgi; then he turned to the wall. When he lifted his head and turned to look at them, they saw that polar bear teeth were already growing out of his mouth. When he looked up a second time, he had the nose and face of a bear. Each time he looked around, the polar bear grew.

Finally it became a whole polar bear and it started to chase them. For a long time they tried to escape the bear and ran on the right-hand side: as you know, polar bears are left-handed. But finally it caught one of the boys and killed him.

The bear placed the body in the meat-cutting depression in the qalgi floor, ate every bit of him, and licked the place clean of blood so nothing would show. The other boy sat and watched from his bench. Then the bear started chasing again, and the boy was scared for he knew exactly what was going to happen to him. Eventually the bear caught him and killed him.

For a long time the boys knew nothing. When they came to consciousness again, they were lying in the meat-cutting depression, and of course they recognized each other. The entrance hole was open now, so they went out and returned to their homes.

The next day when the children were playing kick ball on the playing area [manigraq], and the adults had joined in, the two boys got together and agreed they had made a good start at being shamans, so they had better continue and get their power [qila]. So they went to one of the best-known Tikiġaq shamans: he was the brother of Qaunnaiḷaq, who was originally a marmot spirit. Both brothers had been born to Tikiġaq women and became great shamans.

So they went to Qaunnaiḷaq's brother and found him at home with his wife in their iglu, making something, and they told him they wanted to see the real tuunġaq. The man told them to wait until all the people were asleep.

When the time came, the shaman put on his clothes and led the two boys along the south beach to the edge of the burial place. There he stood between them at the edge of the water and announced that the two boys wanted to see the real tuunġaq.

Suddenly the man pointed to one side and said, "There it is!" The boy on that side looked and fell dead immediately. The other would have fallen into the sea, but the shaman caught him; he too died. For a long time they were unconscious. Eventually they woke up, and not long after they became shamans.

All they could describe about the tuunġaq was that he was very terrible and was wearing a duck or murre [guillemot] parka.

(Adapted from Rainey 1940–41)

Aġviqsiiña's tale is of particular interest for its account of a classic shamanic initiation. Here, as in countless descriptions by other Inuit and Eurasians, the shamanic aspirants are eaten alive by an animal spirit and return from psychic death as initiated aŋatkuqs. The tuungaq which the boys glimpse in the final episode is so *real,* so unlike the humbug tuungaq of Tigguasiña's story, that there are no words to describe it. Herein lies its authenticity and the actuality of their polar bear initiation, without which the spirit would have been invisible to them. (Note also the appearance of a brother to Qaunnaiḷaq mentioned by Asatchaq in story 9.)

In Asatchaq's version, Tigguasiña's developing career, stereotyped though it is, is outlined amid a clutter of wonderfully realistic objects, textures, and voices, inside the qalgi and around the village. The conversation between Tigguasiña and his friend takes place outside, with a view, through the dusk, of lamplit domestic windows, thus providing a new visual perspective on the orphan's marginality. But the storyteller's falsetto impression of the boys' voices ("A *real* spirit?") helps transform the dark entrance-passage intrigue into airy, boyish chatter. The melodrama in the final qalgi séance is in keeping with the charade in the entrance passage. But Tigguasiña's final gesture ("Plaque is strong!" the storyteller said later) is neither boy's play nor the theater of Utkusik's order. Tigguasiña snatches the initiative and ruthlessly steps into Utkusik's place at the center of the qalgi.

Tikiġaq people frequently connected relics they picked up with the details of their oral history. The 1940 excavations gave them an extensive new opportunity to do so. The famous jet-inlaid ivories that filled the eye sockets of an Ipiutak skull came from "the man with ivory eyes," whose story adults used to terrify bad children. Of the present story, Asatchaq commented, "Just east of the old Mission House [on the north side, near Ipiutak], we dug up the bones of a dog buried in the middle of a human skeleton." According to Asatchaq's mother, Niġuvana, this must have been Tigguasiña "because he turned himself into a dog when people were angry with him."

SIĠVANA AND THE OLD SHAMAN:
TERROR IN THE ENTRANCE PASSAGE

Just as the orphans in "Aniŋatchaq" and "Tigguasiña" are later versions of protoshamanic figures such as Tuluŋigraq and Ukuŋniq, so the young woman in this tale is a postmythic "woman who won't marry." Siġvana is a Tikiġaġmiu with no shamanic pretensions who nonetheless combines the persona of an ordinary young woman with that of the archetypal uiḷuaqtaq. Confronted with the challenge of Siġvana's refusal of marriage, an unscrupulous old shaman sets about "taming" her with a display of power which at once reinforces her mythological identity and humiliates her into submission.

11

I'm going to tell a story. Now, I'm going to tell a story.
There was a woman who refused to take a husband: here, in Tikiġaq.
Now, a shaman wants her.
And this young woman has a name: Siġvana.
And she has parents.
Now an old shaman visits her parents and asks for their daughter.
The old man is a shaman.
"It's for our daughter to decide," the parents say.
"If she wants you, you can have her."
That's what they say to him.
And so the shaman comes for her one evening.
"*Naami:* No."
As soon as he comes in, Siġvana walks out of the iglu.
After she's gone out, the shaman stays inside for awhile.
Then he leaves too. He goes to find her.

Well, the shaman doesn't know where Siġvana has gone.
Then he starts asking, and he finds out from the people.
And when he finds which iglu she has entered, he goes after her.

When she sees him enter, she starts leaving.
As soon as she goes out, he follows her.

Then she goes into another iglu.
But as she enters, there's the shaman in the entrance passage.
Just as she enters, there he is, approaching. He's leaving the iglu.

She'd escaped from the shaman,
but now she meets him leaving every iglu that she enters.

Every iglu that she enters, there he is already.

When she sees the shaman, she turns back, and goes out again.
She turns, and doesn't enter; she goes out to another iglu.

This continues.

Every time she goes into an iglu,
she meets the shaman coming out of it.
They meet in the entrance passage.

This young woman's getting weary of the shaman.
But now he decides he'll put a sleep on her.
And when he's made her sleep, he'll start.

Siġvana goes back to her parents' iglu.
She *still* finds the shaman in the iglu entrance passage.

Every iglu that she enters, there's the shaman.
She meets the shaman leaving every iglu that she enters.

And now the young woman is getting sleepy.
The girl who doesn't want a husband is sleepy.
Now she wants to sleep, she goes home and sleeps there.

The shaman does nothing.
The shaman doesn't even sleep with her.
He does nothing. But he will do something.

And during the night, the young woman grows old.
Her hair turns gray, and her teeth fall out on her pillow.

Her parents see what's happened to her.
Their daughter Siġvana has become an old woman.
Her hair is white and her teeth have fallen out.
She's grown old overnight.

Now she's old, the shaman still does nothing.
The man and woman stay in the iglu with their ancient daughter.
They want to see if she can stand up by herself.
The day before, she'd been a young woman.

Now the father tells his wife to fetch the shaman,
so he can make their daughter what she was before.
"When she knows what it's like to be old,
she will decide to take the shaman," says the father.
And he says to his daughter, "The shaman can change this.
Then he'll take you for his wife. But not as an old woman."

So the mother goes out and fetches the shaman.
(Shamans did this in the past, when a woman didn't want a husband.)
The shaman comes into the iglu.
And when he enters, he sees an old woman down there on the floor.

He sees her teeth have gone. He sees her gray hair.
And when he comes in, he sits down and does nothing.
He doesn't shamanize. And as the shaman sits and does nothing,
out of the woman in her sleeping skin a seal begins to crawl.
And as the seal emerges from her, she starts smiling.
But she can do nothing.
She can't stand, she can't move. The seal crawls out.
It comes out of her and tingles,
but she can't do anything.
And once it's come out, it goes back into her.

When the shaman entered, the woman's father said to him:
"Being like this is no good for our daughter:
if she wants you for a husband, she will have you,
but she'll have to change if this is to happen.
This isn't how she wants to be. Make her normal again.
If she wants you, she will take you."
Then the shaman makes her normal, and she's old no longer.
She's back as she was.

Her hair is black, and she's a young woman.
As the shaman starts to leave the iglu, he says,
"*Qanuq?* Well? Well?" says the shaman.
She says, "I will follow."

So the shaman got a wife again without too much trouble.
And when he took her home with him
it is said he restored her completely, creating her youth again.
This is what Siġvana, daughter of that couple, went through.

.   .   .

This elegant story presents shamanism in active, domestic process, though in its numerous parallels with Tuluŋigraq's story, it also has a mythic substrate. But whereas the uiḷuaqtaq in the Raven myth is tricked with guile and magic, here the girl is simply terrorized with a display of shamanic pyrotechnics. The character of Siġvana herself is a delicate mixture of legendary archetype and naturalistic adolescent willfulness. In the context of her parents' acquiescence to the shaman's demand, the girl's refusal is provocative and daring. Asatchaq conveys her immovability with a single word: "*Naami!* No!" This abrupt stop to the proceedings is followed by an eruption of panic and the old shaman's calculated and unhurried chase.

For the period of his pursuit, it is as though the shaman has depopulated the village. Abandoning herself to the dark, semidomesticated subterranean ambiguity of Tikiġaq architecture, Siġvana has nowhere to hide and finds no one to protect her. Old though the shaman may be, he is master of the entire space, and his casual ubiquity is inescapable.

As in the previous story, the entrance passage is the locus of both vision and danger. "The shaman was using a *tuullik* [yellow-billed loon] amulet to dive through the iglu ventilator," Asatchaq later explained. The counterpoint of the two figures shuttling toward each other down successive entrance passages is conveyed with hypnotic repetition suggesting the supernatural sleep for which the unwilling Siġvana is due: "*isiqtuq* [she enters] . . . *aniruq* [he's leaving] . . . *isiqtuq* . . . *aniruq* . . . *isiqtuq* . . . *aniruq* . . ."

All uiḷuaqtaqs of legend are raped or otherwise punished. But in this story the shaman is successful only when Siġvana has succumbed to the horror of both old age and the seal's emergence. "He used a seal-fetus amulet; there's nothing stronger," said the storyteller in later conversation. The slimy nasal emphasis with which Asatchaq conveys the seal's emergence (*paamŋuaq . . . paamŋuaq* ["crawling . . . crawling"]) is one of the high moments of his often dark narrative style. The episode also reinforces Siġvana's character as quasi-mythic uiḷuaqtaq: just as the woman-who-won't-marry is an aspect of the primal old woman (*aana*), so here Siġvana is both virgin and crone. But smile as she does at the ambiguous maternal pleasure of the seal coming through her, she is forced in the end to grim, mundane submission.

AQUPPAK: A SPIRIT TRIP TO THE WHALES

A widely held assumption that the aŋatkuq was a spiritually inspired incompetent **12**
or madman has virtually no truth in the context of Tikiġaq shamanism. Many
of the most successful hunters and umialiks were shamans, and there is no
record beyond Aquppak's story of a link between shamanism and psychosis.
Shamanic initiation often involved, as it did for Aquppak, a temporary loss of soul,
and this condition was sometimes defined as a kind of controlled madness. But for
most shamans, the initiatory "sleep" took just four or five days; Aquppak was
*crazy (*kinnauraq*) for an entire winter. While some, like Tigguasiña,*
eagerly sought entry to the shaman's world, Aquppak was a reluctant shaman, and
his sense of unease with both the human and the spirit world suffuses his story.

The woman was Nanautchiaq, and she was from Tikiġaq. The man
was Aquppak, her older brother.

The man was on the south beach, walking. He was walking toward
the point. And when he got to Iḷutak, he saw some men about to launch
a skinboat. They were at Iḷutak on the point.

Now these people told him to follow them. But Aquppak didn't
want to get into the skinboat. And when he refused, they took his spirit
with them.

Now these men were not people, they were carvings, which are called
quluġuq; they hang from the ceiling of the qalgi. There are many kinds
of quluġuq figures: ducks, whales, people, caribou, skinboats . . . these
are all called quluġuq. They are not real: they are little carvings.

And one of the little effigies of a human had fallen out of its skinboat,
and its place was empty; someone was missing. It was for this reason
that they wanted Aquppak to go with them.

They went out on the water. And when they left, they took Aquppak
with them, those who went out in the skinboat.

So part of Aquppak went out with them, and he became a shaman. Aquppak became a shaman.

They went to the land of the whales. That's where they went. And all that winter, Aquppak lived as a man without consciousness, because his spirit had been taken away. Only when the whales returned, he came back too.

And Aquppak told the people. "The whales always come and check on what Tikiġaq people are doing. The whales send someone to see if the people are ready for them. And some of the whales will return and say, 'They haven't done anything yet. They haven't even gone out to the ice.' That's what they used to tell the other whales when they went back to them." Aquppak knew all about the whales.

Now, that spring they caught a whale in Tikiġaq; the whale was Aquppak, but the people didn't realize it was him, returned home. In his absence Aquppak had turned into a whale. And his relatives were out whaling, Aquppak's relatives. And he rose in the water near their skinboat—they had a skinboat. That is where he showed himself, because they had a boat for whaling. After he revealed himself, his relatives harpooned him and Aquppak returned to consciousness.

The following winter Aquppak learned that his younger sister had been ill-treated by Utqiaġvik people. Aquppak's sister: her name was Nanautchiaq. Aquppak heard they had killed his younger sister Nanautchiaq, at Utqiaġvik.

This was what they had done to her: in the moonlight, after the snow had fallen a little, when the weather was cold, they made her take off her parka and they had forced her hands into a poke of seal oil. They say that seal oil in a poke is very cold. It is colder than whale oil. The Utqiaġvik people made her do it. They made her take her parka off first, in bright moonlight, and forced her hands inside the oil poke.

Then they gathered snow and made snowballs, and they threw snow at her, and when it fell, it cut flesh from her body. The flesh of the woman. This is what Aquppak heard they had done to his sister.

And when Aquppak heard about this, he said, "I will get even with these people. I will do this for my sister. I will starve the people up at Utqiaġvik. They will go hungry. I will stop them catching animals."

Aquppak did what was necessary. And in the winter, the Utqiaġvik people saw a large snowy owl sitting on a meat rack: all winter the owl sat there. And Utqiaġvik had little daylight. Aquppak caused this.

And many people starved in Utqiaġvik. Aquppak avenged his sister. Utqiaġvik people died of starvation.

(My cousin in Barrow [Utqiaġvik] didn't like this story, because of what happened up there . . . Aquppak was a shaman.)

When Aquppak's umialik caught a whale, Aquppak always got his share. Aquppak constantly asked if the crew had brought in his share. For as soon as they brought it ashore, he could make the ice drift out. People who still had meat to haul in would tell him, "Yours is still down on the ice." Then they wouldn't be in danger of the ice drifting out. These people didn't tell the truth about his meat, so the ice would stay put. I think that's the end . . . it is said that Aquppak starved Utqiaġvik people.

AĠVIQSIIÑA'S VERSION

[In this version of the first part of the story, told by Aġviqsiiña (Rainey 1940–41), Aquppak is called Kattuaq.]

Aġviqsiiña knows that Ququk, his contemporary, had a grandfather who was going down along the shore one day toward the point and saw a boat just putting out. This was the day they burned the *puguqs* [ceremonial carvings]. The people in the boat were all strangers to him; they asked him to join them, but he refused. They went out and took his spirit with them. The boat and the men in it were one of the puguqs going out to the place where the whales are. That's why people burn them.

Kattuaq came home and got very ill. He was thin and sick all winter. His spirit was with the puguq, which traveled a long way till it came to a big house. There were thousands and thousands of people in it, and they all had very long faces, so he knew they were whales. He spent all winter there, and in the spring they started to go north. Kattuaq decided that his spirit would go with a small whale. With him was another spirit. When they got tired, they stopped in a crooked place in the open water and collected something like soft moss, to sleep. Kattuaq was still inside the whale.

When they are close to Tikiġaq, they know where they are. All the whales know all the villages. The first whaling boat they see is sideways on and the whales can see right into it; they see all the men, and they are frightened, and go down. The next boat looks black, very black, and they are frightened again. The third boat is very bright, so bright that they can't see it well; it comes close and strikes a whale. They know the whale is dying. Kattuaq doesn't know where to go; he takes the form of his amulet, which is a gull, and flies back to his own body. His body is dirty: it has been sick for so long, it is very weak, it can't move; he has to go into it, though he doesn't want to. The body is sleeping, but it walks and runs around. All spring the boy is well, but the mind is half-cocked. This is generally how shamans in the making behave. Kattuaq was a great one.

.   .   .

Asatchaq's version of the story opens with Aquppak's initiation at Iḷutak, the small bay just southeast of the Point. It is the day when ritual carvings have been brought from the qalgi to be burned during the autumn whaling ceremonies.*

Tikiġaq people believed in a spirit structure of two or three parts: *iñuusiq,* "life force"; *iḷitqusiq,* "personal soul"; and *atiq,* "name" (see the Introduction). Death occurred when the first two of these parts were absent from the body for four days. Shamans on spirit journeys left mind and body in trance-sleep. Aquppak, however, loses a soul for eight months and is therefore, as Asatchaq later comments, "a bit mad" (*kinnauraq,* from *kinnaq,* "crazy").

All sea mammals were thought to have their origin in the south, where they had their own "countries" (*nunat*). Here their souls returned for rebirth when they died. Aquppak joins himself to a whale soul in *aġviġum nunaŋa* ("the whale's country") and returns to his old self when the whale he has entered finally reaches Tikiġaq. The second version of the story gives us a glimpse of how the whales approached Tikiġaq. In a tale not given here, the whales approach their Tikiġaq hunters and discuss among themselves how they'll offer themselves only to umialiks who will distribute their meat fairly.

The next two episodes record the shaman's exercise of power. Aquppak's sister, whose name the storyteller quotes for himself mnemonically at the beginning, is married to a man in Utqiaġvik, 350 miles north of home. Interregional rivalry and conflict, both ancient and more recent, are expressed here. Asatchaq's aside—about his nonkin "cousin" who didn't like this tale—indicates how such stories can stir up loyalist feeling.

---

*Asatchaq calls the ritual carvings *quluġuqs.* These carvings were permanent galgi property. The carvings made each year and burned to release their spirits were called *puguqs.* The practice of making and destroying these effigies died out during Asatchaq's childhood, but the older Aġviqsiiña had witnessed it for longer.

Aquppak's revenge on Utqiaġvik takes the form of *niġġutaili,* "scaring off the animals," Aquppak transforming into a snowy owl (*ukpik*) for the purpose.

The final episode in Asatchaq's version sketches a picture of the whimsical egotism that sometimes went with aŋatkuq behavior. Aquppak's skinboat crew is laboring to haul in tons of whale meat over increasingly insecure sea ice at the end of the season. The shaman tries to ensure that his own meat is safe on land; he then wants to use his aŋatkuq powers to set the ice adrift and thus deprive his own group of their part in the whale. This tricksterish behavior ran directly against the ethic of whaling crew cooperation. Shamans who stepped outside this ethic were dealt with in a number of different ways. In one nineteenth-century history, where a shaman called Maŋŋuyaaluk is held responsible for keeping the sea ice closed and thus preventing whaling, a rival by the name of Nasauŋaluk is engaged to murder the culprit, which he does by sympathetic magic. In "Ayagiiyaq and Pisiktaġaaq" (story 23), a similar battle for control of sea-ice movement at whaling time takes place, but without casualties.

In the present story, Aquppak's nonshamanic colleagues outwit him with cheerfully brazen deceit. It is interesting to note that while some shamans were too frightening to allow such a maneuver, Aquppak was presumably amenable to a certain control. His negativity as a whaling crew member is compatible with his exercise of *niġġutaili* (shamanically scaring off game) in Utqiaġvik. The same destructive supernaturalism is involved in both events. But how this tendency coexisted with Aquppak's socially helpful quality as a whale spirit is one of the paradoxes of Tikiġaq shamanism. *Qila* (shamanic power) could switch from positive to negative according to a shaman's mood or disposition. But that Asatchaq should have described Aquppak as "a bit crazy" perhaps indicates his continuing status in the village. Only one other Tikiġaq shaman has been recorded as being, at any time, insane: see the commentary to story 24, in which the shaman Isuaġalaaq is derided as "Crazy woman!" (p. 192). Aquppak's initial madness may have extended to a more or less permanent psychosis; if so, his condition may not have diminished certain of his powers, but it did perhaps reduce his authority.

UNIPKALUKTUAQ: A WOMAN'S STORY COMES TO LIFE

There were few Tikiġaq stories about women shamans, partly because the female **13**
practitioners were outnumbered by men and partly because women shamans,
visionaries, and healers worked in secret or without ostentation. But the primal
shaman of oral tradition was a woman: this was the aana who created Raven Man
and whose violent, nubile aspect Raven Man married (see "Tuluŋigraq"). The
uiḷuaqtaq appears in many subsequent legends, and almost invariably she is "tamed"
by a wandering shamanic orphan. In this story a shamaness is tempted by her feeble
and unwitting husband to bring her magic into the open. A spectacular eruption
of power ensues, exposing the village to the fury and disdain of the uiḷuaqtaq.

In Tikiġaq there was once a man and a woman. They had no children.
Now, one day when the man came back from the qalgi,
he asked his wife to tell him a story, an *unipkaaq* [legend] or an
uqaluktuaq [ancestor chronicle].
As soon as he arrived he asked her for a story.
And the woman said to him, "*Ilviñ uqaluktuaġin! You* tell a story!
You've been in the qalgi."
The men always used to tell stories in the qalgi.
"You tell me a story!" said the woman.
No, he wouldn't. So he forced *her* to. Finally she gave in. He forced
her.
And she said, "I will tell a story. But you must keep it from the
people. I will tell an unipkaaq."
The man answered, "Why should I tell people what I hear, why
should I repeat the story you are going to tell me?"
The woman said, "Men always gossip when they get together."
The man said, "Women gossip when they come together too.
You can learn a good deal from women's gossip."

The man started to grow angry.

So: "You tell me you won't repeat it, so I'll tell an unipkaaq."

The man agreed he'd tell no one.

"When you go to the qalgi you will describe the things you've heard.

Nonetheless, I'll tell the unipkaaq."

Yes, well . . . the woman took her parka off, and she went to the katak.

She said to her husband, "Now listen!"

When she had taken off her parka, she went to the katak.

She said to her husband, "Now I'll tell my story."

The woman put her arm into the katak;

she moved her hand in a circle as though stirring something.

"Don't be frightened when things start to happen. You asked for a story, and promised me you won't repeat it."

Now when the woman stirred the katak, there came the sound of splashing water.

The splashing came from the katak, and the entrance passage seemed to fill with water.

The man could hear water rising, splashing, as the katak filled with water, as the katak flooded.

"Don't be frightened," said the woman. "Don't be frightened," she said as her husband watched her.

Then there was a bursting noise, and a whale appeared. A whale rose in the katak, and blocked it.

The whale breathed out, it blew through the katak.

"Since you promised you won't talk about this, we can eat some," said the woman.

"But tomorrow, when you return to the qalgi, you must not go back chewing maktak [whaleskin and blubber].

You can't go with any maktak in your mouth."

They ate part of the whale. They cut the whale up right there.

(I don't know what they did with the rest of it. Perhaps they stored it in the passage.

The iglu where that man and woman lived was right opposite to where we are now.

That iglu's in ruins. It was Siqaaluk's. You can't miss it.

His belukha net anchor is there too, by the midden. His belukha net.

I knew that anchor was there but I never took it.

Siqaaluk liked to hunt belukhas.)

They ate together. And when they'd eaten, the wife reminded the man to say nothing.

"If you talk, they'll ask me for it," said the woman.

Now when the man went out to the qalgi next day, he put a piece of maktak in his mouth.

He went to the qalgi chewing maktak, though his wife had told him not to.

His qalgi was next to the game area, at the edge of it.

(The whale's jawbones from that qalgi are still there, marking the place the qalgi was.

This qalgi was next to the place where people threw out their bones.

Dogs running over the top of the qalgi to get bones were always damaging the qalgi skylight.)

So the husband went back to the qalgi chewing maktak.

The men noticed it immediately. They noticed the man was chewing something fresh, something recently caught.

"What's this?" they asked, "What's this you're chewing?"

The man said he was chewing a piece of *ugruk* [bearded seal] skin.

"That's not ugruk skin!"

They could smell the fragrance of fresh whale skin.

The man tried to tell them it was ugruk skin,

but the others answered, "This is something freshly caught!"

"No . . ." Finally they made him show them what he had in his mouth.

"You and your wife have eaten freshly caught whale," they said.

"Yes, we have. We have eaten maktak. My wife told me an unipkaaq, an *unipkaluktuaq* [a story that comes to life].

She told me not to talk about it. But you noticed what was in my mouth."

And they said to the man, *"Ii!* Yes, bring your wife to the qalgi tomorrow so she can tell us her unipkaaq."

When the man got home, he told his wife what had happened.

And his wife said, "I told you not to talk about it."

"They noticed what was in my mouth. They smelled something fresh in my mouth.

Yes—they want you in the qalgi so you can tell your unipkaaq.

Tomorrow we will go to the qalgi together," the husband said. "You will follow me."

"I told you not to tell my unipkaaq. But now you have exposed me," said the woman.

The next day they both went to the qalgi.

The woman started telling them the unipkaaq, as she'd done previously.

She took off her parka and went to the katak.

Then she started stirring the katak.

The sound of water was heard in the passage.

The passage was filling up with water.

There was no way anyone could escape the qalgi.

Now before she told her story the woman told her husband to leave the qalgi and stay up by the skylight.

And while she stirred, a whale rose in the katak.

And the woman called to her husband to pull her through the skylight, so she wouldn't be among the qalgi people.

Her husband pulled her through the skylight.

The qalgi flooded. All the people in the qalgi drowned.

(I know that qalgi. If you want to see the place it used to be I can show you in the summer.

The qalgi where an unipkaluktuaq took place. A woman . . . her husband exposed her to the people.

The people . . . drowned there in the qalgi. The whale's jawbones are still there.

There's a ditch with the jawbones in it.

They stopped using that qalgi because of the dogs.

In those days they threw their shit out one place, and their bones in another.

This was still done when I was growing up.)

So . . . the Tikiġaq people understood this woman now. She was like that.

She and her husband didn't go hungry.

The people hadn't known she was a shaman. But now they knew that she was a shaman.

And the people from *that* side [south of Tikiġaq] heard about her:

they heard about a woman with an unipkaluktuaq.

And when the shamans down there heard about this woman they started to visit her.

But she recognized them whenever they came into her iglu.

These shamans never revealed themselves in person.

Some took the form of duck's down, and floated through the iglu ventilation hole.

Others came in the shape of winter caribou hair.

When they landed on the floor, the woman would say,

"You've come to find out what I am like, that's why you visit me.
Take your former shape and sit down with me."
Sometimes two people would come and sit with her.
They turned themselves to duck's down before entering the ventilation
hole.
"*Ii*, yes, what do you want here?" The woman asked them.
And they answered, "We heard about a whale, and a woman with a
story . . ."
"*Ii!* Yes!" The woman said yes by raising her eyebrows.
And when she had done that, she turned her head sideways,
and the heads of the two shamans sitting with her fell off.
Two men fell, and others followed. The husband used to watch.
Two headless bodies lay there. Later there were four.
Their heads came off as though a knife had cut them.
And the woman told her husband, "This is your work now.
You always wanted work of this kind. Work on them."
And the man went out and buried the corpses.
"I told you from the start I didn't want to tell an unipkaaq.
Now you work on these bodies," said the woman.
The man took the corpses and heads out of the iglu.
Later she told her husband to hang the heads up in the iglu.
One she had him hang by the ventilation hole, the others she had hung
at the corners of the iglu.

Now people from the south turned against this woman and her husband.
The woman was in Tikiġaq. And when people in the south heard
what had happened to their shamans,
they formed a war party, and traveled to Tikiġaq.
There was a battle, and many corpses lay on the ground.
And in the summer, when the corpses swelled, Tikiġaq stank.
When the woman saw that what she'd done was evil, on account of
the bodies, she told her husband to go and watch for more war
parties approaching.
Her husband did this; he went out and watched for people approaching
the village.
And when he told her there were people coming toward the village,
all she did was stretch her arms out, like this.
[*Asatchaq stretches his arms parallel in front of him, undersides of forearms
up, and moves them up and down, swaying them from side to side.*]
When the woman did this, the earth opened, and all the rotten bodies
tumbled into the earth.

A Woman's Story Comes to Life   **99**

She did this so that what had happened before would not again happen.
In doing this, she made the undersides of her forearms raw.
She cut the earth, and skinned her forearms . . .

After this happened, some visitors, a group of men, arrived in Tikiġaq
   by skinboat.
These were the woman's older brothers. They had come to see what
   she was doing.
When they heard she had been killing people, had killed many people,
   this woman with an unipkaaq,
they came to see her, from their own place, where she also came from.
Her own brothers had sent her away from their place because of what
   she'd done there.
She had done things which her brothers felt responsible for.
She had made life dangerous for people.
Her brothers were grateful that someone had married their sister.
She'd been sent away by her brothers, because she had been killing
   people.
(I think this is the end.)
Their younger sister was like that. She was a shaman.
The brothers were grateful there was a man in Tikiġaq who'd taken
   her.
She was the youngest in the family.
(When my mother told the story, she didn't say how many brothers
   there were.)
The heads of the men she killed were hung in the four corners of the
   iglu. And one by the ventilation hole.
The story ends here.

.   .   .

This tale comes from Asatchaq's mother, Niġuvana, and it was the
only story which Asatchaq gave a title. The term *unipkaluktuaq* was
explained variously to me as "another word for 'old story' " (*unipkaaq*),
"power," and "a story that comes to life." "Having unipkaaqs," or the
ability to memorize and tell old stories, was itself regarded as a kind of
power in Tikiġaq. In the story here, the woman sardonically trounces
her husband's feeble attempt at authority by playing on this notion.
"I'll show you what an unipkaaq is," she says in effect. She then
proceeds to enact two major symbols in Tikiġaq's origin myths.

The first symbol is the sunwise stirring of the katak. Sunwise movement of the hand or sunwise circumambulation (see "Asatchaq," story 19) was a routine gesture of shamanic creativity. In the context of the stories in this collection, the woman's gesture repeats the circling motion in the sun and moon myth (story 2). As suggested in the Commentary to "Aliŋnaq," women were ritually associated with both sun and moon. Since the sun sister, like the character of the present tale, was a kind of uiḷuaqtaq, the mythic connection would have been obvious to a traditional audience.

The second symbol links the woman with the Tuluŋigraq myth and in particular with the primal "land whale" which Raven Man harpooned before it transformed into Tikiġaq nuna. The present story is one of a group of five in which either a whale rises through Tikiġaq earth or a woman in an iglu is equated with a whale soul in a whale. In the stories of rising whales, the iglu katak is the locus of the animal's appearance. It was, of course, impossible for anything except burrowing rodents to rise through Tikiġaq nuna. The whale here must therefore be understood as a manifestation of the primal earth-whale, whose soul, or *iñua,* still inhabited Tikiġaq. (The five stories are published separately in Lowenstein 1993.)

In the present story, this symbolism is reinforced by the character of the woman, who turns out to be a partly reformed uiḷuaqtaq, exiled for murder from the Kobuk River. Just as Tuluŋigraq could harpoon the sea beast only after his alliance with the sedentary, iglu-dwelling shamaness, so too is the woman here a magician. However, unlike her mythological counterpart, whom Tuluŋigraq tricks into marriage, this uiḷuaqtaq escapes the domination of a neutralizing man of power. From this imbalance of the sexes flows the catastrophe so artfully developed from the initial, premonitory domestic jockeying.

III. ANCESTOR HISTORIES

14

The saga of Niġliq and Suuyuk constitutes nineteenth-century Tikiġaq's most relentless feuding drama. A tale of catastrophe for all its protagonists, its action unfolds against a shifting series of grand and evocative backdrops. First are the beaches and the stormy Uivvaq headland north of Tikiġaq, then a moonlit winter village and crowded, violent iglu interiors; the final two episodes take place on the Noatak River and the shores of an isolated Tikiġaq seal-hunting site. Looming across this landscape are murderous antagonists and their victims, all imprisoned within tensions that violence can only intensify before finally, and brutally, allaying. Between the killings are scenes of a ritual violence that almost succeeds in maintaining a balance between the feuding parties. More than any other story, this one conveys the stress of living at close quarters in a small, crowded village full of powerful and competitive hunters.

THE DEATH OF SUUYUK

Niġliq and his family . . . Niġliq's house was close to Qaġmaqtuuq.
Across from Niġliq, south of Qaġmaqtuuq, lived Suuyuk.
Niġliq and his younger brother lived together.

Suuyuk also had his brothers living with him.
(I don't know how many of them lived there.)
In the summer, people started leaving Tikiġaq,
they traveled up the north shore, to go hunting caribou.
The first to go were Suuyuk and his brothers.
Suuyuk took his wife with him.
Suuyuk's wife was Niġliq's younger sister.
Her name was Siġvana. Siġvana was Niġliq's younger sister.

And Suuyuk and his family went caribou hunting up north,
and then they left for home in their skinboat.

At this time, Niġliq and his brother were at Uivvaq.
They camped there and set their skinboat sideways, using it as a windbreak.
And when Suuyuk and his family arrived at Uivvaq they beached their skinboat.

As soon as Siġvana came ashore, she went straight to her brothers.
The two brothers also had their father with them.
Niġliq's younger brother was called Kavisiġluk.

But instead of going to her brothers' tent,
Siġvana went into her father's. She went in,
Taamna Siġvana: that Siġvana. Suuyuk's . . . Suuyuk's wife.
And now Suuyuk started calling her:
"Siġvana, we are leaving!" But she took no notice,
she made no move to leave her father's. That Siġvana . . .

Then some of Suuyuk's brothers climbed up
on Iglak, a small hill near Niġliq's tent.

And one of Suuyuk's kin had died while they were hunting.

And one of the men who'd climbed up said,
"I was there when Niġliq and his brother threw our kinsmen on the ice.
I saw it, myself, while we were butchering a whale.
Niġliq and his brother threw our kinsmen on the sea ice."
(This was before he died. He died before the journey.)
"Niġliq and his brother are to blame," he said.
Suuyuk heard what was said, and he called to his wife,
"Siġvana, we are leaving!"
But it was Niġliq who answered, saying to his sister,
"Younger sister, don't go down to them.
They have slandered us, they have not come to talk to us directly, but have slandered us."
This was why Niġliq didn't let his sister go to them.
When Suuyuk had called once more, he left his skinboat and started toward them.
He didn't stop and talk to Niġliq and his brother,
he went straight to the tent where Siġvana and her father were.
Suuyuk entered. Outside, Niġliq listened.
And as Niġliq listened, he heard something going on in there.

Niġliq entered. Suuyuk with his right hand held Siġvana by the hair.
With his left hand, Suuyuk was holding Niġliq's father.
Niġliq's father had a knife: Suuyuk must have grabbed him when he'd
  picked the knife up.
Niġliq saw that Suuyuk held them both, and his hands were full.
When Niġliq saw what was happening, he drew his knife; he stabbed
  Suuyuk in the back.
Suuyuk felt the knife. When Suuyuk felt he had been wounded, he ran
  for his skinboat.
He plunged into the water. Suuyuk had a whale charm.
He plunged into the water.
(Seawater is medicine for someone with a whale charm.)
He swam in the water, and then climbed into the skinboat.
When Suuyuk got into the skinboat, the men took off, out of range of
  Niġliq's arrows.
They went round the point at Uivvaq, and went south to Tikiġaq.
Suuyuk was wounded. And Niġliq and his family also went to Tikiġaq
  by skinboat.

Now when winter was approaching, in the late fall,
Suuyuk started to go out a little and stand beside his iglu.
(I know where that house was; I dug in its ruins.)
Suuyuk had his arms inside his parka:
he kept one glove on, and he held the other glove.
(People used to stand outside their iglus like this prepared for anything
  that might happen.)
And Suuyuk saw Niġliq standing outside too, in front of his iglu.
(Their iglus were close to one another.)

And Niġliq called into his iglu, to his younger sister,
"Siġvana, come outside!"
Suuyuk was standing in front of his house, opposite.
Niġliq said to Siġvana, "We won't let you come to any harm."
And Siġvana went outside and stood between her brothers.
When Suuyuk saw his woman opposite, outside the iglu, he started to
  walk toward her.
(Those two houses were quite close to each other. They were at the
  east end of Tikiġaq.
I know where they were. When I was a boy, they were still standing.)
Suuyuk saw Siġvana. Siġvana saw him coming toward her.
Siġvana saw him. She went in. Suuyuk saw her.

He came close and followed. Then Suuyuk entered Niġliq's iglu.
Inside, Suuyuk started looking for Siġvana.
When he found her, she was sitting underneath the sleeping bench
    beside the oil lamp.
When he was inside the iglu, Suuyuk went up to Siġvana.
Suuyuk went to her; she did nothing.

Then Suuyuk heard Niġliq and his brother coming in from outside,
and he hid behind Siġvana.
Niġliq was first to enter; he saw Suuyuk sitting behind Siġvana.
When Niġliq entered, he drew his knife. He moved closer.
Suuyuk used Siġvana as a shield. Niġliq had come to get him with his
    knife.
But when Niġliq found he couldn't do as he intended, he sat down,
and Kavisiġluk came in through the katak, drew his knife and
    approached Suuyuk.
Suuyuk used his wife to shield himself.
Kavisiġluk couldn't touch him. *Suni nipi:* absolute silence.

And Niġliq's father was on the sleeping bench.
For some time no one spoke. At last, the father spoke.
"Why are you trying to keep her? She's not my only daughter."
He said this to his two sons. And he told Siġvana to go with Suuyuk.
And when they left the iglu, Suuyuk took her home.
When they entered Suuyuk's iglu, Suuyuk went and sat beneath the
    sleeping bench.
Siġvana approached her husband and sat down behind him.
Suuyuk's brothers were outside. Siġvana knew they would come and
    try to hurt her.
Each one of Suuyuk's brothers came inside, with his knife,
and tried to do to her what her own brothers tried on Suuyuk.
But she used Suuyuk as a shield, as he'd used her to shield him.
They stopped trying to attack her once they had got even.

It was after this, later in the winter, when the moon was full,
the brothers of Niġliq and Suuyuk started shooting at each other.
It was night. (Their iglus were not far from one another.
They were close to Qaġmaqtuuq. You can still see the ruins of the iglu
    Niġliq lived in.)
And Suuyuk and Siġvana had moved in with some kin of his,

they moved away from Niġliq's area, they moved to the west end
  of Tikiġaq.
And after they'd moved they heard their brothers had started shooting:
Suuyuk's younger brothers against Niġliq and Kavisiġluk.
(That was what people told Suuyuk about his brothers.)
And during the battle, one of Suuyuk's brothers stole an arrow.
(I forget who the owner was.) He made living arrows.
One of Suuyuk's younger brothers stole a living arrow.
And one of Suuyuk's brothers took the living arrow, and aimed it at
  Niġliq.
(An old man owned that arrow. He owned living arrows.)
And Suuyuk's brother could scarcely see Niġliq,
but he aimed, and let fly.
They saw a man fall.
Niġliq was hit by the living arrow.
Kavisiġluk was the first to reach him.
Niġliq had been hit by the living arrow.

After Niġliq had been wounded, Suuyuk went to one of his own kin,
  and said,
"Listen: we should go over there and side with Niġliq.
We'll become arrows for them."
He wanted to help Niġliq.
And Suuyuk and he went to where they were shooting, approaching
  Niġliq's area.

Now Niġliq's younger brother, Kavisiġluk, was cross-eyed.
And while they were approaching, Suuyuk said to his kinsman,
"I will walk in front of you."
They were approaching Qaġmaqtuuq,
and Kavisiġluk, who was cross-eyed, saw a man approaching.
And when the man was close enough, he shot an arrow.
The arrow hit Suuyuk and he fell forward on his hands:
Kavisiġluk hadn't waited, he'd just shot the man who was approaching.
And he went to join Niġliq, and said,
"I've shot someone. He is on his hands and knees, trying to regain
  strength."

And at that time, Siġvana had a dislocated hip, and couldn't leave the
  iglu.

She was at Suuyuk's brothers' iglu, opposite Niġliq's.

And someone called in that they had killed Suuyuk, and Siġvana heard it.

When Suuyuk's brothers ran out, Siġvana quickly put her clothes on, and she left the iglu chamber. But she did not leave the passage.

She turned into the cooking space and hid there.

And when the women came back, looking for her, she wasn't in the iglu.

They looked for Siġvana, but they didn't find her. They were going to kill her.

And when Siġvana heard the women settle down, she left the iglu.

She didn't go to her father's house, but started going back between the ridges on another path.

At her grandparents' iglu, Niġliqpak and her son were staying.*

They were at the west end of the village. Siġvana went there.

And the son saw Siġvana coming, and called out,

"*Nayaaŋ isiġin!* Go in, younger sister!* My mother will hide you. Go in!"

As Siġvana entered, he called to his mother through the skylight,

"My younger sister's coming. Hide her."

And when Siġvana came into the iglu, she went behind Niġliqpak's back:

she crouched on her thighs, and hid.

Then Suuyuk's sisters and kinswomen came, and called in through the skylight to Niġliqpak,

"We heard Siġvana was here. If she went in, she must still be inside.

Let's go and find her."

Some of them went in and looked for Siġvana, but they didn't find her.

They looked for her, but they didn't see her behind Niġliqpak, that son's mother.

They didn't find her. (It's coming to an end.)

That Niġliqpak could never be wounded. She was invulnerable.

When Kakianaq caught a whale,* and people started fighting for the jawbones,

Niġliqpak got one of the jaws herself. No one could do anything about it.

"Niġliqpak": "Big brant goose," an old woman, unrelated to Niġliq.

"younger sister": Nonkinspeople, as here, often used kin terms to address each other.

"Kakianaq": This name may be a slip for "Qipuġaluatchiaq"; see story 7.

Now I'll continue the story of the two brothers, Kavisiġluk and
    Niġliq.
Niġliq was the older. They lived here in Tikiġaq.
They had an iglu inland from the other houses, close to Qaġmaqtuuq.

And sometimes they got angry with each other.
And when they quarreled, they stayed home from the qalgi.
They used their own iglu as their qalgi, and worked at home.
They hung up a tent skin in the iglu when they quarreled,
    to be separate from one another.
When they quarreled, they didn't even eat together,
    though they shared the iglu and worked in it.
Tainna ittuk: these two lived like this.

And opposite their house was Suuyuk's:
Suuyuk, whom they'd killed eventually.
And because of their violence, they lost all their friends in Tikiġaq:
those two brothers couldn't live with other people, couldn't visit their
    iglus.
That was Niġliq and Kavisiġluk: brothers. These brothers were too
    proud,
and people started to ignore them on account of this.

So Kavisiġluk left Tikiġaq. He left on the south side,
traveled down to the Noatak, where there are trees, and lived there.
He'd ended up with nowhere to stay or people to visit in Tikiġaq.
So he moved to the Noatak River.
And while he was on the Noatak, the men hunted caribou:
they used to herd them into corrals and then snare them.
The Noatak men would chase them between fences and then rope
    them.
But while they hunted in this way,
Kavisiġluk started shooting caribou, with arrows, as they ran into the
    corral.
This is what he did when he lived among strangers.
So the Noatak people saw him as a person to one side.

Because of what he did, they wouldn't have him in their iglus.
They wanted nothing of Kavisiġluk.

So Kavisiġluk and his wife decided to leave that place.
They got ready, and left.
And a Noatak man traveled with them, too.

And he it was who half-cut Kavisiġluk's bowstring.
When they first stopped to rest, he cut halfway through Kavisiġluk's
    bowstring,
so that when he drew the string it would break.
They traveled on, and stopped a second time.
And when they left their second camp place,
the man who had cut the bowstring drew his own weapon:
and pacing up and down, bow drawn, he challenged Kavisiġluk.
With bowstring drawn, he walked up and down, and challenged
    Kavisiġluk.
Kavisiġluk grabbed his bow when he saw what was happening.
But he found the string cut.
Now attached to that bow was another piece of sinew, a spare sinew.
Kavisiġluk ran, unwinding the sinew.
Arrows fell around him; he ran to escape them as he fixed the string.
He stopped to tie it, but the arrows landed close.
Three times he ran and stopped, and tried to mend his weapon.
But the Noatak man was close behind him.
(They say that once a man who's difficult to hit is wounded,
    he can get no further.)
So it was with Kavisiġluk when his enemy hit him.
He shot him with arrows until he was dead.
That was how Kavisiġluk died.

And after the death of Kavisiġluk, the Tikiġaq people wanted Niġliq.
Niġliq had already gone to live at Tapqaġruk,*
by Tapqaġruk creek, this side of Aqalulik.
(Niġliq had an iglu there: I never saw it, but I saw the ruins.)
And Tikiġaq people tried to find someone to kill Niġliq:
someone who'd kill Niġliq for them.
And they found two men who'd do it. The first was Tarruiyaaq.

"Tapqaġruk": Tapqaġruk was one of Tikiġaq's outlying hunting sites, about fifteen miles
north of the village.

But then it took some time before they found a man to go with him.
Then someone mentioned Sukaŋaaluk, a man easy to persuade, who
said yes to anything.
So Sukaŋaaluk was chosen to go.
Next morning they left for Tapqaġruk.
They followed the young ice along the coast.

Now that same morning Niġliq went down to the ice to hunt seals.
Something had happened to his hand that morning,
the sinews in his hand had tightened and he suffered cramp there.
And he said to his wife:
"What's happened to this part of my body?"
And she answered, "Maybe you will get something this morning."
It was the same day Niġliq would be murdered.
Before he went out to hunt, he laid his hand on something, and the
hand tightened.
And his woman told him that she hoped he'd get something.

Niġliq left to go hunting.
Sukaŋaaluk and Tarruiyaaq approached, walking from Tikiġaq.
Niġliq saw them. The men didn't come straight to him.
They stopped by some old breathing holes,
and pretended to be waiting for seals to rise.
Niġliq saw they had approached from Tikiġaq
along the ice between his iglu and where he was hunting.
He knew they'd find him.
And he thought to himself, "They have come to kill me."

Now Niġliq started walking to his iglu,
and the two men started shooting.
They stood directly between Niġliq and his iglu.
Those two men were on his path: Tarruiyaaq and Sukaŋaaluk.
They shot arrows, and they went on shooting at him,
some went wide, not many, and they went on shooting.
They shot Niġliq full of arrows.
But he didn't want to fall there on the sea ice.
Niġliq said to himself, "It isn't a good sight,
the bones of animals and humans, drifted in together.
They don't look good together, mixed on the beaches." *

"It isn't a good sight, the bones of animals and humans . . .": Niġliq fears being butchered
like an animal. The line in his head derives from qalgi lore.

That was his thought. Niġliq tried to get to shore.
To the beach at Tapqaġruk.
He had to reach shore. He was full of arrows.
His mind told him to reach land before falling forward.
Niġliq reached land and fell forward.
But he didn't touch the ground because of all the arrows in his body.
Niġliq died there. At Tapqaġruk. *Tavra isua:* the story ends here.

.   .   .

Niġliq ("brant goose") is an umialik and leader of a group which includes his younger brother Kavisiġluk ("strange fish-scale"). Their sister, Siġvana, is married to Suuyuk, also an umialik and leader of another group of brothers. Each family constitutes a clan whose houses cluster in neighboring units. Before the story opens, one of Suuyuk's kinsmen has been killed in a quarrel with Niġliq over a whale. The two families, linked by Siġvana's marriage to Suuyuk, live opposite each other in iglus built into parallel beach ridges. The tension relaxes in the summer after whaling, when everyone leaves the village to travel north.

The following episodes contain some of Asatchaq's most powerful storytelling. The first scene is set on a beach under the jaggedly eroded Uivvaq peaks. It is early autumn, and Niġliq and his family are set to return to Tikiġaq for the winter. Suuyuk's arrival and Siġvana's silent reassertion of kin loyalty reactivate a tension diagrammed in high visual relief: Suuyuk and his brothers standing by their skinboat; Siġvana disappearing into the conical skin tent; Suuyuk calling up the long gravel beach; Niġliq quietly observing the scenario develop. Once Suuyuk follows the trajectory of his cry, the tensions that summer had dissipated converge, and we are presented with a tableau of violent interdomestic conflict. Niġliq's attack at once cuts this tableau and exacerbates the feud. Having activated his whale amulet in the sea, Suuyuk escapes around the perilous Uivvaq headland, presumably in reasonably calm waters. But he has failed with Siġvana.

The winter scenes in Tikiġaq combine ritual drama with minutely observed realism. While Siġvana suffers as an agent of the conflict, her importance to each side also moderates the violence. Many of the hostilities are thus a choreographed series of feints, each side demonstrating its power without moving beyond threat and submitting in turn to the same ritual menace. Likewise, when Niġliq is saved by a thin seal-skin headband, we assume that the arrows have been blunted, as they are in another major feuding story, and are thus intended to hurt but not to kill. Nonetheless, as Asatchaq said later, Niġliq attacks the old man who made the offending magic arrow, and this cowardly murder completes his isolation in the village.

Suuyuk's motive for changing sides in the shoot-out is unclear. Since a precarious, face-saving balance between the clans has been achieved, Suuyuk seems, in the interests of this equilibrium, to want to temper his brothers' rashness. The shooting episodes are thus perhaps extensions of the shielding scenes in the iglu: each party is satisfied so long as it can demonstrate its power. As in the story of Qaunnaiḷaq, where the joking partners dangerously upset the terms of their friendship with the hero, Kavisiġluk breaks the boundaries of decorum. An all-out feud has so far been avoided, but Kavisiġluk's arrow spells disaster for both families. Suuyuk falls; Siġvana is widowed; Kavisiġluk escapes to the Noatak River, where his fatal compulsiveness undoes him.

Wherever they live thereafter, both brothers are ostracized, and in the final scene at Tapqaġruk, Niġliq's hand cramp completes the story's pattern of decreasing space. From the expansive, open-air hunting world of the beginning, Niġliq is squeezed into ever-tighter positions: first from qalgi to iglu, then to half an iglu; at last, as he lives in virtual exile on Tapqaġruk's sand spit, his own hand contracts on itself (a detail echoing his brother's bowstring trouble). From his socially successful career as umialik and leader of a clan, Niġliq has brought himself to total isolation. As Niġliq's killers move in, even his wife is permitted a detached, unintentionally ironic comment: "Maybe you will get something this morning!" Niġliq's death is a double humiliation. First he suffers the shame of his terror, expressed in a quotation from qalgi lore, of losing human identity by dying alone among the animals. Second, having survived this danger, he dies pierced by arrows, his body propped above the beach on their shafts. A violent life ends nowhere, suspended.

PANIUNAYUK AND AQSAQAURAQ: A FEUD AVERTED

While the saga of Niġliq and Suuyuk shows how interfamily quarreling can **15** *lead to murder, "Paniunayuk and Aqsaqauraq" demonstrates how people can transcend violence. The two main characters are young men tangled in sexual rivalry. As their quarrel climaxes, a convergence of magic and intelligent goodwill conspire to avert bloodshed. For all its lively material detail—its inside-out boots, knives, meat, and iglu furniture—this story of non shamans suggests how thoroughly the supernatural suffused people's lives and helped to explain each lucky survival amid constant danger.*

I'll tell another story. Niġliq is gone. This man's name is Paniunayuk. (I am adding this one to extend the story I've just told.) This man could not be hit by arrows. Paniunayuk was good at everything.

Farther up the Kuukpak River was another man. His name was Aqsaqauraq.

And Aqsaqauraq's wife left the river to go to Tikiġaq. She was going to get some whale meat and blubber from Tikiġaq. Aqsaqauraq's wife. She left for Tikiġaq.

(She wouldn't have had many dogs . . . two or three dogs; she walked in front of them.)

And as she went home to Kuukpak she stopped at Itivliaġruk to see her lover, who was Paniunayuk. And she stayed there with Paniu-nayuk.

Soon he started telling her, "Go home to Kuukpak." But she didn't want to. All through her stay, Paniunayuk tried to talk her into going back to her husband at Kuukpak. No, she wouldn't go home.

Now Aqsaqauraq was getting angry. Aqsaqauraq was at Kuukpak all this time, and now he decided to go to Itivliaġruk and visit his wife's lover. He left his place and went to Itivliaġruk. Now just before he was going to climb the riverbank at Itivliaġruk he sat down and turned his boots inside out, so they wouldn't make a noise, so he could walk silently.

He crept toward Paniunayuk's iglu. When he reached the place, he called to his wife. And Paniunayuk said to the woman, "Listen! Your husband has come for you." The voice had come through the skylight. Aqsaqauraq took his bow and fitted an arrow to it. He aimed down through the skylight and shot at Paniunayuk, who was lying inside.

But Paniunayuk was wearing a breastplate. The attacker aimed at his chest, but he just hit the armor. When he was hit, Paniunayuk jumped into the little entrance passage. The arrow had little to do with it; he simply jumped into the passage.

Now Aqsaqauraq's uncle was in Paniunayuk's iglu at the time. When Aqsaqauraq shot at Paniunayuk, his uncle went out and saw Aqsaqauraq running away in the direction he'd come from. As he ran he looked like he was slipping. His uncle chased him, closed on him, and grabbed him from the back. After he'd taken hold of his back, he called out: "Paniunayuk!" he shouted. "Paniunayuk! Come and get even with him." After he had caught his nephew, he called to Paniunayuk to get even with him. But Paniunayuk didn't come. When Paniunayuk didn't appear, he let go of his nephew.

Now when Paniunayuk was hit, the woman changed her mind and went back to her husband at Kuukpak. Aqsaqauraq got his wife back. After he had shot his wife's lover, he didn't go and see how he was. (That's how it was in those days.)

But after he had done this, Aqsaqauraq lived in fear. He and his wife stayed at Kuukpak for some time, and then they decided to go to Tikiġaq. He was living in fear.

Now Aqsaqauraq was a good hunter. He caught caribou in the winter, and during summer also, and brought back choice caribou meat. He used to travel with his wife.

Now Paniunayuk wanted to get back at Aqsaqauraq, but he couldn't manage it. The entrance to Aqsaqauraq's iglu was blocked with a large piece of slate. No one could come up through the katak from the passage, for the rock was held in place by a pole fixed against the ceiling of the iglu. This was how Aqsaqauraq protected himself. That's how Aqsaqauraq did it. There was no way Paniunayuk could get even with Aqsaqauraq.

Paniunayuk wanted to get even, but he couldn't get through his enemy's katak. It was always blocked with a slab of rock. And it could not be moved on account of the wood pinning it down.

Now he tried to get in again while Aqsaqauraq and his wife were sleeping, and he sang a song to make them sleep more deeply. When he had finished the song he started to work on the rock over the katak. He shifted it a little: and now he was able to take the pole down with his arm, and pull it down into the entrance passage.

Paniunayuk entered the iglu. Aqsaqauraq was sleeping deeply. Paniunayuk got his knife out. He aimed at Aqsaqauraq: but before it reached Aqsaqauraq's body his arm stopped in midair. The knife would go no farther. The knife went halfway down, but no farther toward Aqsaqauraq. Paniunayuk couldn't kill him.

After he had tried using his knife and found it didn't work, Paniunayuk took Aqsaqauraq by the hair—Aqsaqauraq was still lying there—and he beat his head on the floor. And when he had done that, he shouted, "*Yai!* once you tried to kill me, but now you're just sleeping!" Aqsaqauraq got up. How had Paniunayuk gotten into the iglu? He sat down opposite him. And Paniunayuk sat down at the west side. Paniunayuk sat on the inland side.

Not a sound was made. Neither man spoke. Paniunayuk was good at everything: but this time he'd failed to do what he wanted.

For a time they sat there; and Aqsaqauraq said finally, "Listen: after the dogs fight, they eat together!"

And he told his woman to fetch meat, and she went out of the iglu. Aqsaqauraq's woman went out to the meat rack, and when she returned she had a pack full of caribou meat with her. She brought the meat in. It was wrapped up in caribou skin. She cut the lashing and opened it. (The choice parts of the caribou were always kept in the skin. This *iḡmaḡun* [packet of meat] contained the best parts of the caribou.)

Aqsaqauraq's wife put meat between them and said, "Go ahead, eat! After the dogs fight, they eat together!" She called them dogs: that's what she called them. So they ate together. And they told Paniunayuk to take the rest of the meat home with him.

And Aqsaqauraq said to Paniunayuk, "If I live until the summer, you will have another pack of caribou meat when I've come back from hunting. I wouldn't be alive now if you were like other people."

Paniunayuk got his knife out, but he had no stomach to kill Aqsaqauraq. When Aqsaqauraq's mother had carried him on her back, she had put her index finger in her standing excrement and placed it on his tongue. Because his mother had done this to Aqsaqauraq, Paniunayuk had no stomach for him.

. . .

Asatchaq came to the end of "Niġliq and Suuyuk" and at once launched into this tale. Both stories are narratives of conflict; but unlike Niġliq's saga, this one ends in high good humor, with the quarrel transcended and a feud averted.

The problem at issue in this tale is less marital infidelity as such than an imbalance between the parties. If Paniunayuk had been married, the two couples might have exchanged spouses equitably as *aipaġiik,* "exchange partners." As it is, the two men are *aŋutauqan,* "cohusbands or lovers of the same woman," a partnership they find difficult to handle. The tension implicit in this relationship is raised by the woman's long absence with her lover at Itivliaġuk.

A second uneasy imbalance follows. Obsessed with getting even after the attack in his river iglu, the skillful Paniunayuk is thwarted by Aqsaqauraq's magical invulnerability. Aqsaqauraq, with his aphorism from qalgi lore about the despised dog, provides the moment of self-consciousness on which reversal hinges. Violence gives way to silence and then communality. And whereas Paniunayuk—because of his enemy's excrement-tinged flesh—"had no stomach for [killing] Aqsaqauraq," they now seal their friendship with a feast of choice dried caribou and pledge themselves to a trading partnership.

UTUAĠAALUK: A MURDER MYSTERY

The solitary boys of all the previous iḷiappaq tales became legendary shamans. By
contrast, the orphaned and defenseless young Utuaġaaluk is presented simply as
a victim. Beaten routinely by his sister's husband, Utuaġaaluk awaits his moment
of revenge. But as in most Tikiġaq stories of conflict, the gratification of
achieving balance through violence is countered inevitably by reciprocal violence.
The process of renewed revenge is thwarted in this story when the victim's kin
misidentify their enemy. The comic and grotesque discovery of the brother-
in-law's corpse on the tundra leads to a suspenseful unfolding that implicates the
wrong men. The two accused men contrive a situation in which the guilty
Utuaġaaluk is forced to confess but is then tacitly acquitted.

16

This is what they say about Utuaġaaluk; he was raised by his older
sister. His name was Utuaġaaluk. Utuaġaaluk's older sister had a husband
who beat her. And when the man beat his wife, he always included
Utuaġaaluk in the beating. That's how the boy was raised: whenever
his older sister was beaten, he too was beaten.

Now the man who always beat his wife went inland to hunt caribou
one summer. Utuaġaaluk went with him. Utuaġaaluk traveled with
his sister and her husband. They went hunting caribou. And Utuaġaaluk
carried a bow and arrows.

And while they were out there, Utuaġaaluk killed his *niŋau* [sister's
husband] because he could not forget how he had been treated. He
killed him at Iŋaluurat, at the bottom of the hill. And that's where he
buried him: he dug a grave and covered it with tussocks. Utuaġaaluk
left the grave so that no one would see the ground had been moved and
then patched together.

And there were two brothers walking back to Tikiġaq; they had been caribou hunting near the place where Utuaġaaluk and his sister had been camping. They'd come from another direction, but now the two brothers were on the same path as Utuaġaaluk after he had killed his niŋau. The two brothers were traveling back to Tikiġaq.

Now Utuaġaaluk and his sister are already in Tikiġaq. And the news they bring is that Utuaġaaluk's niŋau had simply vanished: he'd been out hunting and never returned to camp where they'd waited for him.

Now after Utuaġaaluk and his sister had left Iŋaluurat, the two brothers who were traveling reached the place where Utuaġaaluk had committed the murder. The brothers stopped there.

Both of them were carrying meat and hunting gear on their backs. And the younger brother walked off to one side to defecate when he couldn't hold out any longer. But after he had defecated he couldn't find soft grass to wipe himself with, so he shuffled to the side until he found some, and he pulled up the grass to wipe himself.

As he wiped, he caught sight of some toes, a man's toes sticking through the ground ahead of him. When he had finished wiping, he dug in the earth and found a body. Then he dug up the corpse; underneath it he discovered an arrow.

(It was the custom for a man to leave an arrow with his victim: the arrow that he'd used for the killing.)

Now these two brothers had caught a lot of caribou. They were packing home the meat. And when the one who had found the arrow looked at it closely, he recognized the owner's mark.

It was Utuaġaaluk's. And that brother knew that Utuaġaaluk had often been beaten by his niŋau, when he beat his wife. He knew this was Utuaġaaluk's arrow.

The two brothers kept the arrow. They carried it with them as they walked home toward Tikiġaq. It was the younger brother who had found it, and he carried the arrow. They crossed from inland to the beach at Isuk: they came to Isuk on the south shore where the cliffs start, carrying their meat and their equipment.

Now as they walked along the south shore toward Tikiġaq, they were met by someone coming from the village who told them they had been blamed for the death of Utuaġaaluk's niŋau; for they, the two brothers, were the only men who'd been out in the same area. Utuaġaaluk and his sister said this.

Utuaġaaluk had not been blamed, for he'd said his niŋau had not returned from hunting. Utuaġaaluk and his sister made everyone believe this, and now the Tikiġaq people were waiting for the brothers.

And the brothers learned from the man who met them on the south shore that the relatives of the dead man were waiting for them, so they could kill them. People had met in the iglu of the dead man's relatives.

Now the two brothers are still walking, and that day they'll reach Tikiġaq, they'll be home in their iglu.

And when they reached Tikiġaq, before they reached their iglu the attack started. People started shooting. The two brothers barely made it into their iglu.

But while these brothers had been on the land, coming home, they had practiced their shooting. They used squirrel burrows as targets. They practiced shooting until both of them always got his arrow in the burrow. "That's how we'll shoot," they said, when they heard the Tikiġaq people were waiting for them.

Well, they made it to their iglu, but their iglu skylight was destroyed by people shooting arrows through it. Those Tikiġaq people wanted war with the brothers. But even though the men outside shot at them constantly, they wounded neither of the brothers.

Now when they grew tired of hiding from attack, the two brothers told their wives to make some *akutuq* [caribou fat creamed with whale oil and dried meat or berries]. They decided they would go to the qalgi even though the people were pursuing them. All the Tikiġaq people seemed to be against the two brothers because of the man who had died out hunting that summer.

So the brothers called out from their iglu and told the people they could do what they wanted with them: but first they should eat together some of what they'd brought from inland. (They could not keep their iglu skylight in one piece, but somehow neither had been hit by an arrow.) The two brothers tried to persuade the people not to hurt them immediately.

And they called out, "We have something to show you. We will bring what we want to show you to the qalgi, and we'll bring some food also." So the brothers went out to the qalgi, and their wives brought akutuq in a large container. They had set up a delaying tactic. And the arrow they had found was laid across the top of the container.

When all the men were seated in the qalgi, the two brothers spoke. "We have this to show you, but you'd better eat some akutuq before you kill us," they said. Then they passed what they had to show around the qalgi: and it was the arrow they had found at Iŋaluurat. It passed from one man to the other.

Now Utuaġaaluk and his sister were also in the qalgi; Utuaġaaluk was sitting opposite the katak. He was seated some distance from the katak, but directly opposite. And the brothers who had found the arrow said, "We brought home this arrow so that we could find the owner. The akutuq comes with it. We are tired of hiding from your arrows."

They handed the arrow to the man sitting next to them, and said, "Do you recognize the owner's mark?" The man said, "This isn't my arrow. I don't recognize the mark." They passed the arrow round the qalgi; each man inspected it and handed it on. No one claimed the arrow.

Finally the arrow came to Utuaġaaluk, who was sitting opposite the katak. The arrow was handed to Utuaġaaluk, and Utuaġaaluk sat looking at it. It was his arrow and he recognized it. He said nothing.

And the brothers who had brought it with them said, "This arrow comes from a body we found buried up there, at Iŋaluurat. Now is the time to show the arrow."

Utuaġaaluk sat a long time with the arrow, looking at it without moving. Utuaġaaluk sat there without moving. Suddenly he sprang from where he sat, and in one leap crossed the qalgi and jumped straight through the katak. He'd been sitting opposite the katak. He did it in one leap and left the qalgi.

He went out. And the people who had blamed the brothers, and shot at them in their iglu, replaced the skylight they had destroyed. And they said, "We made a mistake in blaming you for the murder."

And the younger brother started to tell how it happened. "It was when I couldn't wait to shit at Iŋaluurat, and I couldn't find the kind of grass I wanted, so I shuffled to the side, and found the toes in front of me. I dug up the grave and there was the arrow under the body."

So the feud was over. The people replaced the brothers' skylight. The story ends here.

. . .

"This is what they say about Utuaġaaluk." Like most ancestor histories, "Utuaġaaluk" emerges from three or four generations of talk, and Asatchaq identifies himself simply as its latest vehicle. More clearly than most of the stories, this one exposes the starting point of conflict. Utuaġaaluk and his sister are orphaned and without kin: hence Utuaġaaluk's dependence on his sister's husband. While the husband exploits his dominance, the avengers, as usual in Iñupiaq strategy, await the moment of maximum opportunity.

Part of the story's suspense derives from the texture of its earthy local detail: the owner's mark on an arrow, toes, packs of dried caribou meat, defecation, squirrel holes, bowls of creamed fat, snatches of conversation. The geographical context of the story is also specific, moving from hunting grounds just twenty miles southeast of the village to the path of Utuaġaaluk's leap into the qalgi entrance hole.

The story sketches some interesting aspects of Tikiġaq character. Utuaġaaluk, a historical version of the legendary shamanic orphan, is here portrayed as low in status, marginal, and fugitive. By contrast, the socially attuned hunter brothers are cheerful, resilient, and inventive. Their translation of the feud into an improvised qalgi event is echoed in Utuaġaaluk's confession, which is likewise represented as a qalgi game (paŋiliktuaq, "long jump").

The brothers' proposition to the qalgi and Utuaġaaluk's guilty answer provide both climax and resolution to the story. Jumping from where he sat cross-legged, Utuaġaaluk must have covered ten feet or more. (Asatchaq used the verb nutik-, "to leap like an animal.") "After that he was safe. No one dared touch him," Asatchaq later commented.

There are two implications to Utuaġaaluk's mute confession. First, the qalgi agrees that the boy's grievance is now settled and that there should be no retribution from his victim's family. Second, since miraculous leaping often expressed shamanic prowess (see "Qipuġaluat-chiaq"), Utuaġaaluk's leap through the katak both sets him aside as a possible shaman and provides an escape from accumulated miseries.

TAИNAALUK: SOUL RESTORATION

Death, in Tikiġaq's view, was a two-stage process. After biological death, the
spirit (iḷitqusiq) stayed near the body for four or five days in a condition
called siññiktaq, "supernatural sleep." If a shaman or some other adept intervened
during this period, body and spirit could be reconciled and life renewed. During or
just after siññiktaq, the dead traveled east beyond the Kuukpak River "toward
daylight." Taŋnaaluk, a Tikiġaq hunter—and not a shaman—lived by himself at
Kuukpak, a settlement on the Kuukpak River. In this tale, a woman in
siññiktaq visits Taŋnaaluk, and with heroic sexual prowess, he unfreezes her body,
restores her to life, and—against her inclination—returns her to her husband.

17

I am going to tell a shorter uqaluktuaq. The name in the story is Taŋ-naaluk. This one is for Aniqsuayaaq, for Tom.

Taŋnaaluk was at Kuukpak, alone, by himself. He spent his time fishing. He lived at Kuukpak in the autumn when the ice was forming. Taŋnaaluk was a man. He lived at Kuukpak because he liked being alone.

And one day when he returned to his iglu from fishing, he saw that his skylight was lit up. Taŋnaaluk said to himself, "I must have a visitor. Someone must have come from Tikiġaq."

Taŋnaaluk was bringing home the fish he had caught in a seal-skin bag. He was carrying home frozen fish. Taŋnaaluk was sure he had a visitor, because his iglu skylight was lit up; he saw this as he approached it.

And when Taŋnaaluk entered his iglu, he found a woman there. She was sitting there covered with something.

And this was a dead woman. Not long before, Taŋnaaluk had learned that a woman in Tikiġaq was sick. Taŋnaaluk had heard about the woman.

This woman in the iglu was covered with something. A dead woman had come into the iglu.

And when Taŋnaaluk entered, he brought fish with him, so his visitor could eat *quaq* ("raw frozen fish").

Taŋnaaluk started to eat. And as he ate, he threw a fish to the woman. But when it hit her the fish bounced back at him, alive and writhing. Taŋnaaluk did this for some time, but the fish kept bouncing back to him alive.

Later in the evening Taŋnaaluk said to the woman, "Why are you covered up? It doesn't look good." So he grabbed the skin she was wrapped in and threw it out into the entrance passage.*

But every time he threw the skin into the passage, it returned to the house and landed where it had been before. Taŋnaaluk went on trying to throw away the skin, but it always came back to him in the iglu.

Then Taŋnaaluk said, "You're my only visitor, and you can't even speak to me!" That is what he said.

They spent the evening together. And Taŋnaaluk tried to find out what was happening at Tikiġaq: but she didn't reply to his questions. When it was late Taŋnaaluk said to her, "Since you're not doing anything, we will go to bed."

It was then that Taŋnaaluk found the woman was frozen. So he said, "Come to bed with me." And he took her to bed and undressed her.

(It was said in the past that when a person dies they use a certain path [from Tikiġaq] to go upriver. They used to say that the dead all take the same trail toward Kuukpak. They go straight through Kanigaluk. They don't go around it. This dead woman had taken that trail and passed the place where Taŋnaaluk was living.)

Taŋnaaluk went to bed with the woman, but she was frozen stiff. And at first when he lay down with her Taŋnaaluk found her very cold; in fact, her body was frozen. So he started thawing her. (Some of the stories are like this, but I won't leave anything out.)

Taŋnaaluk knew this was a woman, so he got on top of her. All night he made love to her. He pulled out his penis when it started freezing inside her. But he continued all night.

Finally Taŋnaaluk thawed the woman out, and when she had warmed up he saw that she could move her joints. But the woman still wasn't breathing. When she was completely thawed, and no longer stiff, her corpse came alive.

The woman came alive, and at last she spoke to Taŋnaaluk. "Come back to Tikiġaq with me!" she said. But Taŋnaaluk refused: he didn't want to go to Tikiġaq.

"We can get there fast," she said, "by the path I came on. When we

"he grabbed the skin she was wrapped in": This is the woman's caribou-skin grave wrap.

get to Tikiġaq, we'll live together, because you brought me to life again. I won't go back to my husband."

The woman wanted Taŋnaaluk for her husband. "*Naami!* No!" Taŋnaaluk didn't want to leave Kuukpak. The woman tried talking him into it because he had restored her to life. But Taŋnaaluk just went to bed and to sleep.

Taŋnaaluk slept. And while he was asleep, he started to feel cold, and he woke up. He found he was in the entrance passage. The woman had swept him out into the passage as she was leaving the iglu.

That's why Taŋnaaluk didn't get a wife for himself. It was his own fault; he refused to take that woman when she passed through Kuukpak. He could certainly have had that woman.

When Taŋnaaluk woke up he was sorry, but the woman had gone already. A corpse had traveled through his iglu, while he was living at Kuukpak.

When Taŋnaaluk went to Tikiġaq, he told the woman's husband what had happened, and the man was sorry. "If you had agreed to have her as your wife, she would be alive now," he said to Taŋnaaluk. Instead, she passed on because he had refused her. The story ends here.

.   .   .

Some Tikiġaq people were based year-round on the Kuukpak River; others spent the fall and early winter there, fishing through the ice and taking caribou and the smaller fur-bearing mammals. Removed from the intensity of Tikiġaq itself, river life was a haven for old people and solitaries. But there was no such thing as complete self-sufficiency in even the most isolated of Tikiġaq's settlements, and Kuukpak residents relied on contact with other Tikiġaq groups for supplies and company. Folklore apart (an analogue of the fish episode crops up in Grimm's folktales number four, "The Boy Who Left Home to Learn What Fear Was"), Taŋnaaluk's character is ambiguous and intriguing. Although he was not a shaman, his resuscitation of the woman's corpse expresses the fakiristic element in Tikiġaq spiritual athletics.

Ququk (born circa 1875) told the following variant, which reveals the blurring of the soul elements *iñuusiq* and *iḷitqusiq* after the introduction of Christianity:

When a person dies his *iñuusiq* [spirit] "goes somewhere." There is a story told in the qalgis: In Uyaġaaluk's house there was a sick woman. One day when a man was returning from caribou hunting, he saw her walking out along the north side of the lagoon [Tasiq]. She tried to get away from him but he pushed her back. People watching saw only the man pushing something. Finally he pushed her or it up to the house and down into the skylight, which was steaming. He looked in and saw people crying and the dead woman's body. He went in and pushed her over toward the body. Suddenly she came alive again. Later she wanted him to be her husband because he brought her back to life. He was no aŋatkuq. [Qukuq] thinks he pushed back her iḷitqusiq [soul or spirit].

(Rainey 1940–41)

SEA-ICE STRANDINGS: TWO STORIES

Tikiġaq people, often victims of the sea, were always scholars, and lore about the **18**
ice and didactic survival stories could fill a separate volume. Young hunters
learned ice lore both from elders in the field and from anecdotes and stories, many of
them couched in the harsh tone of alġaġuun *("warning"), as though youth were*
being preemptively scolded for not knowing better. Nevertheless, correct
procedure on the sea ice had its rewards, and the first of these texts evokes a
hunter's survival through sheer stamina and ingenuity. In the second story, a
young man who abuses old people is punished when the elders use their
supernatural power to make the ice drift away while he is hunting seals.

NUYAGRUAQ: THE RESOURCEFUL HUNTER

Now I'll tell an ancestor story. Nuyagruaq was the name. He was a
man. He lived here in Tikiġaq. And he drifted out on the ice. That
Nuyagruaq . . . All winter he was stranded on the sea ice and couldn't
reach land.

And as Nuyagruaq walked on the pack ice, he came to a pressure
ridge which was hollow and had two sloping sides which met at the
top. And there was an entrance to the hollow. The inside of the pressure
ridge was hollow. Nuyagruaq stayed the night in there and slept.

And after he had been there a while, Nuyagruaq heard the sound of
feet approaching, the sound of something on the thin snow of the pack
ice. Nuyagruaq was still in the hollow. The noise came closer; it climbed
to the top of the ridge where Nuyagruaq was sheltering; he could hear
it moving around.

After it had been up there for a while, it said, "*Yiia!* My *niulu* is
broken!" * After it had said that, it walked away. Nuyagruaq came out

---

"My *niulu* is broken": *Niulu,* "twisted tooth" (the canine?), is almost always shamanic in
connotation. In a protoshaman story analogous to "Ukuṇniq," a wandering shaman

of his shelter: he wanted to see what had been up there. He saw a polar bear retreating. A large polar bear. And in the place where he had heard talking, he found a tooth. A polar bear tooth. Somehow it had broken. The polar bear had been talking about its tooth. It had known there was someone in the pressure ridge, but it had left him alone.

All winter Nuyagruaq was stranded on the sea ice. When spring came, pools of meltwater formed on the ice. That Nuyagruaq . . . He had nothing to chew on by this time: not even a piece of line or sinew.

And when spring came, and pools of meltwater lay on the surface of the ice, all he had left was a *nuġlu* [a buckle of bone or ivory]. He had eaten his harpoon line; there was nothing else he could eat. So he put the nuġlu in his mouth, and since it couldn't be chewed, he swallowed it.

It was many days before he could shit it out. And when it came out, he washed it in meltwater and swallowed it again. It was many days before it came out in his shit again. (I don't know how many times he swallowed that nuġlu.) He swallowed the nuġlu so as to have something in his stomach. (I think it was the bone that kept him alive.) And he reached land.

All he'd had to eat was the nuġlu. When he shat it, he washed it and swallowed it again. Nuyagruaq was that kind of man.

THE MALICIOUS YOUTH

Here in Tikiġaq lived a man who lacked nothing. He didn't have a wife. But he had every material thing he needed: stores of meat, caribou skins for parkas, and also finished clothing such as parkas and caribou-skin trousers. He had sets of clothes for both men and women.

One evening when this man had nothing else to do, he invited two old men to eat in his iglu. He had no one to help him; he didn't have a wife to cook for him. And after he had fed the old men, he said, "You two, play games." He told them to play games. So the two of them played.

Now when one of them lost, the young man tried to make the loser angry. He told him to do all he could to beat the other man in the next round.

So the two old men played for a time: this is what they'd been told to

---

transforms into a polar bear. When he returns to Tikiġaq, his son walks out on the ice and is destroyed by a circle of niulus that have been placed so as to fall inward on him.

do. And the second time around, the man who won the first game lost. Then the winner of the second game tried getting the loser angry to get even with him. And when he did this, the iglu owner, who was watching, sided with the winner to get the loser more and more angry.

Now when this happened, the man who had lost flew into a rage, and when his blood was up, the host started goading the winner to do something: to get hold of the other and fight him. So fight each other they did; tearing each other's clothes off, they fought to win, while their host sat and laughed at them . . . That young man.

Only when they were done fighting and had torn off all their clothes, he gave them each a new set to put on before they left. That young man was like that.

And some time later, when he was finished with the old men, he invited two old women to his iglu. He gave them food, made them eat, and then he told them to start playing games.

It was as before: when one of the old women lost, the young man started making the loser angry. And she did get angry: she didn't like losing and so she started fighting. As they fought, the women tore each other's clothes off, and pulled out each other's hair; white hair lay all over the floor. When they could fight no more, they stopped. They got too tired to go on. When they were done, they had hardly any clothes left. Then the young man gave them clothes which were ready to wear: parkas, trousers, boots—all new. That was how the young man behaved.

All winter he made them take turns playing games. He liked watching them.

Now one day that winter when the weather was fair, the young man went out onto the sea ice to hunt. The ice was thin. And when he had finished hunting and it was time to return, he started back to Tikiġaq. He could see land as he walked. But the ice was thin. And just as he put one foot down, the ice cracked off in front of him, and he floated out to sea.

So the young man was stranded. He drifted on the sea all winter. When the weather was good, he thought he might reach land. But every time he put out his foot to step onto safe ice, the ice cracked off again, and he drifted out farther.

This continued all winter. There was no way the young man could get to shore. Finally, summer came, and he had to keep traveling from one ice floe to another. He did everything possible to move onto the largest ice floes. But as the ice melted round him, all he could get firmly underfoot was a small piece of ice.

(That man was like that . . . which is why old people always told the young not to harm the old or make fun of them; they told the story of this young man as an example.)

Finally when he could feel nothing under him, he was up to his waist in water, and the ice seemed to hang from his feet. He could do nothing at all, so he let the current just carry him along. Occasionally he saw floating driftwood. The ice was hanging from his feet and wouldn't melt, and he was up to his waist in water. But now, suddenly, in front of him he saw the trunk of a tree on the surface, and he was being carried toward it.

When he got close enough to the trunk, he saw there was a hole in it above water level, just big enough to crawl into. So he grabbed the tree and climbed into the hole.

All summer he stayed there. Finally the sea started freezing in the autumn. And from where he was, he could watch the seals, but he had no weapon to get one with. When he had started to drift he had left his gear behind, in his hurry.

This is how he suffered; and it was because of what he had done to the old people. He suffered greatly. And it wasn't the young man's fault that he couldn't get to shore: the old men and women in Tikiġaq saw to it that he stayed out there. It was the old people who made him suffer.

And as he drifted along in that tree trunk, he finally caught something. He knew how to hunt. He knew very well how animals could be taken. But while he was at sea, he never saw anything that came from land: for he was living at sea.

Now he decided to leave the tree trunk he was living on; but before he left it, he checked the wind direction. He didn't leave his driftwood shelter until he was sure he would reach land. And since he had no one to tell his plans to, he made plans on his own.

So he left the tree trunk, he made it to shore, and returned to Tikiġaq. And when he reached Tikiġaq, he gathered the people; he called the men to him and told them what had happened. He told them about himself: he used himself as an example.

He told the men they should never behave as he had. When he was young he had been cruel to old people. He had made old men and women fight each other. And he in turn had suffered much at sea because of what he had done to them. He told the men they should never do what he had done. Maybe it ends here.

.　　.　　.

As these and other survival stories illustrate, the Tikiġaġmiut's expe-
riences with travel on sea ice led to interpretations of its movements
that combined the pragmatic and the mystical. The details of ice
topography in Nuyagruaq's story hint at the conditions hunters had to
comprehend and negotiate. But such knowledge was seldom at variance
with a supernatural element, and there is thus no discord between
Nuyagruaq's methodical tactics and his encounter with the speaking
bear. On the contrary, psychic sensitivity was regarded as an asset that
paralleled and supplemented practical skill.

Although Nuyagruaq's experience with the bear is incidental to the
central matter of his survival, this same apparently tangential detail
suggests another truth. Certainly the hunter's supernatural or hal-
lucinatory perception takes him no nearer to safe ice and home. Rather,
the event tells us something different. Isolated miles out on drifting
floes, Nuyagruaq has entered a separate world with nothing between
him and the phenomena that surround him. The bear wanders in; it
grumbles; it moves on. It is the hunter, still a socialized and thinking
being, who overhears the complaint; it is not the bear who communicates
it to him. Issues of identification with ancient shamans whom animals
addressed and the shamanic experience of those who saw or heard an
animal's iñua are left to our imagination. Nuyagruaq returns to the
work of survival, and the rest of the story is severe and didactic. "If
that man could survive by swallowing a buckle, make sure you follow
his example!" is the unspoken implication.

The second story, also an alġaġuun, links survival on the ice to the
conduct of life in general. While the fate of the hunter in the first tale is
presented as simple bad luck, the young man in the second is punished
for his cruelty and folly. Part of this folly lies in a naïve disregard for
the consequences of antisocial behavior. However decrepit the old
might have appeared, all elders were believed to have shamanic power.
A number of stories describe the revenge old people could take for the
most insignificant offenses. Thus, if only for his self-protection, the
rich young hunter should have known better. But then the young man
is clearly an eccentric, and his story describes reversals of convention.
Even before he embarks on his sadistic entertainment, the audience
knows that something is amiss. Conventionally, a rich and skillful
hunter became an umialik and, with his wife, distributed surplus
property to his skinboat crew and village paupers. But this man is

alone; he abjures the whale hunt; rather than support a family and his qalgi, he abuses his power to humiliate the very people to whom he should be paying a debt of gratitude.

The story contains other reversals. First, it was the young, not the old, who competed in Tikiġaq's strenuous and often violent games. Second, it was the elders who monitored young people's conduct. The old were revered and well looked after; geronticide was seldom if ever practiced in Tikiġaq. There is a third, psychologically subtle ambiguity in that the elders initially collude with their tormentor only to reveal their latent power by contriving his accident. In the end we are led to acknowledge both the young man's hunting skill and his capacity to change.

Once he has transcended his ordeal and can cite his folly as a warning, he emerges as a model Tikiġaġmiu. But while sea-hunting accidents were often thus attributed to moral lapses or to vengeful shamans, Tikiġaq people knew well enough that the ice could kill without supernatural intervention.

IV.   THE LAST TIKIĠAQ SHAMANS

ASATCHAQ: THE LAST GREAT TIKIĠAQ SHAMAN

This story centers on Asatchaq, a shaman active in the late 1870s and 1880s. The tale is of particular interest when we compare it to that of Ataŋauraq (see story 22). Asatchaq was Ataŋauraq's slightly older contemporary, and the events in both texts took place during the above period, by which time Euro-American culture had penetrated Tikiĝaq life. But while Ataŋauraq's world is filled with artifacts from nineteenth-century North America, Asatchaq's story is bare of contact reference. Instead, Asatchaq inhabits a timeless realm of voyages, of shamanic gestes and confrontations that echo the picaresque supernaturalism of hero sagas such as "Ukuŋniq." The younger Asatchaq (born 1891), who told most of the stories in this collection, was named after the shaman; part of Asatchaq's own account of his great-uncle's history appears in the commentary.

19

ASATCHAQ IN TIKIĠAQ

Asatchaq warned my parents against teaching me to become a shaman. Asatchaq was a great shaman, and for this reason he was blamed for many things that happened. For example, if a man was not getting on with Asatchaq and his wife died, then Asatchaq was blamed; that was why he warned me not to become a shaman.

I saw Asatchaq performing: sometimes this was just for show. Once he took a woman's murre-skin parka. In those days the women very much liked murre-skin parkas for their warmth. Asatchaq laid his drum on the floor, and walked around it several times holding the parka, and singing. I didn't understand the song. Then he held the parka by the hood over the drum—somebody else sat drumming and singing—and a murre's egg fell onto the drum without breaking; then Asatchaq carried the egg round the qalgi on the drum, showed it to everyone, and swallowed it.*

"a murre's egg fell onto the drum": Murre's eggs are large, sky-blue, and splashed with black markings.

Asatchaq had a *kikituk*. Asatchaq kept his kikituk on the drying rack above the oil lamp in his iglu. This is where he kept it. When he intends using his kikituk he has somebody to sing and drum for him. He goes around in a circle and rubs his belly. His belly swells, he turns down his pants and kneels facing the audience as though he were having a baby, the old way. He puts his hand between his legs, and holds it up: there is blood there. Now he calls for a new fawn-skin parka, and somebody brings it; then he just shows the head of the kikituk sticking out of the fawn-skin parka sleeve. He always works with someone in the group who is ill when he performs with the kikituk: he has the kikituk bite the place that is sick and it heals. When he's finished with the kikituk he eats it.

This is how Asatchaq gets himself ready to fly. He takes off his parka and skin pants. He takes off one reindeer sock and ties it round his middle. Next he's tied up with *ugruk* [bearded seal] line. He puts boy's skin pants around his shoulders. Then the people lay him on the floor and extinguish the lamps. After a few moments they hear something flapping round in the qalgi. Then everything goes silent: he seems to be out. He is out for quite a long time. Before they hear the flapping they hear a bang. When the lamps come on again there is Asatchaq still tied, but now he had those little pants on his arms, even though he was still bound. His hands are tied behind his back and his neck bound to his knees with a sealskin line: always ugruk around his neck, but ugruk or seal around the wrists.

ASATCHAQ'S TRAVELS

Twice before the birth of Aġviqsiiña Asatchaq went down to Qikiqta-ġruk [Kotzebue] with his family for trading. He went a third time when Aġviqsiiña was a little boy. Many people used to come together to trade at Kotzebue, from Diomede Island and the Kobuk River every spring.

The third time he went to trade, Asatchaq didn't return. He was taken to Little Diomede Island [Imaġliq] by a one-eyed man who was able to lift two stones in one hand in the qalgi. Twice he took Asatchaq down to Little Diomede.

The second time he was on Diomede, a man called Uŋariuk went to St. Lawrence Island to trade some caribou skins and stayed there a long time. The young man had once killed a St. Lawrence Islander, so his father was worried about him. He gathered all the Diomede shamans and asked them to find out whether his son was living or had been killed.

All the shamans gathered in the qalgi. The first shaman took a bead and walked round and round the entrance hole.* Then he hung up the drum, put the end of a parka over his head, held it out in front of him, and looked out through the face hole at the far end "to see where the bead was going."

"The bead's going to St. Lawrence Island," he said. The bead arrived at St. Lawrence, circled one tent, then a second, and finally all the tents. Then the shaman said the bead was returning: "I see it coming! It's here!" The shaman took the parka off his head and tried to catch the bead; no one could see it, only he. The shaman caught the bead, took his drum, laid the drum on the floor, and shook the bead onto the drum from his parka. Holding the bead in his hand, he walked round the qalgi lamp, moving his hand in circles by his ear so the bead could tell him where it had been.

The bead told the shaman that the young man was dead. It had seen red spots, like blood, by those tents on St. Lawrence Island. When he heard this the father was very sad, and told the other shamans he'd had enough and went home.

Asatchaq was staying with the father—the village strongman—and the strongman asked Asatchaq's wife if Asatchaq could fly: he had heard that Tikiġaq shamans had done a lot of flying. Asatchaq's wife said, "Yes, my husband can fly." So the strongman asked Asatchaq if he could go to St. Lawrence and really find out whether his son was dead or alive. Asatchaq said yes, he could do that: but it must be at night, with everyone abed, not a single person running around. So they waited until everyone was abed. Asatchaq said they must all be inside; stray dogs had to be tied.

Now Asatchaq got his spirit to work, summoned his power by walking around his drum.* Then he was tied up as he was the day before, only this time he had just one reindeer sock tied around his middle in front.

Then they extinguished the lamps, and the people in the tent heard a noise like a duck flying, and they seemed to hear Asatchaq right in there, in the tent flying. (I've made a mistake: it is the next night at the

---

"The first shaman took a bead": Blue, white, and green glass beads made in Central and Eastern Europe started coming into Alaska via Siberia in the seventeenth century. They were used as personal ornaments, amulets, and shamanistic objects.

"Asatchaq . . . summoned his power by walking around his drum": Sunwise circumambulation was a means of generating trance and power. For its mythological analogue, see "Aliŋnaq" (story 2).

qalgi that he does this. Asatchaq said he didn't see that the boy was in trouble; he thought he was all right.

A shaman away from home had to be careful not to show too much power or the local aŋatkuqs would get angry with him.)

After Asatchaq had finished, another shaman performed. This next man didn't have the lamps extinguished: he just walked round and round the lamp to get his power. The he *saw;* he told them that every time he looked at St. Lawrence Island it was red; this made him think that something had happened to the boy who had not come home.

Then the strongman said to Asatchaq, "Nephew, our shamans can't fly, but they have the power of seeing, and they see very clearly." *

Asatchaq was angry; the strongman seemed to be saying he was no good. So when they went home Asatchaq told his host that next night he would try again, and this time he really would fly away.

(To travel from Little Diomede to St. Lawrence Island you go on the ice, and they hunt there in the same way we do here in Tikiġaq.)

The next day some of the men who had been out hunting came into the qalgi as was their custom and said they had seen a dog on the other side of an open water lead; it looked just like the lost young man's dog. The father said, "That means he is dead." When night fell, they went to qalgi and all the stray dogs were again tethered.

And Asatchaq was angry that all the local shamans said one thing and he another. It was as though they thought he was lying.

Shamans who were going to do some genuine flying were always tied to some heavy object. Sometimes they were tied to one of those heavy stone clubs they use for seals or ugruks, but Asatchaq's line was tied to a heavy jade adze.

And on one side of the qalgi there was an old woman with a lamp all to herself because she was half blind.

Then Asatchaq called his spirit: he started to do this by singing, and others sang and drummed. And to fly, Asatchaq stretched one leg out behind, and wings grew under his armpits because his hands were tied behind him.

The lamps were all put out again. When the lamps were out Asatchaq was in such a hurry to fly that he started immediately; but when the old woman, who had put a stick down on her lamp wick to extinguish it, lifted the stick the light flared up again, and everybody could see Asatchaq, who had already left the ground and was flying. When the light came up again, Asatchaq dropped back.

"Nephew": Here, "nephew" is a term of friendship applied to a man from another village.

There was a big wooden dish over the entrance. And just as Asatchaq got to the skylight he felt something pull him back. This was the adze, which caught under the dish and lifted it up. This made a noise; they had tied all the dogs so there wouldn't be any noise, for shamans can't fly when there's noise. Asatchaq was too anxious to get out, that was why he had all this trouble.

But on the third attempt he got out through the ventilation hole, and flew once round the qalgi; then instead of heading for St. Lawrence Island, he started toward Siberia.

(I forgot to say that Asatchaq had two tattoos reaching upwards about one and one-half inches from the corners of his mouth and when he flew his mouth always grew to the extent of these lines.)

So now because the men said they'd seen a dog on the ice, Asatchaq flew toward Siberia to see how the ice was. But he found nothing till he approached the shore. Then he followed the shore and he came to some tents.

Now up from one of the tents flew a man with his hands bound just like Asatchaq's. This man was flying like Asatchaq, only he had both legs stretched out. Asatchaq had one leg bent in front of him. The two shamans flew toward each other as if they were going to meet. And Asatchaq saw the other man had tattoos, in the shape of hands, each side of his mouth, and he was holding something in his mouth.

And each time Asatchaq started to speak as he flew, his mouth stretched wide, and a flame emerged before each word. The other man was afraid, and flew off at full speed. Asatchaq had wanted to ask the other shaman if he had seen anyone from Diomede there. Several times Asatchaq tried to catch up with this man to ask his question, but the other man always flew away.

So for a while the two shamans circled the village, and then the Siberian flew down again to his tent, and Asatchaq was afraid he would do something to kill him, so he got up speed and flew down the coast until he came opposite St. Lawrence Island. Asatchaq cut inland, and when he came to a village he circled it and then he looked down the holes at the tent tops. And down one tent hole he saw Uŋariuk lying on the floor, and when he had recognized him Asatchaq put his face down to the tent hole so that the young man could see him; then he flew back to Diomede.

Meanwhile the strongman on Diomede had grown worried because he didn't know much about shaman flying, and he thought something must have happened to Asatchaq. He asked Asatchaq's wife how long he usually stayed away when he flew, and she said, "Sometimes he comes right back, but when he has farther to go, he's away longer."

When Asatchaq got back to Diomede he flew round the outside of the qalgi several times, and then came down in through the ventilator and tried to get to the floor: but he had such power in him that the first time he tried, he couldn't make it, so he flew several times round the room, and the breathing of all the people who didn't have any spirit helped him to come down.

For a long time after they kindled the lamps again Asatchaq was unconscious and the people in the qalgi sat him up, put his drum in one hand and the drumstick in the other, and gradually Asatchaq revived: first he made one beat and slowly more; then he started beating the drum faster, until he returned to consciousness.

When he had come to, but before he moved, Asatchaq said to the strongman, "Uncle, these shamans of yours have been fooling you all along. Only a while ago I saw your son lying on the ground in a tent, and I showed my face to him through the tent hole so that he could see me. I don't know whether or not he saw me, but you can expect him back after a few days of good weather; if he did see me, then he will tell you, and that will prove that I flew there, and that what I tell you now is the truth."

Next day was a fine day: no wind, a fine day. Toward evening, all the people came out and shouted, "Strangers!" as they do here for the plane, and there was a dog team coming from St. Lawrence Island. And it was that same young man, Uŋariuk. People didn't shake hands in those days, they just watched; and when he had tied up all his dogs, he went inside. While the young man ate, his father said, "Why did you make your uncle [i.e., Asatchaq] so worried?" and Uŋariuk said, "It's all my fault; it was I who first brought uncle here from Qikiqtaġruk, and now I've caused him trouble. But the weather was so bad I couldn't come sooner. But then last night I could not sleep; as I lay in my tent and looked up through the hole I had a vision; it was your face, in the hole."

ASATCHAQ'S THIRD TRIP TO DIOMEDE

Asatchaq stayed on Diomede for the rest of that winter and then came back to Tikiġaq for a few years.

When Asatchaq went to Diomede the third time, everyone there was talking about the great power he had. Up till then Asatchaq hadn't heard about a shaman on the Siberian side who was also said to be very powerful. Asatchaq wanted to take me with him on the third trip to Diomede to show me to people, because I am him; but my mother wouldn't let me go. I was about three and a half feet high then, eight or nine years old.

The third time Asatchaq traveled to Little Diomede, the strongman had been killed. Asatchaq [arrived in the autumn and] spent the winter there. Now two dog teams came from St. Lawrence Island with two Siberians; one was a shaman called Algaq ["Hand"] while the other could speak both the Diomede dialect and Siberian. This man acted as interpreter for the shaman.

Now Algaq and his companion came and visited the house where Asatchaq was staying, and that same evening someone came to the house complaining he had a sore back from having walked a long way with a pack. So Algaq made the man sit in front of him and take off his parka; then he put his hands on the back, and blew on the sore spot, which began to bleed. The shaman let it bleed for a time, then he licked the man's back, and the blood stopped flowing and it was well. That was how Algaq used his medicine on the man with a sore back.

After this Siberian shaman had arrived, the Diomede people warned Asatchaq that he was a bad man and would kill someone with his medicine any time he wanted. And the Siberian said through his interpreter that the reason he'd come was that he heard there was a strong shaman here and he wanted to compete with him.

So that evening, without drums or singers, Algaq started to perform; he just sat in the qalgi and taking his knife, cut round the base of his tongue, removed it from his mouth and held it up to the audience. Then he started eating it back, and ate all but the tip.

Then he threw the tip of his tongue through the door of the qalgi to the dogs, and you could hear them fighting for it.

Next, Algaq took hold of his eye and cut round it with his knife, and removing it from the socket, held it up; the people could see quite clearly that he had no eye in his head, and the blood was streaming down. Then he did the same thing as before: he started to eat it—all but the little round thing in the middle—which he also threw to the dogs; and you could hear them scrapping for it.

I forgot something: a draught was blowing in from the qalgi entrance, and Algaq waved the air toward him, opened his mouth wide, and his tongue came back.

Now Algaq asked Asatchaq to sit down close to him, and he made all the other people lie on the floor, and then extinguish the lamps. Now Algaq started to drum, and his spirit appeared and the spirit came up behind them and laid a hand on the shoulder of each. Asatchaq felt the hand cold as ice on his shoulder, and he tried to grab it, but quickly it went away. Then they lit the lamps. It was not Algaq but his spirit [tuungaq] which had touched them. Then Algaq said, "Now I want to see you perform."

So Asatchaq took his drum and jumped around in a circle to get his spirit, but made no other actions. He just wanted his helping spirit: no other action. He was clever that way. Then he sat down by Algaq.

Algaq put out all the lamps again and started moving around in a circle. Soon people heard that he had someone with him; sometimes they laughed and sometimes there came a shout of joy.* Then Asatchaq heard his wife calling to him, saying she was going to die; Asatchaq went to her and she was already unconscious.

So he dragged his wife outside and bit her crooked little finger, and pulled her hair hard to make her know, but she was still fainting, and Asatchaq's tears were falling already. At last she revived and said she felt better and that they should go back inside, because she was cold. They went back, but Asatchaq didn't sit with Algaq again; he sat with his wife.

Then Algaq boasted that he could kill anyone he wanted to, that he had greater power than Asatchaq, and that before the three Tikiġaq people got home, one of them would be dead. When he'd said this, the interpreter added that Algaq had in the same way killed many people in his Siberian village. He knew this because he had lived with him there, and if Asatchaq had anything to kill him with before someone else got killed, he had better use it. Then Algaq said through the interpreter, "Now you perform!"

Asatchaq stood up without turning the lamps out, and started to rub his left arm. He could kill a person like this immediately. He used to produce his kikituk through the armpit and out through his mouth, the hand opening and closing, and pointing it at someone, killed them. Now as he rubbed his arm he said to his wife, "I am going to kill that man over there." But she replied, "You'd better not; we are strangers here and someone might avenge him." So Asatchaq stopped rubbing his arm.

When a shaman rubbed his left arm, it was to kill someone at once; when he rubbed his right arm it was so that no hunters in the village would get any animals.*

Now Asatchaq started rubbing his belly, and it swelled up, and he

"sometimes they laughed": The cries are from the shaman and his helping spirit.
"no hunters . . . would get any animals": the practice of niġġutaili, intended to scare away game.

removed the kikituk [from his body] right opposite Algaq, and put down his hand, and his hand came up all bloody. Algaq was happy because he'd wanted to see Asatchaq perform.

Then Asatchaq put the kikituk in the sleeve of a new fawn-skin parka and he walked round the qalgi stopping at anyone who was ill, and made the kikituk gnash its teeth at the sick person, and that person was cured. Then he did this with the kikituk a little at Algaq, and said, "You'll want to travel tomorrow, if the weather's good. I'll go outside now and the kikituk will make sure the weather's good tomorrow." "Good!" said Algaq.

Now instead of going outside, Asatchaq got between the double tent skins, and came round until he was behind Algaq, and then he jabbed the kikituk back and forth several times into Algaq's back. And the kikituk's teeth came out red with blood, and then Asatchaq suddenly threw it at Algaq and came back into the tent saying, "The weather will be fine tomorrow."

Then Asatchaq began to pull on his socks. Shamans used to perform in short skin pants: no parka, no socks. Then he put on his *maklaks* [boots] and parka, and leaned over as though he were ill. Then he went outside, and everyone thought he had gone to shit or something, but he never came back that night.

The people waited a long time, but he didn't come to that [tent] so they went to bed. Asatchaq's wife and two children were staying with them. The children were adopted; one a boy, quite big, and the other was a little girl: she's still alive, and lives at Point Lay [Kali].

Asatchaq didn't sleep very well; he was keeping watch. In the morning Asatchaq's boy went to visit a widow who lived by herself in an iglu. He visited her every morning, but when he got there, he saw Algaq on the sleeping platform.

And Algaq told him [and the woman translated], "Tell your father to come over here; it is time to perform!" The boy stayed for a while before leaving; the woman followed him and in the entrance passage told him not to say anything to his father. So he went back and said nothing.

The same day, in the afternoon, they heard that Algaq was dead. But the people who knew him said that he had done this several times in his own village and that they expected him to revive in a few days. They buried him almost the same way they do here in Tikiġaq.

They took off Algaq's clothes, wrapped him in an umiaq [boat] skin, and carried him out. They didn't bury their dead in winter; they just laid them on the snow.

Asatchaq went along to see where they put him. In those days people believed that a man's soul stayed in the village four days, and if it was going to return, it would come on one of the first three days.

Now on the fourth day two men from the iglu where Algaq died did this: one man outside the house took a whale's shoulder blade and the other, inside, took a big stone hammer, and they knocked once on the outside wall of the iglu with the whalebone,* and then on the inside with the stone and then at each of the other corners, and then four times on the lower [sloping] edge of the skylight. After a woman's death they did this on the fifth day. This was to send the spirit of the dead where it should go.

Asatchaq left his kikituk in the dead man's body for about half a month, but then he was worried he wouldn't be able to get it back. He left the kikituk that long to be sure the man was dead. Then late one night while everyone was sleeping, he lay awake for a while, put on his clothes, got up, and went to the place where the body lay.

Now he started to walk round the body in the direction the daylight goes because the shaman's rule is that you should move the way the daylight goes; then he made a little noise to make the kikituk come out; at first he walked slowly, but then faster and faster, and at last the kikituk began to show itself: first at the mouth of the corpse—peeping out and then retreating—then at the base of the neck both sides, where there is no bone, then under the arms, and finally beneath the ribs. At last the kikituk came out and began to follow Asatchaq around, but it ran back into the corpse. The third time it appeared, Asatchaq caught it under his parka and swallowed it quickly.

So they sent the Siberian's dog team back, and almost everyone said they were glad to hear he was dead; and they also heard everyone in Algaq's village was glad, because Algaq had killed people whenever he'd wanted to.

So Asatchaq stayed on Diomede all winter, and during the winter another visitor came from Siberia and stayed with Asatchaq. And they had an interpreter so they could talk to each other. The Siberian said he had come because he wanted to see a Tikiġaq man: he had never seen one, and he said, "Whenever people travel they like to go home with stories to tell," and the Siberian said he would tell the Tikiġaq man a story which he could tell his people when he went home.

"they knocked once on the outside wall of the iglu": The narrator, born 1875, said, "I have seen this done many times." His son and interpreter, born 1903, commented, "I have never seen it."

"Asatchaq" was told by Aġviqsiiña (circa 1875–1945); I have edited his narrative from Froelich Rainey's 1940 field notes (Rainey 1940–41). Asatchaq, the main storyteller in this collection, recorded a shorter version of this history of his great-uncle and namesake, extracts from which are given below.

The older Asatchaq was Aġviqsiiña's spiritual guardian (*qumnaaluk*), as Aġviqsiiña himself explained to Rainey: "When I was born, Asatchaq came to me bringing a polar bear's nose. He always had with him a polar bear spirit, and spat in my mouth because he wanted me to be named after him. *Asatchaq* is the name I don't use—people usually have at least two names—and *Aġviqsiiña* was the name Asatchaq didn't use. He spat in my mouth so that *I would be him*, and also would inherit from him the spirit of the polar bear" * (Rainey 1940–41).

As this account indicates, the shaman perceived the storyteller to "be him"; likewise, Aġviqsiiña's father, Umigluk, was also a shaman. Thus Aġviqsiiña might have been expected to follow both of them into the profession. However, in the opening statement of the story itself Asatchaq suggests that he wanted his namesake to "be him" but without the aŋatkuq element. Many candidates, even in the traditional period, backed away from the stresses of the shamanic life. Standing at the threshold of the Christianized American era, the old man perhaps saw that new choices were possible. Like many of his contemporaries, he appears to discriminate between two strands of religious life. On the one hand is shamanic practice, which he advises his young namesake to abjure. On the other hand are the spiritual beliefs whose actuality he wishes to perpetuate in the transfer of his name and personality to Aġviqsiiña.

Asatchaq was Tikiġaq's last great kikituk adept. The kikituk, a shaman's familiar carved from ivory or wood in the shape of a fabulous ermine or weasel, functioned as a *tupitkaq,* a shaman's animal power-object. When not in use, the kikituk lay in the aŋatkuq's iglu "to keep it warm." Otherwise, it traveled under the shaman's parka or "inside his body," entering and leaving through the mouth or armpit when magically animated. The creature had the curative power of "biting" the spirit that was causing a client's illness. The kikituk was also

---

*Word, name, and identity were transferred in saliva. The shaman's names were Asatchaq/Aġviqsiiña, and the boy's were Aġviqsiiña/Asatchaq.

used in sorcery, being made to burrow into an enemy's body until it reached the heart.

Kikituk practice, on a minor scale, survived Tikiġaq's other major shamanistic institutions. In the late 1950s a kikituk was hidden in the house of a missionary by someone he had offended. By that time, kikituks were also made commercially and found their way into Native Alaskan crafts stores and museums. The storyteller Asatchaq carved the present writer (Lowenstein) a kikituk from gray whalebone. He explained how to use it and assured his non-Iñupiaq colleague that the creature would not turn on its owner.

The paragraph in Aġviqsiiña's text about shaman flight (*uilmaq*) makes no mention of spirit journeys to the moon (*tatqilaqtuq*). The younger Asatchaq gave me the following account of his namesake's moon flights:

> Getting power from his drum, Asatchaq used to travel to the moon. He did this from Uŋasiksikaaq qalgi. To prepare Asatchaq for flight, the men in the qalgi would tie him up, putting short skin pants around his neck and anchoring him with a stone ax [to ensure that his body did not follow his spirit]. One of his legs was tied up bent in front of him; the other he kept straight. This was the position in which he flew.
>
> When he reached the Moon Spirit's iglu, Asatchaq saw tiny caribou running in circles around the posts at each corner of the house. There are four posts in the house: on the north, south, east, and west sides. When people in Tikiġaq wanted caribou, they would ask the spirit for them. They would do this at new moon, and the Moon Spirit would let the little caribou fall to earth for people. But not all of them went directly to the hunters. The Moon Spirit would do the same with whales.
>
> While he was on the moon, the shaman saw a huge container full of small whales. When a woman umialik asked for a whale and held up her little pot with water in it, the Moon Spirit would choose a whale and drop it into the woman's pot. Some women held their pots right up to the moon, and these could be filled easily.

The younger Asatchaq also told me how his namesake met the Qikiq-taġruk shaman Ikiññiq on the moon. Ikiññiq appeared blindingly white, so Asatchaq was afraid of touching him. According to the storyteller Paul Green (Aġnik) of Tikiġaq and Qikiqtaġruk, Ikiññiq independently told the same story. (See story 3 for another nineteenth-century lunar experience.)

The overt rationale for binding the shaman during flight was to prevent his soul from taking his body with it, but the binding also implied birth and death symbolism. While the aŋatkuq was bound with sealskin rope to the iglu interior, his spirit was born into the outer world. Shamanic flight also involved a symbolic death: the shaman "died" into trance while the spirit flew from the body. Some shamans never woke from trance and died in fact as well as in ritual. The birth symbolism was reinforced by the suggestion of the seal-line umbilicus connecting the shaman to the inside of the iglu. The shamanic alternation of birth and death was also repeated in the two villagewide amulet groups, one of which was associated with birth goods, the other with grave goods. (For a discussion of the iglu as a symbol of the female and a locus for birth, see *Ancient Land: Sacred Whale* [Lowenstein 1993].)

The older Asatchaq's journey starts with a summer trading expedition to Qikiqtaġruk (Kotzebue) and Sisualik. There he meets the Imaġliq (Little Diomede) strongman and strikes up a partnership. The place of tobacco in this cross-continental adventure is of interest. In his 1976 version, Asatchaq describes the Diomede man going to St. Lawrence to barter fawn skins for tobacco. These skins he would have obtained at Sisualik, while the tobacco came from Siberia. The Diomede Islands and St. Lawrence were both entry points for tobacco, which had been introduced by the Cossacks to Siberian natives in the early eighteenth century and which was, by 1750, available to mainland Alaskans via native middlemen on the Bering Strait islands (Foote 1959–61). The Siberian natives who brought this potent leaf occasionally traveled as far as Sisualik, but usually they did their trade halfway across, safe from the hurly-burly of the interregional fair.

The Inuit used tobacco as an intoxicant, mixing it in small quantities with wood shavings or dried fungus; the mixture was smoked from pipes in a long, single inhalation until the smoker passed out. The Diomede man in Asatchaq's 1976 version of the story embarks on a sled trip of extraordinary risk over some of the worst sea ice in the Arctic: such was the intensity of the desire for tobacco.

SUUYUK THE ELDER: THE LAST TIKIĠAQ FEUD

The story of Suuyuk the Elder, which dates from the 1870s, outlines the last blood feud in precontact history. The storyteller here is Asatchaq, whose great-grandfather Suuyuk is murdered at the outset of the story. (A diagram of the relationships in this and the following two stories is given in the commentary.) The shaman Suuyuk has flown into a rage—the cause is forgotten—and he threatens to shamanically starve the rest of Tikiġaq. Quliuq and his associates kill Suuyuk before he can take his revenge; in turn, Suuyuk's son Kunuyaq uses Quliuq's past stinginess as a pretext for his own revenge. The feud did not stop there. Partly because of his role in Quliuq's murder, Kunuyaq's partner Ataŋauraq was murdered about ten years later (story 22).

20

From here in Tikiġaq, he [Suuyuk] went to the north beach and left by skinboat. Perhaps he told someone he was leaving. And he went to Uivvaq. He left because he wanted to starve Tikiġaq people. He was an aŋatkuq.

And when they discovered that he wanted to starve them, some men formed a plan to kill him. Suuyuk traveled to Ayagutaq, east of Uivvaq, and lived in a tent there.*

And a group of men left Tikiġaq to get him; among them were Quliuq, Kayuktuq, and Samaruuraq—those. They went north to kill him.

The shaman they were chasing had his two wives with him. They were living in a caribou-skin tent at Ayagutaq. And the night the men arrived, they sang a sleep song [siñiŋnaq] to make the shaman sleep deeply. And as he slept with his wives, they took hold of the tent skins and pulled the whole thing up.

They pulled up the tent and laid it to one side. Then they struck him

---

"Suuyuk traveled to Ayagutaq": Ayagutaq, one of Tikiġaq's winter settlements, consisted of three or four iglus.

with two spears. (This is what my father said when he told me the story.) On each of his sides they pierced him with a spear.

But the shaman stood up. The two spears did not bother him. He ran toward the sea. He had a whale charm, and saltwater is the medicine that goes with that whale amulet [aġviqtaq].

They watched him run to the sea, and when Quliuq saw him, he said, "If he sees who we are, this thing will go against us. If he finds out who we are when he regains consciousness, there will be trouble for the people."

Now Quliuq took his bow and arrow and ran in front of the shaman. (I knew Kayuktuq when he was alive. Quliuq was his father.) And Quliuq ran in front and shot him. He killed him there, at Ayagutaq. That's where they killed Suuyuk.

(It is not good to be woken in a tent by something unexpected.) The attack was at night. And one of Suuyuk's people in his hurry to dress couldn't get into his caribou-skin trousers. He kept putting them on backwards. It took him several tries to get his trousers on. He was one of the people in the tent . . . It was at Ayagutaq that they killed Suuyuk.

Now Suuyuk's son was Kunuyaq, and Kunuyaq knew where his father had been murdered. And some time later, in the winter, Kunuyaq was at Uivvaq with his family.

And Quliuq was staying at Ayagutaq. It was Quliuq who had murdered Suuyuk, who had shot and killed him. And Quliuq had found a stranded whale at Ayagutaq. But he'd told no one about it.

And at Uivvaq, with Kunuyaq, there were men who heard about the whale. Ataŋauraq was among them. So they came together and planned what to do. Those people at Uivvaq were all related to each other. (This is what Ququk told me: these men were all descendants of Aġnapa-guuq.)* And the Uivvaq men started talking together: they tried pushing Kunuyaq into action, because Quliuq had killed Suuyuk, who was Kunuyaq's father.

And there at Uivvaq they decided to visit Quliuq and appear friendly. (Kamik was with them at Uivvaq too. He was my uncle.) Then they discussed the whale that Quliuq had found beached at Ayagutaq. Quliuq had said nothing about it: he'd told no one about the whale.

It was at this point they started talking Kunuyaq into avenging his

---

"Aġnapaguuq": Aġnapaguuq, born circa 1810, was the shaman Suuyuk's father and the storyteller's great-great-grandfather. His name is the earliest in Asatchaq's family genealogy (see fig. 1, pp. xxii–xxiii). Dives Ququk, whom Asatchaq credits as his source, was born circa 1875 and was thus a contemporary of Asatchaq's parents. His vast knowledge is apparent in Rainey's 1940 interviews with him.

father's murder. One evening when the men had gathered, Kamik said, "When we were children, Quliuq kept food from us when we were hungry." This was the moment Kunuyaq gave in and decided to act. Kamik said, "When we were small, he didn't give us food when we wanted to eat." This was what made Kunuyaq decide to take action. And Kamik said, "Come on: let's do it!" And they got ready to leave early the next morning.

Next day they started off toward Ayagutaq. They were going, as they said, to "butcher the whale." Kunuyaq followed. He was not the leader. But it was Kunuyaq who took the whale knife [kaugaq]. Atanauraq also went with them. They went to Ayagutaq to "butcher the whale."

But on the way to Ayagutaq, they met Quliuq and his family, who were traveling to Uivvaq. Kunuyaq and his group let them pass. Then Kunuyaq shouted, "Quliuq, we hear you have a whale at Ayagutaq! We're on our way there now to get some meat." Quliuq replied, "Yes, there's plenty of meat. You can have the whole thing!"

Now Quliuq had not previously mentioned the whale. The subject had to be raised with him. And Kunuyaq was carrying the whale knife. Quliuq continued on his way to Uivvaq. And Kunuyaq's party went on to Ayagutaq.

When these men arrived at Ayagutaq, they found the whale, and started butchering. But they did very little: they just pretended to work on the carcass. And shortly after their arrival at Ayagutaq they started back toward Uivvaq, following Quliuq and his family.

Quliuq was with his wife. Kayuktuq, Aniqsuaq, and Qayugaq were also with him. There were five of them. Qayugaq was riding on the sled: he couldn't walk because he had no testicles. Kayuktuq and Aniqsuaq had a woman with them; her name was Nasuaq.

Now when the two groups met earlier, Kayuktuq's woman was running in front with the dogs. (In those days, someone always went ahead leading the dogs.)

But now they took turns. Quliuq went in front with the dogs and his wife pushed the sled from behind. (What was her name, the wife of Quliuq . . . ?) They were traveling on young sea ice. It was late autumn.

Now when the men from Ayagutaq drew level with Quliuq, and the two parties traveled together, Kunuyaq chose his moment to attack. While Quliuq's wife was in front with the dogs and Quliuq was pushing the sled, Kunuyaq could strike from behind.

This is how it was. Quliuq was pushing and Qayugaq the boy was on the sled when Kunuyaq plunged the whale knife through Quliuq's backbone. Quliuq fell. When Quliuq was down, Kunuyaq shouted to the men who were with him, "Quick, get the children! If they grow up they might take revenge!" Kunuyaq said this just to test the others.

Then Kunuyaq took his bow and fitted an arrow. But none of his party made a move to the children. Kunuyaq held his arrow ready. It was only Quliuq he wanted. Now he was prepared to take on his own men if they touched the children.

(My grandfather Kunuyaq was always coughing. He would fill a fruit can like this from his lungs in a single night. [*Asatchaq points at a can on the floor beside him.*])

After they killed Quliuq, they cut open his body. But Kunuyaq didn't want to cut up the loins. (That's why he coughed so much in later life.)

The other men started to work on the corpse. (When anyone was killed, they used to cut up the body, just like an animal's. But because Kunuyaq didn't want to work on the loins, he contracted his cough.)

So they murdered Quliuq. My grandfather Kunuyaq gave my father the name Quliuq too: he gave his son the name of his own victim.

.   .   .

The diagram on the next page delineates the relationships between the parties involved here and in the following two stories, the events of which took place in the 1870s.

Although the present story mentions no motivation for Suuyuk's anger, the attempt to starve a village (*niġġutaili,* "to scare off game") was a common gesture of generalized shamanic retribution. (See also stories 12 and 23.) Here, Suuyuk goes north in unexplained fury to effect his revenge from the Uivvaq region. Uivvaq, Tikiġaq's major satellite village, was a seal- and polar bear–hunting area of great importance during the hungry decades around the turn of the century.

Rather than enlist a rival practitioner to thwart him, as sometimes happened, a party sets out to kill the shaman. At first the wounded Suuyuk attempts to deploy his whale amulet, activating it with saltwater (a detail perhaps borrowed or displaced from story 14). In shooting the wounded man, Quliuq decides to risk a blood feud rather than incur supernatural revenge. Kunuyaq is goaded to carry out the second murder only when his enemy's stinginess—a major Iñupiaq crime, but not usually a capital offense—is adduced.

To block the vengeful return of a murder victim's spirit, the corpse was sometimes dismembered and the bladder attached to the truncated neck. Kunuyaq's cough, in old age, was attributed to his refusal to

FIGURE 2. Kin Relationships in Stories 20–22
(Dotted line indicates nonkin relationship.)

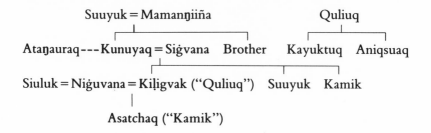

Quliuq killed Suuyuk, in revenge for which Suuyuk's son Kunuyaq—Asatchaq's grandfather—murdered Quliuq with the aid of his associate, Ataŋauraq. Quliuq's sons, Kayuktuq and Aniqsuaq, later murdered Ataŋauraq to avenge their father's death.

perform this ritual. But Kunuyaq did take the precaution of giving his victim's name as a protective amulet to his son Kiḷigvak. As "Quliuq," Kiḷigvak was thus putatively safe from his murdered namesake's kin. Asatchaq was given the name Kamik after his uncle, who was also involved in the murder. His name connected him with the personalities in the story but had no implications so far as the feud was concerned.

SUUYUK THE YOUNGER: A SHAMANIC ATTACK

The shaman Ataŋauraq, who appeared in the previous story as an associate of **21**
Kunuyaq in the murder of Quliuq, here suddenly and inexplicably turns on
Kunuyaq's sons and allegedly attacks them. This story represents a further stage in
the cycle of violence that eventually led to the murder of Ataŋauraq himself
(story 22). In the later story, Ataŋauraq is presented in the almost purely secular
role of strongman and trader. Here we meet him as a shaman, still engaged in
the traditional activities of the Tikiġaq aŋatkuq. But the beauty of this story
lies in Asatchaq's evocation of the rites that attended the revival of a dead or
dying man. The precise outcome of these rites is uncertain. Presumably Suuyuk
died quite soon after his return, half-dead, from hunting.

This is about my father, Kiḷigvak, and his brother Suuyuk. Ataŋauraq
wanted to kill them. Ataŋauraq called them ducks: he said they were
young ducks, easy to kill from the shore. This is what he called Kunuyaq's sons. He saw them when they were on the beach, and said that.

One morning in winter when they woke up, Suuyuk and Kiḷigvak
got ready to go out on the ice together. They were going to hunt seal.
Then they separated on the sea ice. And when Kiḷigvak saw a seal [after
Suuyuk had left him], he could feel the inside of his body growing hot.
Kiḷigvak had an amulet: I have seen it. It was a wolf's snout given him
by Uyaġaaluk.* Uyaġaaluk used this amulet himself when he fell off
the cliffs at Aglikuq [south of Cape Lisburne]. It was a wolf's snout.
He described his fall to Kiḷigvak when he gave him the amulet.

And when Kiḷigvak felt himself getting hot inside, he put the amulet
in his mouth and chewed it to make it wet; then he rubbed himself with

"Uyaġaaluk": Uyaġaaluk ("Big [old] rock") was Ataŋauraq's brother. As we see later,
Kunuyaq goes to Ataŋauraq to ask him to get a shamanic sighting of the very man Ataŋauraq
is suspected of attacking.

it.* He rubbed the place he felt the heat coming from. When he had finished rubbing his stomach, the heat left him.

And at the same time, Suuyuk was hunting in another place and sat down on the ice by open water when he saw a seal. But it wasn't a seal: it only appeared to be one. Suuyuk aimed and shot at it. And as he started to get up and fetch it, he felt his stomach getting hot. He felt heat in his stomach: and when he felt this, he spat on the snow. And he found that he was spitting blood. Suddenly he began vomiting blood.

And there were two men also hunting on the ice who knew where he was. One of them was Anaġlun, a man from Kiṇit.* The other was a Tikiġaq man, called Apaayuaq. No: it was Saalaaġruk. These two men put Suuyuk on their backs to carry him home. They took turns, but Anaġlun did most of the carrying. Saalaaġruk didn't do much for Suuyuk because of his relatives in the village [misfortune?]. So he carried Anaġlun's rifle for him.

Suuyuk died out on the ice because he was vomiting blood. Anaġlun wanted to bring him ashore: but he didn't make it. Suuyuk died before they reached land. He [Anaġlun] laid Suuyuk on his back and left him there with his mittens under his head for a pillow. He arranged his feet so they pointed toward land. They left his body in burial position.* Then they went back to Tikiġaq, for there was a wind rising from the north.

When they reached Tikiġaq, they went to Suuyuk's parents, Kunuyaq and Siġvana, and told them they had left Suuyuk out on the ice. He had died there because of the blood he had been vomiting.

And when Kunuyaq heard his son had died, he told his children and everyone in the iglu not to make a noise [apsalliq].* Because Suuyuk had died out on the ice.

Now while Suuyuk lay there, he came back to consciousness. And he started crawling around on his knees and elbows in the direction the sun takes, following the air and sun. He crawled in larger and larger circles. Then he completely regained consciousness and found he was crawling on his knees and elbows, so as not to get his hands frozen. But he couldn't tell where he was or how far out he was.

"when Kiḷigvak felt himself getting hot inside, he put the amulet in his mouth": Saliva activated amulet power, while abdominal heat was regarded as a common sign of shamanic attack.

"Kiṇit": Kiṇit (Kiṇigin) was the village at Cape Prince of Wales, two hundred miles south of Tikiġaq. The man here had temporarily settled at Jabbertown.

"burial position": The knees of the dead were bent and the feet pointed inland so the soul would travel in that direction.

"apsalliq": Apsalliq was a mourner's rule of silence observed for four or five days after death.

Now his mind told him to get back to Tikiġaq. I don't know how he got his direction right. But he used his own shadow in the moonlight. And when he fell in the water he climbed back out again, keeping his hands inside his parka. When he fell in the water, he used his elbows to climb out again.

And when Suuyuk saw his own shadow by moonlight, he saw he'd turned into a polar bear. He had four legs like a polar bear. But inside he was still human. He headed for Tikiġaq. His mind told him to hurry. He didn't stop for the night. He just went on. Even when he fell in the water he climbed back out again.

Suuyuk reached land between here [Tikiġaq] and Jabbertown. There was a huge driftwood log at the place he landed. Everyone in the village was asleep. But Siitchiagruaq saw him, I know that. Siitchiagruaq saw the polar bear come ashore and watched it go toward Kunuyaq's iglu.

When the bear reached the iglu, it called in through the skylight: "Kunualuŋa" (this is what he used to call Kunuyaq), "Kunualuŋa, I've come home." And when he'd said he'd come home, his father called back, "Have you really come home? Are your feet on the ground?" "Yes, I've come home. My feet are on the ground." And to prove it, he stamped on the rocks surrounding the skylight.

When they heard this, Kunuyaq and his wife started to come out, but not before they had rubbed themselves with soot and burnt lamp oil to keep their son alive.* They rubbed themselves with used oil from the lamp: they wore nothing above the waist where they'd oiled themselves.

When my father Kiḷigvak heard Suuyuk had come back, he went to see how he was: for he had heard that he had died vomiting blood. He expected to see him covered with blood.

When they came out of the house, Kunuyaq went first. He approached his son. Suuyuk was standing by the skylight. Kunuyaq put his arms around him. Then Suuyuk stamped his feet again: but his father wouldn't let go of him.

When they started to go inside, Suuyuk went first. But he almost failed to get inside. The katak lifted, and he almost fell through the gap. He hit the edge of the katak with his head.

When Suuyuk died, his father paid shamans to find out where his spirit [iḷitqusiq] was. His father went to Ataŋauraq to find out where his spirit was. But Suuyuk's mind rejected Ataŋauraq's search, and the

---

"soot and burnt lamp oil": See the commentaries to stories 1 and 2 for the magical properties of burnt lamp oil. If a man's soul approached home within four days of death, his elders attempted to clasp him to them and thus, providing they had blacked themselves, restore him to life. In the Tikiġaq legend of Apikiiña, the lost man's parents are successful.

shaman could say nothing. This was because of what Ataŋauraq had done earlier: he had made an animal to use against the two brothers, Kiḷigvak and Suuyuk. But Kiḷigvak hadn't been affected, because he had a wolf-snout amulet. I know amulets like that one: they come from the old days. But I used one myself: I rubbed my body with it when I was sick.

.   .   .

Suuyuk, Asatchaq's paternal uncle, was named after his grandfather, who had been murdered some ten years before the events of this story.* The rationale for Ataŋauraq's attack in this story is not clear. On the face of it, Ataŋauraq had every reason to maintain good relations with Kunuyaq's family, for he had accompanied Kunuyaq at the murder of Quliuq, who had himself murdered Kunuyaq's father, Suuyuk. Perhaps this assault was later attributed to Ataŋauraq in the context of his increasingly irrational behavior. Thus Ataŋauraq's boast at the beginning of this story could either represent uninhibited verbal behavior or flow from some particular quarrel with the two young men. If the latter, it perhaps explains why Kunuyaq might still approach his former associate Ataŋauraq for help when his son went missing. Rainey (1940–41) provides the following synopsis of the story, which he heard from Aġviqsiiña, a junior contemporary of Suuyuk the younger:

Anyone who died on the ice or who was drowned might come back to life. This happened to Aġviqsiiña's wife's brother Suuyuk, who had a haemorrhage on the ice and died. The two men with him gave him up and left him. The ice broke up and went out; but that night new ice formed. Suuyuk woke up, and the first thing he was conscious of was the wind blowing around his face. Then he got up and walked, and when he fell through the ice it was easy for him to climb back up. He looked at his footprints and though he felt like a person, his prints were not like those of a real person. When he got to the driftwood on the south beach, he came ashore. He then came back to his parents' house after four days, and his parents rubbed their hands with lamp soot and went out and brought him in. If they hadn't done this he would have taken the way under the house [on the soul's journey to the east] which he saw was open and easy for him. It would have been hard for him to come up

*See story 20, "Suuyuk the Elder," and the diagram on p. 152 for further information on the relationships here.

through the katak. Many spirits want to come home: but if no one helps to bring them in, they go straight ahead under the iglu, as this is easier. Aġviqsiiña said: "Many times, when a person dies, the aŋatkuq brings back his life, and these people tell the story of what happened to them. They left the body and started down the slough [running east-west on the spit], then along the lagoon and the south side of the Kuukpak river. It is all dark during this time. They feel strong and run without any trouble. Then far to the east they see like the daylight breaking up. They hurry toward the light, but somebody comes in front of them and makes them come back to life. This is the spirit of the aŋatkuq."

This history of Asatchaq's uncle Suuyuk dates to the early 1880s, the high point of Ataŋauraq's power and a correspondingly low point of Tikiġaq morale. Tikiġaq had been penetrated by the material culture of the Euro-American whalers and traders, and the population had been drastically reduced by disease and emigration; nevertheless, the local systems of thought were still intact.

Of special interest are the symbols and motifs that dominate the story: the sunwise movement associated with Suuyuk's recovery; the application of soot to help restore his soul; finally, in the version from Rainey's notes, the eastward voyage of the soul toward the realm of daylight. All these symbols are represented in earlier stories: the creative shamanic movement of sunwise circling has its fullest expression in Aliŋnaq's story, and it also occurs in stories 13 and 19 as a life-generating gesture. The magical, creative properties of lamp soot figure in "Tuluŋigraq," "Aliŋnaq," and "Women's Moon Rites." The legend of Apikiiña, a hunter stranded on the young winter ice, shows Apikiiña's spirit returning to the family iglu, where his parents, with the help of soot, restore life to him precisely as Suuyuk's parents do. Finally, the image of the soul running east also appears in "Taŋnaaluk." In Suuyuk's story, these motifs follow one another in a coherent, intermeshed pattern. The element connecting all the symbols is fire and the rejuvenating energy of heat and light; its mythic and cosmo-logical analogue lies with the sun and, by mythic association, the soot-smeared moon (see commentaries to stories 2 and 3).

The transition between this story and the next one is astonishing. In Suuyuk's story, Ataŋauraq, for all his disastrous flaws, functions as a recognizable Tikiġaq shaman within the inherited system, a view of Ataŋauraq that perhaps arises partly because we witness events from the point of view of Suuyuk's highly traditional Tikiġaq family (see the Introduction). But a decade later the shaman is dramatically transformed. No longer primarily an aŋatkuq, he is a trader, strongman, and entrepreneur in a new cultural and economic epoch. Suuyuk's story, with its elegant symbolic pattern, demonstrates the narrative unity we have come to expect from earlier Tikiġaq stories. But the fragmentary nature of Ataŋauraq's saga reflects the social turmoil no doubt present, but not expressed, in Suuyuk's history. In Suuyuk's story, both Ataŋauraq and his victims still participate, albeit painfully, in an autonomous belief system. In the later text, we are shown how an ambitious individual brought up within the tradition could first manipulate and abuse it and then rampage through its debris.

JABBERTOWN AND ATAŊAURAQ: EURO-AMERICAN TRADERS AND THE TIKIĠAQ "CHIEF"

All the preceding stories were recited in forms learned from a previous story- **22**
teller, and each tale had a structure that was the story. No such shape
existed for Ataŋauraq's saga, which is pieced together from anecdotes and
conversations that Asatchaq heard from his elders before the continuity of the
oral tradition lapsed. This telling was therefore improvised in a number of
sessions which the storyteller found particularly demanding. Once he
had started, Asatchaq spoke much of the saga in a voice of musing
reminiscence; a perambulation past traders' stations along the now deserted
south shore was his point of entry to difficult and painful material.
This history in fragments evokes a time of fragmentation. But for all
the narrative disjunctions, the accelerating force behind each of the
episodes—which bring to a climax the feuds in the last two stories—raises
them to an intensity which is grand as well as depressing.

JABBERTOWN PEOPLE

I'll start from the east end where the [timber] houses were first built.
I'll name the ones I know.

Nelson and Andrew were at Piŋutchiaq.* Andrew was the first there.
Then came Nelson. Andrew was the first white man to build a house.
The second house was at Ayagutaq, where Jaana [John] built. They had
a house at Ayagutaq; then they moved west to Jabbertown.

And next to these Ayagutaq people were "Cooper" Koenig and Jaana.
I don't know John's last name. He had a beard; they said he was German.

"Nelson and Andrew": The whaler/traders Rustan Nelson, an American of mixed descent,
John Kelly, and the otherwise unidentified Andrew built houses at Piŋutchiaq, a high
bluff between the south beach and Ayagutaq lagoon, about twelve miles from Tikiĝaq.
A group of southern Iñupiaqs working for them built iglus into the bluff. The iglu ruins
and graves of this settlement survive.

And at Jabbertown too was Mr. Lieb. Max Lieb was his name.* He was in the next house. Between Jabbertown and Beacon Hill there was a schoolhouse.* They built it there for the children of Jabbertown and Tikiġaq, for both places. For schooling. The first teacher was a man called Walter . . . Walter . . . teacher . . . [last word spoken in English].

The school was next to Max Lieb's house, west of it. They settled near the ponds where people get ice [for drinking water]. The white men built their houses where there would be ice. That's what I worked out: they built their houses near the drinking water.

And Jaanauraq [diminutive of Jaana] lived at Jabbertown. He lived by himself. He was the father of my qataŋun [exchange sibling]: my qataŋun's mother slept with Jaana. They had a daughter together; her name was Q——.*

Then there was Yiiguraq [Jim], and Tom George, a black man. They took a house abandoned by someone who'd left Jabbertown: this was Unŋulik, who had a wart on his chin.* He was Roy's father, and Aqivgaaluk was pregnant at that time by Unŋulik.

And a woman called Sinŋaurauluk married someone who'd arrived with Unŋulik; he too was a white man; I don't know his name. They also moved into an empty house. And there was a woman called Anaq ["excrement"].* And a man and woman arrived from Imaġliq [Little Diomede Island]; they too were put ashore at Jabbertown so they could go whaling. Their names were Pivsuk and Itiqqaq. They came with a

---

" 'Cooper' Koenig," "Jaana," "Max Lieb": For more on "Cooper" Koenig and Jaana (Johannes Hackmann), see the commentary. Max Lieb, a German and relatively late arrival (1903?), married Atuagana (?) in 1905. He was sometimes in partnership with Koenig, with whom he owned the schooner *Jessie*. Each summer this ship brought them a year's supplies from Seattle (Foote 1959–61).

"Beacon Hill": Beacon Hill is high ground just northeast of Jabbertown where a number of graves and iglu ruins from this period survive. The schoolhouse was moved to Tikiġaq in the 1920s and was used successively as a school, a community hall, and a nursery until half of it was taken to a new site in 1975. It is now derelict.

"Q——": Asatchaq's qataŋun (exchange sibling) was the daughter of Jaana and a woman who also had sexual relations with Asatchaq's father, Kiḷigvak.

"Yiiguraq," "Unŋulik": Yiiguraq (Jim) was a white trader, who drowned returning with coal from Cape Lisburne circa 1900. Unŋulik was Ward Vincent of Martha's Vineyard, father of Roy Vincent, born on Herschel Island but a Tikiġaq man until his death in 1981. Ward Vincent may have received his local name via the pronunciation of his own first name. There being no d in Iñupiaq, Ward would be pronounced "wart," which was perhaps translated by some wag into "Unŋulik" ("has a wart"). Maybe, as the storyteller says, he had a wart, too.

"a woman called Anaq ['excrement']": No negative or comic connotation attached to names such as "Anaq." Another example is the name Anaqulutuq, which means "chamber pot."

complete whaling crew, but they didn't catch anything that spring. They were related to Anaq. And Anaq had a son by the name of Luke, and they also had a house. There was Nuuk.*

Jonah moved west from where he was [tape unclear]. Jonah had a wife whose name was Avayiq, and they had a son called Kiasik ["shoulder"]: Charlie Jonah, Charlie-Marlie . . . [Kiasik's nickname].

And there was Yiiguraq, and he was the brother-in-law of Tarrauluk. His wife was Siitchiagruaq; they had no children, but they adopted some. Siitchiagruaq was barren for some reason: before she went to Yiiguraq she had had another husband [presumably a Tikiġaq man], and she had no children by him either.

And it was Siitchiagruaq who saw Suuyuk [uncle of storyteller] coming home from the ice when he turned into a polar bear.

She was going home to her parents' iglu when she saw the bear coming in from the sea ice. Her father was Sisailaq and her mother was Anasugaq. These were their daughters: Siitchiagruaq was the oldest, then Qavaan . . . who was the next . . . [Tukummiq: "Naunaġiña?"] Yes, Naunaġiña . . . and who else . . . and Naiyuk now, and also Kippauġan. Five daughters in all. The only boy was Tarrauluk . . .*

And [a white trader]* was of great help to Siitchiagruaq's parents. He also owned a little store, which was supplied by the Coast Guard. This was of great help to her parents. They had their own frame house and they caught a whale . . . Yiiguraq disappeared when he went north to Uivvaq to fetch coal.

ATAɊAURAQ AND PETER BAYNE

The white men I knew didn't seem to harm the Iñupiaqs. But there was one man called Piini.*

"Nuuk": Nuuk was Captain Edwin W. Newth, master of the steam brigantine *Jeanette;* he wintered at Herschel Island in 1893–94 and 1895–96. He regularly passed through Tikiġaq and was notorious for his traffic in Iñupiaq women (Bockstoce 1986: 277).

"These were their daughters . . .": Here Asatchaq reflects on a late nineteenth-century genealogy. Naunaġiña (Eddie Lisburne, born 1893) was translator Tukummiq's father. He was drowned off Piŋu in the 1920s.

"a white trader": The name is unclear on the tape.

"Piini": Peter Bayne, master of the schooner *Silver Wave,* wintered at Sea Horse Island in 1890–91 and subsequently (1893–94) at Tikiġaq's Marryat Inlet in the *Emily Schroeder,* which was wrecked in the great storm of October 1893. Bayne returned in the *Silver Wave* in 1894, wintering again in Marryat Inlet, but ran the ship aground and abandoned it in the spring (Bockstoce 1977). It may have been Bayne who maliciously taught Ataŋauraq how to distill liquor.

Bayne lived over there at Jabbertown. One spring Ataŋauraq told Bayne to take his whaling boat to the north side so that he [Bayne] would not be ahead of the other whalers [southeast of the Point].

Bayne had a small whaling boat. Ataŋauraq didn't want him in the line of the first whales. Bayne was a white man. And he put his boat out on the north side, near the *pisiktaġvik* [archery practice ground]; it was also near the iglus . . . That Bayne . . .

So that Ataŋauraq goes to Bayne, and Ataŋauraq has no weapon. But behind his back, Ataŋauraq holds his long tobacco pipe, holding it behind his back with both hands.

Bayne thinks that Ataŋauraq's carrying a pistol. And when he gets to Bayne, Ataŋauraq wants to talk to him. I don't know where Ataŋauraq learned English, but he talked with white people and understood them. It was the same when he went aboard the whaling ships. When he boarded ship, he went straight to the captain. I don't know how he learned English. He always wanted liquor [*taaŋŋaq*] from the captain. He didn't stop for anyone.

So Bayne thought Ataŋauraq had a pistol. And he struck Ataŋauraq with his own pistol and cut his head. But Ataŋauraq didn't have a weapon. And he bled from the cut . . . Ataŋauraq *taamna* . . .*

There was a woman who knew Ataŋauraq's medicine.* She went over to Ataŋauraq's iglu and dressed his wound using the skin of a weasel, because that was what would heal him.

Suŋitchuq Ataŋauraq taamna, suŋitchuq . . . That Ataŋauraq did nothing.* If he had had a pistol, perhaps he would have hit Bayne or shot him. But he was carrying nothing. And anyway, Ataŋauraq had simply been visiting the white man.

After he'd attacked Ataŋauraq, Bayne took his crew whaling. They started on the north side of the point. When the ice opened, they went far out on the water, beyond rifle range, and then came round to the south side [i.e., they circled the village and hunted where Ataŋauraq had ordered them not to, only farther from land] . . . That Bayne . . .

Bayne was the first white man to build a house here in Tikiġaq [in the village itself, not in Jabbertown]. His house was in the middle of the village. He paid my father, Kiḷigvak, a wolverine skin in exchange for the first whale Kiḷigvak caught [i.e., in exchange for the baleen, or

"*Ataŋauraq taamna*": The phrase "*Ataŋauraq taamna*" ("that Ataŋauraq") recurs frequently, in a tone of nostalgia mixed with awe and revulsion.

"Ataŋauraq's medicine": The loan word *marrasiq*, "medicine," refers to Ataŋauraq's amulet. The term for liquor, *taaŋŋaq* (above), is a loan word from "tonic."

"*suŋitchuq*" ("does nothing"): A narrative device used frequently in the story to suggest a pause before or after violent action.

possibly half of it]. The whale was an *iŋutuq* [a young, fat bowhead].

Kiḷigvak, my father, ate rice and molasses when he visited Bayne's house.

There were Kuuvak people, Kivaliñiq people, Qikiqtaġruk people, and they came from other villages also. They arrived from Imaġliq and Tapqaq too.* They came to work for the white whalers, and for white men's food which the whalers brought with them. Many ships went past Tikiġaq, but few spent the winter here.

[Tukummiq asks a question about wintering.]

Yes, there was one man called Yuuguraq,* and he put his boat in the lagoon near the inlet for the winter, though not in the path of the spring ice as the river takes it out to sea. He spent the winter frozen in there. Bayne, too, spent his first winter here in his boat. I saw the broken pieces of it myself.

Yuuguraq had a whale crew of people from the south. Kalinaq was among them; Kalinaq was a Kobuk man. Yuuguraq didn't mind where they came from. These southern people came more for white goods than for whaling. And when they came here, they brought furs with them to trade for rifles.

ATAŋAURAQ AND HIS TRADING PARTNERS FROM THE NOATAK RIVER

At that time Ataŋauraq lacked nothing. And one thing he did was to take fox furs from the Kobuk people and trade for them.

Ataŋauraq had a partner called Tikiligauraq, who was Kumatchia-gruaq's father, and he had another partner by the name of Aullagrauluk, who was the grandfather of Kippaurauraq.* Both Tikiligauraq and Aullagrauluk were from Nautaq [Noatak]. These men were Ataŋauraq's partners.

One day Tikiligauraq was talking to Aullagrauluk. He said. "When we reach Tikiġaq you will be shy."

Aullagrauluk said he wouldn't be bashful in the presence of an Iñupiaq

---

"Kuuvak people, Kivaliñiq people . . .": Residents of the Kobuk River, Kivalina, Kotzebue, Little Diomede Island, and Shishmareff.

"Yuuguraq": Joe Tuckfield, from Cardiff, Wales, was called Yuuguraq, "Little Joe." He married a Tikiġaq shaman.

"Kippaurauraq": Antonio Weber of Noatak, who settled in Tikiġaq in the late 1800s.

like himself, in front of someone not a white man. But Tikiligauraq said, "When we get to Tikiġaq and go to Ataŋauraq's place, it will be just like visiting white people." This was when Ataŋauraq was living in his first house; it's not there any more, it's been washed into the sea.

If Tom Brower had come here before those ruins had been washed away, I would have shown them to him.* But he visited after they'd been destroyed.

That's what they said before they reached Tikiġaq. Tikiligauraq had white fox skins he wanted to trade with his partner Ataŋauraq.*

In those days women wore nothing above the waist in the iglu. Inside the iglu they wore nothing [above their skin pants]. Later they wore dresses.

Tikiligauraq and Aullagrauluk went inside Ataŋauraq's iglu. Tikiligauraq had been there before, but it was Aullagrauluk's first visit. Tikiligauraq went in first. And when they arrived, the family was about to start eating. They were served on a table.*

It was Siḷauyaq who served the food; she was Ataŋauraq's first wife.

There would have been five people at the table: Ataŋauraq and his wife, Aullagrauluk and Tikiligauraq, and one other.

Throughout the meal, Aullagrauluk didn't say a word. When he traveled to Tikiġaq he said he wouldn't be shy. But now he was too bashful to speak. It was because Ataŋauraq and his family were like white people.

And apart from them was a group of women who were also eating. Some of these were Ataŋauraq's wives. They were eating maktak [whale skin and blubber]. Aullagrauluk wanted to join the women eating maktak. But he didn't say a word.

After they had eaten, Ataŋauraq said to Aullagrauluk, "There are rifles over there." In those days, they kept the guns standing on their butts in a corner of the iglu. Ataŋauraq told him to go and look at them and pick one out for himself. "Choose one," he said.

But Aullagrauluk didn't take the best or the largest of them. He took a smaller rifle which was called a .44.

"Tom Brower": Son of Charles Brower. Charlie Brower was a white whaler/trader who settled in Barrow and the author of *Fifty Degrees below Zero*. He spent the winter and spring of 1884 in Tikiġaq and went whaling with Ataŋauraq. Both Browers maintained a keen antiquarian interest in the region.

"white fox skins": Ataŋauraq wore a white fox-skin parka for camouflage against attack when he traveled on the ice.

"table": Asatchaq uses the loan word *taivlu* for what was probably a board on the iglu floor.

While he was traveling to Tikiġaq, Aullagrauluk said that if Ataŋauraq offered him a gun, he'd take a long-distance rifle for caribou
hunting. He had a hard time choosing when the umialik told him to
pick one. He hadn't thought he'd be shy, but when he went in, he found
it hard to say anything at all. Perhaps it was the women who made him
bashful.

And Kiñaġun became Tikiligauraq's wife. She was Ataŋauraq's wife,
but after Ataŋauraq was murdered, Tikiligauraq claimed her. He was
not the only man who found it hard to speak in Ataŋauraq's presence.
There were others too. Ataŋauraq was like a white man.

THE FIRST BREAD BAKED IN TIKIĠAQ

And when the Coast Guard came, there was a Japanese cook on board;
I saw that cook, and my mother saw him too.*

When the Coast Guard was leaving for Utqiaġvik [Barrow], Ataŋauraq wanted them to leave the cook at Tikiġaq, so that the women
could learn to bake. He wanted his women to learn to bake bread from
him.

The Coast Guard left for a week, and when they returned, the Japanese cook got back on the ship. Ataŋauraq kept him for a week, and
some of the women learned to bake from him.

And when the Coast Guard returned [some other year], my mother
recognized the Japanese man: even though she didn't understand what
he said, they just recognized each other, and somehow they talked together, my mother and the Japanese man. No one ever had a cook as
Ataŋauraq did.

ATAŊAURAQ'S STOVE AND TIMBER

After Ataŋauraq was killed, the lumber he had ordered for his frame
house came to Tikiġaq on the Coast Guard ship. Ataŋauraq was killed
around March, and the following summer the timber arrived. He was
murdered when the days started to get longer.

They asked Siḷauyaq [one of Ataŋauraq's wives] what they should do

---

"a Japanese cook": This may have been Kyosuke ("Frank") Yasuda, who traveled to Barrow in the Revenue Marine Service cutter *Bear* and who later established a settlement,
with his wife and other Barrow Iñupiaqs, at Beaver and Fort Yukon (Keiichi Murai,
personal communication).

with the lumber they'd brought up with them. Should they unload it in Tikiġaq? Siḷauyaq said no, because Ataŋauraq had many relatives, and she thought they wouldn't let her keep anything. She said, "If they unload it here, his relatives will leave me nothing." There was also a large coal-burning stove, and this they unloaded at Barrow for Charlie Brower. I saw that stove when I went to Barrow. Pauyuuraq and I went to eat at Brower's when we were working for Stefánsson.* It was a big stove. And it was a big house. Siḷauyaq refused the house on account of Ataŋauraq's relatives. She was sure they wouldn't let her have it. Ataŋauraq was like that.

ATAŊAURAQ AND A WHITE TRADING PARTNER

He [Ataŋauraq] always went straight to the ship's captain. And he had a [white] partner, whose name was Mickie Lee. He was a small man. He was Ataŋauraq's partner. And once Ataŋauraq chased him right into the ship with a knife. Ataŋauraq had been on board drinking, and his partner refused to fill his cup again. So Ataŋauraq drew his knife and went after him. He chased him all over the ship, but couldn't catch up with him. Sometimes they went down through a passage under the deck, Ataŋauraq chasing him with his knife. Ataŋauraq didn't want much: but it wasn't given. If Ataŋauraq had caught up with his partner, he would have used that knife. The little man ran to the front deck, with Ataŋauraq following, but he never caught up with him. He didn't harm anyone there.

TRADE IN ARTIFACTS

Charlie Brower lived at Utqiaġvik, and he was an umialik. But it was here in Point Hope that Brower worked for [went whaling with] Ataŋauraq, when Ataŋauraq hit Brower in the face, and his face swelled up. When Brower went back to Utqiaġvik, he told people that he'd been an umialik when he was in Tikiġaq.

But it was only after he left for Barrow that he became an umialik. Before, in Tikiġaq, Ataŋauraq hit him in the face.

Maybe Brower also had some stories to tell about those days. They

"Pauyuuraq and I": Pauyuuraq ("Jerry") and Asatchaq ("Jimmie") joined Stefánsson's 1913 Canadian Arctic expedition and were on the *Karluk* before it sank in January 1914. They stopped in Barrow both on the way out and before they returned home.

might be different from our stories. But these were the people, Bayne especially. Ataŋauraq got most of his supplies from Bayne, particularly when he ran out of molasses. It was baleen that the whites were trading for. These men were successful traders. Also Cooper [Koenig].

And Cooper was the first to start trading for artifacts. Cooper and his wife Pausana bought up a lot of artifacts. He and his wife used to go to the old graves, taking sealskin bags with them and filling the bags from the old graves.* Pausana knew which graves would have hunting weapons on them. They didn't have to dig for them. They took what they'd found to Jabbertown, returning to Tikiġaq with what they had traded for on their backs.

And here, in Tikiġaq, it was Pausana who first dug for artifacts. Pausana was a woman. She was cutting some *qaattaq* [rectangular sections of sod used to insulate the iglu exterior] to the east of my house, where there'd been a midden.

And when she rolled up that sod, underneath it she found an adze made of jade and knives. Then everybody started digging. They found arrowheads. It was at the midden they started digging. I was among them. There were many arrowheads under where the school is now. Just west of the school. Arrowheads were buried with the corpses. When someone died, many of the things they owned were buried with them. Lots of arrow points. And broken lamps were found in some graves too. They were buried with the things they owned in those days. That was how the digging started.

Later it was Rainey who got us to dig here at Tikiġaq and Ipiutak. When Rainey was here, we dug in the old iglus. He put me in charge of the Tikiġaq digging and someone else was foreman at Ipiutak.* I was chosen because I knew the old houses well. When they [Rainey, Larsen, and Giddings] were looking for artifacts, I was the foreman. The money wasn't very good, it was five dollars a day. Rainey took away many of the things they found here. We found many good things in the ground here. We found graves that were placed side by side, close together. They never dug under the graves, which is where all the arrowheads had been found. George Omnik was in charge of the diggers at Ipiutak.

"filling the bags from the old graves": The reference is to artifacts left with the dead on burial racks. In an earlier period, the Tikiġaq people also buried their dead in shallow graves. Koenig initiated a casual trade in artifacts that continues today.
"the Tikiġaq digging": Larsen, Rainey, and Louis Giddings arrived in the summer of 1939 to excavate old Tikiġaq. By chance, they then discovered the Ipiutak site, and local people were paid from WPA funds to help with both digs. Their finds are in the Danish National Museum, the New York Museum of Natural History, and the University of Alaska Museum, Fairbanks. One cargo of Ipiutak material sank on a barge in the Bering Strait.

For some reason, Rainey didn't want the bottom of the graves disturbed.

I know the place where those bodies were found side by side. Rainey took the bones out. But they didn't put all of the bones together. The bones of each grave were numbered and laid together in one piece.

And in some of the graves, there were skulls with long jawbones. I never understood why those figures with long jaws were buried side by side. And in one grave we found the bones of a walrus under a human skeleton. I don't know what kind of person would be buried like that.

ATAŊAURAQ'S HOUSEHOLD

Now I'll tell a bit of uqaluktuaq about Ataŋauraq. I heard this from my mother, Niġuvana. She used to live with Ataŋauraq's family. Ataŋauraq had her move into his household to be his *ukuaq* [daughter-in-law]. She lived with Siuluk, Ataŋauraq's son by adoption.

While my mother lived at Ataŋauraq's house, she saw that there was one wife [among Ataŋauraq's six] whom he most liked to beat. This was Kumatchiagruaq's mother. He beat her up because of something that had happened between her family and Ataŋauraq's. The woman's name was Qiñuġun. The two families were feuding. That's why Ataŋauraq beat Qiñuġun. The trouble had begun with Suuyuk, my great-grandfather. Suuyuk had been killed by relatives of Qiñuġun.

She was beaten for this reason. Ataŋauraq struck her on the head once. She used a weasel skin as medicine.

What had been done earlier [the feud], they kept alive.

And to Ataŋauraq, all the people were alike, relatives or not; he'd kill anyone he pleased. But by doing this, he turned everyone in Tikiġaq against him, and they grew to be afraid of him and hated him.

But before Ataŋauraq killed anyone himself, Kayuktuq and Aniqsuaq acted against him because of what Ataŋauraq had done to their ancestors. Suuyuk was their ancestor.*

"Suuyuk was their ancestor": "Suuyuk" is a slip of the tongue for "Quliuq." See the commentary to "The Death of Suuyuk the Elder" (story 20).

This is how they killed Ataɳauraq. It was on account of what had happened in a previous generation.

When Ataɳauraq went hunting on the sea ice, men used to lie in wait for his return. When he went hunting, he always wore a parka made of white fox skins. They used to say Tukummiq made his fox-skin parkas for him.* He always wore these fox-skin parkas on the sea ice.

There were many who wanted to kill Ataɳauraq. Even his nephews, who were Qaiyguaq's uncles. Ataɳauraq had been a danger to the whole village.

They killed him because of the fear he inspired. They were not the only ones who wanted to kill Ataɳauraq. My uncle Samaruna was among them. Samaruna had some red fox skins that he saved for someone. And Ataɳauraq sent someone to fetch Samuruna's fox skins. Samaruna had saved these fox skins for a white man who had given him a good blanket for his family. The white man came from a four-masted ship and had given Samaruna the blanket. An excellent blanket.

And Samaruna had ten red fox skins. More than once, Ataɳauraq sent a man to get the fox skins. But Samaruna wouldn't part with them. And he told the man who'd been sent to get them, "Let him come for them himself!" Ataɳauraq wanted those red fox skins badly.

And Samaruna sat by his umiaq which was on its side as a windbreak. He sat with his rifle ready. He was prepared for Ataɳauraq if he came for the fox skins. This is as far as the story of Ataɳauraq goes.

THE MURDER OF ATAɳAURAQ

It was March when they murdered Ataɳauraq; this was when my mother said it happened. My mother had married into Ataɳauraq's family: she was ukuaq to them, having been given to Siuluk, the adopted son of Ataɳauraq.

So it was in March they planned the murder.* They surrounded the skylight. Umittaqpak was among them. Umittaqpak fired his gun into the iglu.

And on the evening they planned to kill him, Ataɳauraq was drunk; he was sleeping off his liquor.

"it was in March": The murder of Ataɳauraq actually took place in February (1889).
"Tukummiq": A female shaman who was Ataɳauraq's younger contemporary.

And it was Aniqsuaq who went inside the entrance passage. He had his rifle with him. And when he came up through the katak, he saw Ataŋauraq. Two of his wives were with him. And Aniqsuaq shot Ataŋauraq.

As Aniqsuaq told it, he didn't think the men outside by the skylight opened fire. Aniqsuaq was the younger brother of Kayuktuq.

THE FATE OF ANIQSUAQ

After they'd killed Ataŋauraq, Aniqsuaq found an old rifle barrel, and he was going to use it to distill liquor. So he pushed the chamber of the gun into the stove to burn out something that was stuffed inside it.*

But the chamber was full. It has been loaded without being fired. Aniqsuaq was working with it in his house. He had put the whole chamber in the fire, with the barrel facing outwards. He wanted to use it as the distilling pipe [*kusiqtuq,* "it drips"] for the liquor to drip through. (I have seen those stills for making liquor.)

This is what Aniqsuaq was doing. And when he was right in front of the stove, the chamber went off. It roared and exploded. It hit Aniqsuaq in the chest. When people talked about it, they said the gun had been timed just right.

The gun inside the stove that shot Aniqsuaq was loaded. He was killed instantly. This is what happened.

And the Coast Guard went after Kayuktuq.

.   .   .

JABBERTOWN

At the height of its prosperity in the 1890s, Jabbertown was a village of rough timber houses, iglus, and tents above the beach five miles south of Tikiġaq. The first Jabbertown camp was established in 1887 by Peter Bayne, who had worked at Barrow in 1884–85 on the first Arctic shore-based whaling station (Bockstoce 1977). Unlike most of his European colleagues, Bayne quarreled unpleasantly with the local people, as Asatchaq's account of his meeting with Ataŋauraq reflects. The most successful shore-based operation was started in 1889 by

---

"into the stove": A few of Tikiġaq's wealthier families had acquired wood-burning stoves by the 1880s. Before long, the stoves caused a serious depletion of south beach driftwood.

the Westphalians Heinrich "Cooper" Koenig and Johannes Hackmann (both had been coopers on American whaling ships). Jabbertown business was twofold. The main business was to hunt bowhead whale from skinboats and wooden dinghies each spring. For this work the Europeans required crews, and since Tikiġaġmiut refused to work in boats which directly competed with their own whaling effort, the commercial hunters employed Iñupiaqs from the Kobuk and Noatak Rivers, the Seward Peninsula, and even the Diomede Islands. By the mid-1890s, there were often two hundred people each spring in the Jabbertown community, almost double Tikiġaq's year-round population.

All the Jabbertown bosses were small-time operators who had abandoned the big ships to make their fortunes by shore-based whaling; most, if not all, at least broke even by selling baleen in Seattle and San Francisco. Their secondary, year-round business was to trade for skins and other local goods with the Tikiġaq community. Koenig's journals reveal quite well the nature of his operation. While the Tikiġaq economy disintegrated around him, the methodical hand of the trader recorded a various and constant business. Here, for example, are nine of the thirteen dealings with Tikiġaq hunters Koenig noted for July 1889 (Koenig trade journals, Archives of the University of Alaska, Fairbanks). In the left-hand column are native goods received; to the right are Koenig's items of exchange:

July 23	whalebone, 25 ft. [quantity illegible]	425 lb. flour
	dogskin boots	1 yd. drill
	1 large and 1 small sealskin	250 primers [gunpowder ignition caps]
	1 coil seal line	5 yd. drill
	6 deer skins	50 lb. flour
July 29	whalebone, 16 lb., 5 ft. long	75 lb. flour 4 [?]
	seal line	1 package matches
	1 sealskin	1 small tin cup
July 30	large sealskin	25 lb. flour

Koenig worked in Jabbertown until about 1908. Baleen remained the central item of exchange, but as the value of baleen declined, the trade in polar bear, fox, and lynx skins grew. As the transactions recorded by Koenig suggest, Tikiġaq's primary needs were food, cloth, and firearms; tobacco was the major luxury good. Throughout the subsistence crisis around the turn of the century, an extraordinary flow of imported material poured into the village: shotguns, rifles, lead shot, powder, steel knives, harpoon irons, files, planes, saws, stove pipes, steel traps, lamp gear, kerosene, coal oil, candles, turpentine, calico, mattress ticking, blankets, tea, coffee, molasses, rice, beans, dried fruit, pepper, yeast. For each of these items the locals coined a term, many of them witty, some still current a century later: mustard was "baby shit"; beans were "fart makers"; sausage was "like a penis"; oatmeal was "ear dandruff"; a rifle was "caribou windpipe." A few nonlocal words, such as "tea" (*tii*) and "pepper" (*papa*), which could easily be fitted into the phonology of Iñupiaq were brought into the language.

In the absence of comparable trade journals, it is hard to assess how representative Koenig's dealings were. But since local people were hardened interregional traders, one may assume that within the limits of their dependence, they bargained to their satisfaction. A number of traders, including Koenig and John Backland, earned considerable trust. In exchange for baleen and polar bear skins, Backland imported lumber for Asatchaq's father in 1913. Similarly, in July 1906 Koenig bought eighteen pounds of large whalebone for forty dollars, and twenty-six pounds of small whalebone for thirty-nine dollars from a local man called Ququk. In consideration, "Henry King" (Koenig) drew up a letter of agreement with "Koko (a native)" to purchase in Seattle "sixteen sacks of flour, one hundred pounds of sugar, fifty pounds of butter, fifty yards of calico, one hundred pounds of lead, twenty-five pounds of powder, two thousand no. $2\frac{1}{2}$ primers, two thousand no. 2 primers, one thousand no. 1 primers, and one dozen sixteen–ounce tins of baking powder." Any balance of the seventy-nine dollars due to Ququk would be repaid thereafter. The deal was witnessed by the trader Joseph Tuckfield and the missionary Edward J. Knapp, who composed the letter. Everyone, including "Kookwarook" (Quqauraq, the diminutive of Ququk), signed the agreement.

Of special interest in these journals is the record of how Tikiġaġmiut and traders met each others' immediate needs. The traders required seal line and caribou and sealskin clothes to support their hunting effort. Tikiġaġmiut needed manufactured goods to make up for the diminished scope of their own activities. The scarcer the game, the greater the need for imported technology in the form of firearms and steel traps; the less meat that hunters could bring in, the more essential the import of carbohydrates, flour in particular. Equally revealing was the way in which local goods acquired an exchange value set by Europeans. However benign any trader may have been, the new value assigned to local goods subtly altered their identity, just as imported goods began to overlay the material culture of native Tikiġaq.

Koenig's life at Jabbertown was relatively successful. His wife, "Daisy" Pausana, bore him six sons and a daughter, and the family sustained good relations with both Tikiġaq and the Jabbertown community. For most of the Jabbertown period, circa 1887–1916, the missionaries exercised a moderating influence on the practice of trade. John Driggs was both keenly interested in village welfare and a close friend of Koenig and other Jabbertown traders. The manufacture of and trade in alcohol were banned. As the document drawn up by Knapp suggests, the native population continued to have its independent advocate.

The majority of Koenig's contemporaries did rather poorly, and their lives remain obscure. Most of them, including Driggs and a few natives, joined a gold prospecting venture on the Pitmigiaq River and went so far as to stake out claims, but nothing came of it. Following the collapse of the baleen market, Jabbertown declined, though some of the Europeans who had married locally stayed on. Koenig went south before the baleen trade dried up and switched from whale hunting to rabbit breeding in Washington state. Tuckfield removed to a houseboat on the Kuukpak River, where he subsisted quietly until his death. By the 1920s the traders had all gone, and their houses were hauled by skinboat into Tikiġaq. At least six of these houses were used until recently, and a few of them were even moved to the new town site in 1975.

ATAŊAURAQ

The fragmentary story of Ataŋauraq is the last uqaluktuaq in the purely local tradition. Ataŋauraq was not Tikiġaq's last shaman, but this first and last Tikiġaq "chief" preeminently embodied the forces that were to change Tikiġaq society forever. Most of the story takes place in the late 1880s, Ataŋauraq's final years of power. It ends abruptly with his murder in February 1889 and is followed by a postscript on his assassins.

Ataŋauraq's career evolved in the context of the Euro-American trading presence. A bold and successful trader, his patronage spread through Tikiġaq until he was acting as broker between the big ships and the whole village. Along with this economic power, Ataŋauraq set up an improvised fiefdom based on vastly exaggerated umialik status and simple terror. Status like his was unprecedented in the western Arctic, although other "chiefs" established themselves in the widespread social and economic collapse that followed contact. The best-known and most successful of the new trading bosses was Goharren of Indian Point, Siberia, and Ataŋauraq may have heard of him at the Sisualik trade fair and been inspired by his example (Bockstoce 1986). Like Goharren, Ataŋauraq did well for almost a decade, and his initial success in bringing trade goods to the village helped stabilize Tikiġaq's subsistence crisis. However, Ataŋauraq overreached himself. He stole wives (there were five in his iglu on the night he died) and murdered almost at random when he was thwarted. His own assassination was delayed only because the villagers feared his henchmen, his (moderate) shamanic power, and punishment by the U.S. Coast Guard;* not least, the villagers stood in simple awe of the man.

Another factor was at work against Ataŋauraq, one that might well have destroyed him earlier. The feud sparked off by the murder of Suuyuk the Elder (story 20; see also fig. 2, p. 152) still smoldered, and since Ataŋauraq had been one of Suuyuk's associates and was at the very least witness to the subsequent revenge killing, he remained a target of the anger of his victim's sons. Thus Ataŋauraq's assassins had a double motive, which was well understood in the community. "Kayuktuq and Aniqsuaq acted against him," said Asatchaq, "because of what Ataŋauraq had done to their ancestors" (that is, to their father, Quliuq). Asatchaq's voice, if not his private view, remained impartial. Stories of Ataŋauraq's life and murder had filled his childhood; but since the assassins were related to his great-grandfather's murderer,

---

*The U.S. Revenue Marine Service had, since 1879, patrolled the Alaskan coast to suppress the production and sale of alcohol, and had at least once uncovered and smashed large numbers of stills in Tikiġaq. The Coast Guard's brief was the enforcement of U.S. law among the indigenous and European communities; one previous summer, a group of desperate Tikiġaq men had asked them simply to take Ataŋauraq away with them. Ironically, the Iñupiaq term for the Coast Guard was aŋuyagukti, "one who wants to harm."

his retrospective allegiance was divided. Still, Ataŋauraq's death saw the end of blood feuds in Tikiġaq, and thus the havoc that he had fueled at last climaxed and burned out.

With news of Ataŋauraq's death current throughout northwest Alaska, the Coast Guard arrived to arrest his killers. When the officers of the *Bear* came ashore in August 1889, they identified the culprits but found that Aniqsuaq was dead and that Kayuktuq had traveled to Uivvaq (Cape Lisburne) in advance of the Marine Revenue Service. The *Bear* steamed north in pursuit. But when the Coast Guard anchored off the beach and a dinghy was put out, Kayuktuq disappeared into his tent, loaded a shotgun, handed it to his wife, and pushed her out with it. There she stood, gun leveled, as the Americans landed. "But," said Asatchaq, concluding this episode of the saga which had started with Suuyuk on the same Uivvaq beach, "when they saw her standing there, they went away again." As in stories 9 and 14, there is a suggestion of ritual drama here: Kayuktuq could, after all, have vanished into the interior.

Born in 1891, the storyteller Asatchaq owed his life to Ataŋauraq's destruction. In the year leading up to the assassination, Asatchaq's mother, Niġuvana, aged about fourteen, lived in Ataŋauraq's house: she was to marry Ataŋauraq's adopted son, Siuluk. As soon as Ataŋauraq was dead, Asatchaq said, "Niġuvana was taken by my father's mother to marry Kiḷigvak." Tikiġaq's hatred and fear of Ataŋauraq were encapsulated in Asatchaq's family's experience. "Suuyuk the Younger" (story 21) describes Ataŋauraq's presumed shamanic attack on Asatchaq's father, Kiḷigvak, and paternal uncle Suuyuk; years earlier, Ataŋauraq had assaulted Asatchaq's grandmother and forced her family to flee up the coast into temporary exile. Asatchaq's maternal uncle Samaruna had his life threatened for withholding some fox skins Ataŋauraq wanted. Such incidents became commonplace. As Asatchaq remarked in the tale: "To Ataŋauraq, all the people were alike, relatives or not; he'd kill anyone he pleased. But by doing this, he turned everyone in Tikiġaq against him, and they grew to be afraid of him and hated him."

Beyond these speculations about Ataŋauraq's place in late nineteenth-century history, the "chief" remains an enigma. For all the unprecedented hatred he stirred in Tikiġaq, he is remembered with a certain respect. Perhaps the closer he is to the modern age, the harder he is to see. Aŋatkuqs of the precontact era, mysterious as they remain, performed within a native system whose theories were compatible with what the shamans did; thus their actions are coherent and readable from the outside. Because Ataŋauraq so powerfully embodied the confusion of rapid historical change, the structures through which to perceive him are fewer.

Umigluk (David Frankson), the narrator of "Ayagiiyaq and Pisiktaġaaq" (story 23) and the son of Aġviqsiiña, who belonged to Ataŋauraq's clan, provided perhaps the most succinct analysis of Ataŋauraq's career. "He started all right; he helped Tikiġaq people; he brought them things and fair trade with the white man. But after a while he went bad." Alcohol abuse, said Umigluk, was one important factor, and few old Tikiġaġmiut would disagree with that diagnosis. But then Umigluk drew on an archetypal figure of legend who appears in several stories not represented in this collection. The figure is that of the *iñuqaġnaiḷaq*, "the man who habitually murders people." Like Ataŋauraq (perhaps), the iñuqaġnaiḷaq starts his career in a reasonable and orderly way; he then loses a favorite child and in his grief embarks on a course of indiscriminate murder. "This," said Umigluk, "is what happened to Ataŋauraq. His youngest daughter died, and he started to kill people."

Whether or not the story is true, it nonetheless suggests that some Tikiġaq people did see Ataŋauraq both as a new man ("Ataŋauraq was like a white man," as Asatchaq's story expresses it) and, perhaps retrospectively, as a representative person of legend. And perhaps there were other traits belonging to the recognizable shamanic persona. How, for example, might Ataŋauraq's own ancestor Qaunnaiḷaq, or the adult Aniŋatchaq or Aquppak, have responded to the demands of cultural adaptation? Many of Tikiġaq's remembered shamans were larger than life, huge in energy and reckless of opposition, and it is difficult not to see Ataŋauraq's career in terms of the same bold figuration. While one function of the old shamans was to enforce certain inherited codes, another was to modify or disrupt them, thus setting new precedents. In transferring the focus of his interest from shamanism to trade and "local government," Ataŋauraq, for better or worse, forced open new areas of potential experience.

While he certainly did not renounce his own shamanic practice, Ataŋauraq boldly and self-consciously took large steps toward the freedom of a new secular order. For example, one eyewitness recorded how Ataŋauraq at a stroke dissolved a complex of whaling taboos by ordering one of his wives to bring a coal-oil stove onto the sea ice during the whale hunt, although both women and fire had long been proscribed during whaling (Brower 1950: 55).

In the commentary to story 21, Ataŋauraq is described as "rampaging through the debris." Images of breakdown and reintegration suffuse shamanic discourse (see the commentary to "Tigguasiña"). The aŋatkuq's initiation involved removal both from a functioning self and from the routines of secular tribal life. Without a conventional self and an ordered society to return to, the shaman could never put his initiatory crisis to creative use. Tikiġaq's traumatic induction into nineteenth-century American life was far from being a shamanic experience. It was, nonetheless, a dizzying, disorienting period of collective breakdown. But in contrast to the crisis of shamanic initiation, there were no positive structures to grasp on the other side. Ataŋauraq may not have become an iñuqaġnaiḷaq because he lost his favorite daughter. His personal drama seems, nevertheless, to have been an emblem, and a personification, of Tikiġaq's collective trauma. Unlike his predecessors, whose creativity reinforced—and whose destructiveness could on the whole be contained within—traditional organization, Ataŋauraq's personal explosion of bravura took place within the communal explosion. There was nothing to contain him. Assimilating the disorder, he converted it to his own law. When the consequences of his actions—and the laws of retribution stemming from the Suuyuk feud—brought him down, an uncanny peace descended on the village. This left the survivors—of continuing famine and disease as well as Ataŋauraq's terror—to work painfully at reconciling what was left of their tradition with the pressures of a modern order which the "chief" had done so much to further.

AYAGIIYAQ AND PISIKTAĠAAQ:
SHAMANIC CONFLICT AT WHALING TIME

"Ayagiiyaq and Pisiktaĝaaq" was told in English by Umigluk (David Frankson), **23** *grandson of the shaman Ayagiiyaq, with occasional comments by his wife, Aviq. The events of the story took place around 1900, at whaling season in Tikiĝaq: but the sea ice was closed, making it impossible for hunters to take their skinboats to open water. By this time Christianity had become well established in Tikiĝaq, so the local shamans no longer performed in public. Five miles south of the village, however, the Kobuk shaman Pisiktaĝaaq was working for the Jabbertown whalers. Some Tikiĝaq umialiks sent for Pisiktaĝaaq to change the wind and open the sea ice. Ayagiiyaq, a local shaman, intercepted Pisiktaĝaaq's first dangerous and exposed attempt at his work, thus demonstrating that Tikiĝaq shamanism was still very much alive beneath the Christian surface.*

I'll tell the story. First, everyone called him Ayagiiyauluk ["little old Ayagiiyaq"]. He was a small man. And that Ayagiiyaq was my grandfather, my mother's father.

One time in those days, a lot of people from Kobuk, Kivalina, Kotzebue, Noatak—they came down with dog teams with all their equipment to whale at Jabbertown. And there were a lot of people at Jabbertown. And Pisiktaĝaaq from Kobuk was among them.

And in the spring when the whaling season came, the lead, the lead wouldn't open, it was closed all the time, and the Point Hope people are getting worried that there won't be a good whaling season: no good whaling this spring.

So they sent word down to Jabbertown, sent somebody down to tell Pisiktaĝaaq that Point Hope people would like to have him come down to Point Hope sometime, so that through his *aŋatkuaq* [shamanizing] the lead would open, and they would pay him for doing that.

And the messenger came back, and he said he'd do it, just to help everybody, because he's anxious to get paid too—maybe sealskins, seal lines, things they need down there [in the Kobuk River region], maybe blubber, maybe *maktak* [whaleskin and blubber], things like that, you know, that are precious to him.

So next day—he told the messenger he'd come the next day. So the next day everybody gathered at the Point. There's a bend at the Point [southeast of the tip]. Everybody gathered there, at the bend. The Point goes this way [*narrator gestures*] on the south side. Everybody gathered there . . . everybody gathered.

And when they gathered, Pisiktaġaaq told the young men, not too far away from the beach, on the ice down there where the level is, the level ice, he told them to dig a big hole. And the young men started to make a hole. They made it, and they take all the ice out, and make it really clear. Taking all the slush ice out, and making it really clear.

After they'd done this, he put up a little tent . . . what are they called? *Akiivik*, that's bearded-seal intestines sewn together, which makes a pretty good-sized rain shelter for traveling. So he told them to make a little tent out of the akiivik right alongside a skinboat. They did it, and everybody sat. And Ayagiiyaq [the rival shaman] put his parkie, he took his arms from the sleeves of the parkie, and bent his legs and put his parkie over his knees. They call this *umiumak*. And he sits there alone. And he watched.

When they were ready, Pisiktaġaaq told them, told his helper to tie *aliq* [a long seal line] all around him. And he wants one small dead puppy. And they gave him that, one that's just been born and died.

And he goes into the tent, into that little tent he's had made. And everybody's watching while he starts getting his power there. They can see the little tent move as he starts to get his power. Not too long after he's got his power. He didn't use a drum. [Aviq: "Just singing."] Just singing. Everybody watched silently. A lot of people.

Then he told one of his helpers to get hold of the seal line. And when he'd got his power, he came out of that little tent, and he starts to walk round the hole in the ice. After he'd gone round, probably four times, he wanted to jump in. Then he jumped. In that hole. He didn't go in. As though it's solid. Can't go in. Can't go through. He just *pigliq*-ed [bounced], you know, bounced. [Aviq: "Bounced."] When he jumped in that hole, he bounced. He can't get in.

He tries it several times and he can't do it. And he says, "I can't do it." He says to the people, "I can't do it. I'll try tomorrow again. I can't get through today, I'll try again tomorrow." And after he said that, he put a *long* look at Ayagiiyaq. A *long* one. [Aviq, softly: "*Long* . . . time."] He didn't say anything. And everybody went home.

Next day they gathered down there again, they came down and gathered down there again. He's kind of mad [angry], you know, that Pisiktaġaaq. So he tried it this time, and he made it. He goes through. And they hold him. And the line's moving and one person's holding him. And finally he came back, came up. There he has that puppy in his one hand. And it's cut in half. [Aviq: "In the middle."] That dead puppy. [Aviq: "*Napik:* broken in half."] That means the ice is going to break.

He came up, and when he gets good, he tells the people, "Tomorrow morning, early morning, the ice is going to break, and everybody will go out and whale." [Aviq: "And catch whale."] Yah . . . yah . . . And Point Hope would catch a whale when the sun was there. Then everybody goes home.

It breaks next day, and they catch a whale. You know what he did, Ayagiiyaq? Played trick on that first day, you know, on that hole, so *he* wouldn't go through. And Pisiktaġaaq is really mad . . . that's why he got mad at him, and he's trying to kill him . . . for that reason [*spoken very softly*]. That's what the story is, see, for that reason, because Ayagiiyaq had played trick on it [the ice hole] and he couldn't get through. And he was trying to shame. And he got mad at Ayagiiyaq and tried to kill him. After they went back [to the Kobuk River].

[Lowenstein: "Was Ayagiiyaq jealous of him?"]

No . . . No . . . He wanted to show how much power he had to prevent him from doing a thing like that.

[Aviq: "Just to show him how much power he had."] Just to play it. But Pisiktaġaaq didn't like that. Ayagiiyaq didn't try to kill him. He just did it to discourage him. He was a pretty strong aŋatkuq.

[Lowenstein: "Why did these aŋatkuqs fight?]

It was like men in the past who sometimes used to say, "I'm a good fighter. I'm a good hunter. I'm a good singer." Something like that. It was the same thing with all aŋatkuqs, they wanted to trick each other, each one wanted to be best himself, to be best aŋatkuq. That's how they acted.

. . .

The present story records Tikiġaq's last public shaman conflict. The background to the conflict was familiar to Tikiġaq whalers. A south wind had brought the pack ice and the shore-fast ice together, closing the channel through which whales migrated. Until there was a north wind to force open a lead, the whale hunt could not begin. Control of the sea ice by supernatural manipulation of the wind was an important shamanic specialization. Some shamans dealt only with the south wind; others were "north wind aŋatkuqs." The right wind direction was so vital to all kinds of hunting that many nonshamans also practiced raising or allaying wind.

Asatchaq remembered the names of ten shamans still working in Tikiġaq at the time of this story, and three of them, including Ayagiiyaq, were highly regarded. At least one, Tiguatchialuk, was, like the Kobuk shaman in this story, an adept in spirit flight; another, Anaqulutuq, was an early convert to Christianity. However, after Dr. John Driggs established himself in the village and started to preach the new religion, both shamanism and village ceremonialism quickly declined. Driggs had been stationed in Tikiġaq to alleviate the social and medical effects of contact. His work as a doctor helped stem the worst imported diseases, and in confronting abuses by Euro-American whalers and the trade in alcohol he brought Tikiġaq into the realm of American civic order. The disorder that preceded Driggs's arrival had already done much to undermine the local religious system. The commercial hunters had demonstrated how efficiently they could catch whales without recourse to ritual and taboo observance, and the shaman Ataŋauraq was one of the first to follow their example. A decline of qalgi ceremonies accompanied inroads on whaling ritual. As the village population dropped, the qalgi buildings themselves collapsed, and only two were left by the turn of the century. In the circumstances, it took little persuasion from Driggs to convert Tikiġaq, almost wholesale, to Christianity within the first two or three years of his ministry.

Despite these factors, shamanism somehow prevailed for another decade. Some aŋatkuqs converted but continued to practice in secret. And even as the new religion became established, traditional ideas coexisted alongside it. This might have appeared an agreeable balance were it not for the fact that Christianity claimed no sway on wind direction and sea-ice dynamics. These matters, as several texts show (see stories 8, 12, and 18), were the sphere of the shaman; and since the whale hunt was a communal event, the shaman was expected to perform in public to induce a north wind and to keep the ice steady. But since the aŋatkuqs could no longer practice in the open, Tikiġaq whalers faced a major dilemma.

Five miles down the south shore, the Jabbertown hunters were, like the Tikiġaġmiut, waiting for the ice to open. The Kobuk shaman Pisiktaġaaq had come there to work for the commercial whalers. Evangelical Christianity had in fact arrived on the Kobuk and Noatak Rivers before the Episcopalian mission reached Tikiġaq, and although the majority of river-dwelling Iñupiaqs had coverted to Christianity, the rhythm of their nomadic existence made it easy for shamans such as Pisiktaġaaq to continue their practice. Thus, while Pisiktaġaaq was at Jabbertown to work within the new secularized dispensation for cash and European goods, he was still well known as a practicing shaman and was, moreover, conveniently beyond the power of the Tikiġaq mission.

Pisiktaġaaq takes the stage in this story with all the gusto and bravura of a north Alaskan aŋatkuq. Many elements of his performance and Ayagiiyaq's intervention were familiar shamanic business. Iñupiaqs often secluded the shaman in a little tent as he went into trance, and Ayagiiyaq's arm-rubbing gesture was a well-known means of generating hostile power to keep game from hunters. Here the gesture may imply that Ayagiiyaq was helping to maintain unfavorable conditions, but more likely, he was deflecting the course of his rival's *qiḷa* (shamanic power). The shaman's intimidating, eye-to-eye confrontation was a local version of the "evil eye," and for lay people such a stare might constitute shamanic attack. Pisiktaġaaq's leap was preliminary to a journey beneath the sea ice. Both leaping and seabed spirit journeys were characteristic shamanic gestures, and to bounce back from the water surface, as in "Qipuġaluatchiaq" (story 7), was a sign of incompletely generated or interrupted power. The business with the dog had double meaning. In the first place, a symbolic connection existed between wolf or dog and whale, as we saw in "Aniŋatchaq," where the chief of the whaling spirits has a dog's or wolf's tail (see the commentary to that story and, more fully, Lowenstein 1993). Most Tikiġaq skinboats carried wolf and/or dog amulets during the whale hunt: perhaps the exposure of a newborn but dead puppy was a way of enticing whales to visit a kindred soul. The second level of symbolism lay in the splitting of the puppy's carcass, which would induce a sympathetic response in the sea ice.

Beneath this story's jaunty tone and entertaining theatricality lie darker, unspoken issues. The primary issue is the paralysis of the

Tikiġaq shaman community, its incapacity to perform at a moment of crisis. The personal humiliation of the shaman Ayagiiyaq, expressed in his bitter and pointless interruption of a séance designed to help his own community, indicates how deeply this impotence was felt. It was doubly insulting that a man from inland who had come to work for Tikiġaq's whaling competitors should take over from the sea-ice hunters' own spiritual adepts. Unspoken, too, is the crisis of subsistence that lay behind this particular, temporary hitch to whaling. Asatchaq related a Tikiġaq story from about one decade earlier that explains the situation in bleaker and more peremptory language; here, though, the absence of whales caused by the commercial hunters is attributed to a Tikiġaq shaman.

> The shaman Maŋŋuyaaluk made the animals disappear. No one could find anything. People were starving. They were growing skinny. It was springtime. No whales. And the people were starving. People were dying. And here is Nasuaŋaluk, another shaman. And people paid him to shamanize and make the game return. And so they pitched a tent for him, on the gravel on the south beach, and he started singing:

> *Sumun makua tililagitch?*
> *Aġvitvitchli tilailagitch?*
> *Uvuŋa imma Tikiġaġmun imma!*

> Where shall I sweep them?
> Where should I sweep the whales?
> I want to sweep them in to Tikiġaq!

The story ends with the death of the guilty shaman and the onset, as in the present text, of a successful whale hunt. Tikiġaq hunters did continue to catch a few whales in the early years of this century. But in the context of the general subsistence collapse, these few were never enough. Stories such as "Ayagiiyaq and Pisiktaġaaq" and Asatchaq's tale of Maŋŋuyaaluk are painful but uncomplaining expressions of decades of hardship, of refusal to give up, and of faith in human power to transcend large and uncontrollable events. After all, if a shaman was capable of keeping whales away, then he could also bring them in. But to add to the poignancy, because of accumulating outside intervention, the shamans' days were also numbered.

PISIKTAĠAAQ: A SHAMAN ON HIS DEATHBED

Pisiktaġaaq, the Kobuk shaman of the preceding story, died in 1931 in the **24** *Kotzebue clinic; there, in his last illness, he was baptized by Aviq, who told this story in English. By the time of Pisiktaġaaq's death, Euro-American institutions, including a rudimentary public health service, were well established in the Arctic. Like many other young Tikiġaġmiut, Aviq was literate and Christian and, despite possessing traditional healing powers of her own, accepted Western medicine. Aviq's firsthand account of Pisiktaġaaq's death is an electrifying evocation of a shaman's mind in the grip of a terror he himself once inspired.*

And that Pisiktaġaaq that we were talking about, he died in 1930 . . . no, it was '31. That year there was a lot of flu, and I went down to Kotzebue. The field nurse took me down because I wasn't feeling well and I went down for an operation. And after I was there for a while I got heavy flu.

I arrived there in March and I stayed until July. And after I got over the flu, I was walking round the hospital when they brought in an old man from the Kobuk, and it was Pisiktaġaaq. And they had three Eskimo nurses. One of them was Charlie Rich's daughter.* She was the best one. She died long ago.

And they always used to tell me that Pisiktaġaaq was a real medicine man, a *bad* man, they called him a bad man. Every summer in the Kobuk villages or in Kotzebue, whatever she liked, he told his daughter to go get it. "If you like it, go get it, and if they don't give it to you, through my power I'll kill them. Or make them sick or cripple their legs." That's why they were scared of that man. White things too, white man's clothing. The daughter would just go and get them from the store without paying. That's why they don't like him.

"Charlie Rich": Rich was a Kobuk River Iñupiaq.

And they told me that Pisiktaġaaq was really sick. I could hear his voice and tell he was having a hard time from his voice like this, "Ohhh . . . arriii . . . Ohhh . . . arriii . . ." He was having a hard time. "I won't make it, I'm going to die!" And one of those girls told me, "He won't make it through his power even, he's going to die."

So one night around six . . . one of the nurses and Doctor Smith . . . I always had my prayer book and my Bible. I always read them, my prayer book and my Bible. And they know this. One of the nurses came over and said, "The doctor wants you to come over to that sick person, that old man."

"*Irrigi*," I said [an exclamation of fear]. "He's aŋatkuq . . ." Yes, he's real aŋatkuq. But I go over there and pray for him. He doesn't know how to pray, the aŋatkuq. He's asked for someone to pray for him. "I need someone to come over and pray for me." He'd sent through those nurses. So I grab my prayer book and I go over to his room.

The doctor was there and the doctor's wife and two native nurses. Pisiktaġaaq looks at me. "*Aŋaiyullaviñ?* Do you know how to pray?" He was having a hard time . . . gee whiz. And I say, "Yes, *aŋaiyullaruŋa,* I know how to pray." "You pray for me. I want *paptaiguruŋa,* I want baptism." "*Paptainiagitpiñ,* I can baptize you," I said. So I tell the doctor and the nurses, "Get the water for me in a little bowl." They go get it for me. And I take the prayer book. And before everything I start to pray and talk to him in Eskimo.

[Here Aviq inserted a passage in Iñupiaq in which she urges Pisiktaġaaq to renounce shamanism and embrace Jesus. Pisiktaġaaq replies that he wants to be baptized and go to Jesus. His vision is darkening.]

[Pisiktaġaaq:] "I know my trail when I close my eyes, as I try to die, no light, all dark, no place to go. *Dark! Aaqqaa!* [a cry of disgust]. That smell! It really stinks! I don't like that!" And then he starts to cry. And while he's crying, he tells us: "All over! Barrow, Wainright, Point Hope, all through the Kobuk River, Diomede, Nome and other villages! Through my power I killed them. I . . . *killed* lots of people through my power." And he cried and cried. "I confess. After you baptize me I will vomit up my power. You will see it."

And after he confessed all his sins, then he asked me, "What's your name? Who are your parents?" And I told him about Samaruna, my uncle, and my auntie Niġuvana, and my mother, Tarruq, my father, Uvigaq . . . and he started to cry more: cri-i-i-ed *loud*. "Yes, I tried to kill your mother once—two times. Your mother's legs swelled all over, I made your mother's legs swell and go rotten. I did this through my power."

I know what he meant. He was right. It was true. My mother, when I was a young girl, before I got married, my mother's legs were swollen a-a-ll over. And a woman called Aġġiik treated her, using a piŋutaq.* She wasn't an aŋatkuq. She was Jimmie's uncle's wife, she was crippled. Kunuyakauluk's wife. And that woman saved my mother. She qapuk-ed [cut] 'em, and the bones came out rotten and she began to heal and she got better. "That was the second time. The first time, I tried to swell her face." My mother's teeth were swollen.

And the reason for this was that one summer, Aġġiik and my mother, when they traveled to Kotzebue to trade, every time they met that medicine man, he wanted to shake hands. And Aġġiik and my mother got tired of this. Tired of shaking hands with him. So one day when they were shaking hands, my mother qavlumairuq [raised her eyebrows]. And next day when they passed each other, the medicine man turned away so as not to meet them. After that my mother's legs swelled. He didn't like that qavlumairaq.*

So when he knew me, after he'd confessed and he knew my parents' names, I started to pray for him and I said the Lord's Prayer. Then after I'd prayed, I opened my prayer book and gave him the baptismal prayer and I baptized him with water. And after I baptized him—he was having a hard time you know—his face was like this [radiant upward gesture].

"Taikku-u [thank you]! God-mullasituŋa [Now I can go to God]! I see my light! God will receive me! I will go to heaven! I thank you. All my sins are forgiven. I am sorry for all my mistakes. I can go to heaven now. Thank you!"

Then he started to vomit. "All of you see my power!" And Doctor Smith was there and his wife. And I told them, "Get some of that heavy white paper. He wants something to vomit onto." So they got the paper, really heavy paper, and we put it there, and he started to vomit.

"All of you see my power, that I used so much." And he started vomiting. And he vomited. And it was this long [about two inches], that arrowhead he vomited. A kukigralik [arrowhead]. It was of white, bright stone that's like glass. A long arrow point, well shaped all over, a good shape, a real long one. And he put it there.

And he told us, "Be sure to burn this. It's not good. It was used for killing people everywhere, in all the villages. Be sure you burn it. Destroy

"piŋutaq": A piŋutaq was a small flint blade used to release "bad blood" (augluk).
"qavlumairaq": The gesture of raising one's eyebrows signifies "yes" or "all right." The shaman correctly interprets it as a comment on his behavior: he is being treated as a child or a lunatic.

it." And he gave it to me. And the doctor grabbed my hands. Doctor Smith grabbed my hands. So he could destroy it himself. So he and his wife took it over to another room, you know, to boil it. That's what I figure. [Umigluk: "Sure, he kept it. He wouldn't destroy it!"]

Then after I baptized him, he began to sing. "I'd like to know how to pray. Ah! Lord God! I am now one of your members. I'll be in you. Forgive all my sins. Thank God. And this woman: when she goes home to Point Hope, give her all kinds of animals, through her husband. Give her all the jobs possible throughout their lives. I don't like to see them heavy, God, in your power, those two, she and her husband. So it's right." And that evening he died. Smiling he died. Yes, that's a true story.

.   .   .

In "Jabbertown and Ataŋauraq," we saw how Euro-American culture entered the Arctic. In the events of the present story, which occurred about 1930, we witness the way the Iñupiaq world had been penetrated by Euro-American institutions. It is important not to exaggerate the changes that had taken place. Iñupiaq life remained at subsistence level. Most people still lived in iglus or small sod-insulated cabins heated with seal oil. Everyone spoke Iñupiaq, and most people over thirty were probably monolingual. But even on the evidence of the present story, the changes were real. Qiqiktaġruk has become Kotzebue; Tikiġaq is Point Hope. The shaman Pisiktaġaaq dies surrounded by Iñupiaq nursing aides and prayer books and in the care of an American medical professional. Wonderfully evoked are Dr. Smith's possession of basins and heavy paper and—in Umigluk's interpolation—his supposed greed for curios. In Dr. Smith's equipment we see, for the first time in these stories, imported goods at work within a small enclave of institutional American life, the tiny Kotzebue clinic that served a vast area of northwest Alaska. Nevertheless, the Euro-American presence had undergone a marked transformation of style. Thirty years earlier, when Pisiktaġaaq was shamanizing in Tikiġaq, the traders, missionaries, and doctors were free-lancers, or at least solitary. By 1930, schools, churches, stores, and clinics had been become established. Because they were imported to serve a public institution, the "basins and heavy paper" of the Kotzebue clinic were somewhat different from the goods that flowed informally between white men and Iñupiaqs at places such as Jabbertown. The improvised barter between natives and traders recorded by Koenig continued, but by the time of this story there were village stores even among the previously nomadic Kobuk River people, and Pisiktaġaaq's shamanic intervention in the business of these stores tangled anachronistically with new economic processes.

In the transformation of Pisiktaġaaq's flint to the status of a curio, we witness an ironic value reversal. As suggested in the commentary to "Jabbertown and Ataŋauraq," many Iñupiaq goods had already been given a new exchange identity. But while most bartered Iñupiaq wares had a local utility that made the white trader's interest in them functionally and economically explicable, we also saw at the end of Ataŋauraq's story how Koenig and his wife began to trade in local artifacts. In the present story, the magical and spiritual value of the shaman's amulet is thus observed from two divergent points of view. Pisiktaġaaq's perhaps opportunistic rejection of the arrowhead is echoed by Aviq's all-too-comprehending horror. But as the storyteller's husband points out ("Sure, he kept it. He wouldn't destroy it!"), in the eyes of the white doctor the amulet acquires a new complexion. The culture, partly obliterated by traders and condemned by the church, returns with a curiosity value. What Iñupiaqs had lost is thus reflected back on them through the window of a museum of their own past selves. The amulet itself is distanced and made impotent: once revealed in the clinic, it is a dead thing, impotent but fascinating because of its provenance, and thus collectable. We are witness to a further dual process. As the shaman vomits, the power drains from his tool. The doctor boils it, and the flint is sterilized. The two facts are parallel. In native theory, the shaman's body is emptied of power by the act of vomiting. In Western terms, the amulet is neutralized clinically and thus initiated into the sphere of its new culture. Whether the arrowhead gathered dust in a desk drawer with rubber bands and paper clips or found its way to a museum, its supernatural identity was effaced forever.

It would be redundant here to comment on Pisiktaġaaq's earlier shamanic province. The features of his practice were similar to those we have seen in previous stories, and his character in these two stories may no more be reduced to a psychopathy than may the characters of earlier shamans. In Iñupiaq societies, it was often the unpleasantness and sometimes the evil of shamanism that provided the spindles of incident around which narrative gathered. But shamanism, for all its acts of psychological terror, likewise ran lifelines through society; the lines went beyond its human members through the world of myth, the spirit realm, and the ethereal cosmos, the earth and the moon lying on an axis to which the shamans alone had access. It is thus impossible, from the vantage of a different time and culture, to put a moral value on the shamans' practice. The larger characters provided the best stories and were thus remembered even as ritual life declined; by contrast, the quiet lives of healers and those who inconspicuously subordinated themselves to ritual were largely forgotten.

Feelings in Tikiġaq and the Kobuk region about the demise of shamanism remained ambiguous. As we shall see, Iñupiaq Christians of the first half of this century often abominated the old aŋatkuq practice; but they invariably believed it to represent a power of which Christianity was a separate manifestation. The shaman's *tuuŋġaq* ("helping spirit") was real but fiendish. However, after the introduction of Christianity, Jesus and the prayer book could be invoked where the tuuŋġaq alone once operated. But this conversion of spiritual allegiance provoked problems with regard to the Iñupiaq people's relationship to their own ancestors. On the one hand, the ancestors remained objects of unblurred reverential focus; on the other, for all their knowledge and power, they were shown to have been pagans, living in a criminal darkness of spirit. For some professed Christians, such as the storyteller Asatchaq, this duality presented no problem; the two systems simply coexisted. But for many others, even today, the paradox remains agonizingly unresolved. Indeed, a sense of retrospective shame for the non-Christian past was one of the factors which most seriously undermined the self-confidence of Iñupiaq society.

Pisiktaġaaq's act of renunciation—the physical and shamanic intensity of the vomited white stone—leads us to contemplate the nature of Iñupiaq shamanism. First embodied in, then disembodied by, the shaman, who palms the arrowhead into his vomit in a grisly act of conjuring, the artifact itself is a powerful symbol of aŋatkuq energy. Shamanism, as represented in these stories, was a kind of psychic hunting. Its purpose was to send symbolic energy toward another being and penetrate that being; to capture a helping spirit and drive out rival souls in the act of healing; to magnetize animals with magical songs and lure them to the hunter; to turn the wind around; to bring in or send out the ice; to locate by clairvoyance lost travelers, dogs, or essential equipment. The shaman was one who saw through obstacles or across great distances or who traveled in spirit through space, underground, or beneath the surface of the water. All such sending, traveling, extending, and projection were acts of connection. And just as the hunter connected his prey with the extension of himself that a weapon represented, so shamanic acts diminished separation between humans and animals, self and object, life and death. The shaman Pisiktaġaaq's arrow, like Asatchaq's kikituk or any familiar, was his psychic hunting tool. But its power to connect him, for good or ill, to beings within the Iñupiaq cosmos was now over. The shaman died happy. Disconnected, he floated off into a cosmos free of arrowheads and tuunġaqs. It was a world both alien and blissful. But Pisiktaġaaq was canny enough to disengage from his past at the very last moment; for him the Christian sphere was nonfunctional, passive, and non-Iñupiaq; no Iñupiaq shaman could hunt within it.

In Tikiġaq itself, the institution of shamanism seems to have died out in the first decade of this century, but individual adepts continued to practice. Mostly healers, visionaries, and witches, they were not initiated into the spirit world their ancestors believed in, and they abandoned aŋatkuq singing and drumming in public. Thus their entry into trance was largely deritualized and often involuntary, and with certain exceptions they made no attempt to practice spirit flight. Many of these visionaries lived comfortably within a syncretic spiritual realm and carried the shamanic process into Christianity. For example, Asatchaq's mother, Niġuvana, described being taken in her dreams "to the 'singing people's' country" where she learned new songs for the postwhaling celebrations. In church, which she attended regularly, Niġuvana had visions of angels and the souls of departed Tikiġaġmiut hovering above the altar. Niġuvana also practiced traditional healing and, with several other Tikiġaq women, trained as a community midwife. A modified variety of precontact medicine, largely involving massage, laying on of hands, bone setting, and prayer, remains today a significant feature of life in Tikiġaq.

The storyteller Aviq is one such tribal doctor. It is therefore perhaps no coincidence that she, like other psychics before her, should have fallen afoul of competitive or malicious practitioners. The best known of these practitioners was Isuaġalaaq, who was credited with killing Asatchaq's father, Kiḷigvak, around 1925. Though several old people described Isuaġalaaq as an aŋatkuq, the old woman was perhaps closer to being an *ilisiilaq,* "witch, caster of spells," the term *aŋatkuq* being used loosely and perhaps in a slightly pejorative sense. By contrast, Niġuvana and, to a lesser degree, Aviq were each described as *qiḷaqaqtuaq,* "one having power," or *qiñaligaaq,* "one having vision."

Aviq's first encounter with Isuaġalaaq was as an observer. Here the old lady comes across as a victim both of her own trance and also of other aŋatkuqs:

When my mother took me to our fishing camp, we spent the night with Isuaġalaaq. When it was dark, she began to aŋatkuaq [shamanize]. I was sleeping. She started hollering. No words, just "Yeh-yeh-yeh-yeh! Yeh-yeh-yeh-yeh!" Her husband Kunaaluk said: "Light the lamp!" The old lady got better. "*Hauk!*" [an exclamation of fatigue]. Ah! I come back again! Thank you!" Her husband said: "Where have you been?" "Another aŋatkuq after me! She tried to kill me."

In the next two accounts, Aviq provides a vivid firsthand description of what it was like to feel persecuted by a shaman. Perhaps this sensitivity to psychic invasion is also an aspect of the shamanic character itself. The incidents here happened in the early 1930s, when Aviq and her husband were both operating a whaling boat and running the village store. During the spring whale hunt, while her husband was on the sea ice, Aviq had this dream about the shaman:

I was dreaming in the storeroom, in our place in the village store. I was working inside the house in my dream; working, working, cleaning up the room, and I swept the floor. I went to the storeroom and I swept it. And the door was open and I looked at it. The door was open—this wide [about a foot]. Then when I opened the door, somebody was in there, somebody with mouth open; she lay under the stores. I was scared. So I made the sign [of the cross], and when I'd made it I saw Isuaġalaaq, the medicine woman. She was putting something in my iglu, in my home. The door closed and I woke up. In my dream I'd made the sign of the cross like any person who tries to lead a good Christian life. I made a sign before I ever touched the mouth I saw. Before I stamped on it. I recognized her. I could only see the face lying just like this with the mouth open.

The persecution by Isuaġalaaq was to grow more intense. Aviq continued:

When I had my second pregnancy, I [already] had a baby girl. Said Isuaġalaaq, "Name your son Agliġauluk!" That was her son's name; he became a walrus; he went back to the walrus people. But we wanted my uncle's name, Isigraqtuaq. My husband said, "No, I don't like too many names." The aŋatkuq got mad. Two years later I was pregnant again. I was twenty-nine years. It was twins. That man came from Kotzebue. Superintendent. Vaccinating. I was seven or eight months pregnant. He wanted to give me a shot. He did. I had a hard time. It killed the babies. They were dead born, ten pounds each. I started to get sick. Even when I woke I see the aŋatkuq's face come into our house. The placenta never come out.

Niġuvana, my auntie, and one other tried to get the placenta. Both worked together. I was unconscious. In the end they took it out. More: that mother woman bother me again. *Arri!* All over. When I closed my eyes I saw her. Really dirty. Black skin parkie. Funny hair all scattered. People were stretching out all over to my body, praying for me. Hunters were all outside that February. When they came in they kneeled outside the store—we kept the store. All men all around. Lord's Prayer.

That helped me a bit. That woman went back a bit. But still she was after me. So I never change. Same thing. My husband said, "Put all the Bibles, all around her!" They did. And prayer books all round. Then I slept. Our Savior, his power coming in. I rested and slept. I slept, slept good.

But she still came in. I could see her. How stop? My father one night, he sat down by the store door. Warm clothes. He sat outside. He sat with crossed arms. He went home. It was late. My mother came to check me. His mother came to check me. They went home. My father came back. He was going to stay all night. Night watcher. I cry, "*Aapaŋ!* [Father!] She's coming again!" I knew she was coming. We *tupak* [were startled] in our room. My father was sitting there. Suddenly the door closed, hard. *Arraa!* [Too much!] And my father shouted: "*Tavralu kinnaġasuna!* [Crazy woman!] Go away! Die!" Suddenly the door closed. She'd gone. I felt better. I tried to sit up when the door shut.

Next day my mother's people, they saw the aŋatkuq. "How's Aviq?" they asked. "She's getting better." And she said she wanted me to die because we didn't want her son's name for our boy. And Kunaaluk was her husband. He said, "I had a hard time last night. I thought she was dying. She was unconscious a long time." And Kunaaluk prayed hard, and took the Bible. He prayed; he made her come back again. He took the Bible and made her come back. And he told his wife, "If you do that again to anyone, I won't try to help you. That's the last time you give me a hard time. You'd better stop *aŋatkuaq* [shamanizing]. It's no good for you now. Jesus only. Jesus only. He told her that. So she was stopped. She lived. But never bothered somebody.

The man regarded as Tikiġaq's last shaman was Masiiñ, who died in 1958. Still highly respected in Tikiġaq memory, this story about him, told to me by Alec Millik, remains current:

It was 1953, wintertime. My wife invited Masiiñ to supper. And after we had eaten, the old man told stories. Then he called me by name, and told us he'd been traveling last night. He'd been to Russia. And when he'd flown round for a while, he saw the Russian boss. "That's a bad man," said Masiiñ, "so I killed him." Next day, at three o'clock—we had a battery radio—I listened at my coffee break. The news announcer said Stalin was dead."

But Masiiñ knew no English. He died five years later without ever having learned a word of the language.

SIĠVANA AND THE OLD SHAMAN

Transcribed in Iñupiaq and translated by Lawrence D. Kaplan

Uvva . . .	unipkaaġniaqtuŋa
Here now . . .	I shall tell a story

uiñigulaitchuamik		uvani	Tikiġaġmigaluaq,	aanaaqaġluni
of one who never wanted to take a husband		here	long ago in Point Hope,	and she had parents

aasii.	Aasi uvva	aŋatkum	nuliaġuksimagaa.	Aasi taamna
too.	And so	a shaman	wanted to marry her.	And that

aġnaq atiqaġluni	Siġvamik.	Siġvamik	atiqaġluniguuq,
women had the name	Siġvana.	Siġvana	was her name, it is told,

aanaaqaġluni	aasiiñ.
and she had parents	too.

Aasi	aanaak	uqallautimagaluaġik	nuliaġuglugu,
And	her parents	he told	that he wanted to marry her,

aŋayugliatchiam,	aŋatkuuvluni	aglaan.	Patchisigimagaak
an old man,	who was a shaman,	however.	They left it up to

paniktik.	"Tasamma ki	ilaa uiñigukkumi,	uiñikkisigaatin."
their daughter.	"So then	if she wants a husband,	she will take you for a husband."

Tavra aasii	ullakkaluaġaa	unnuŋman,	naami	aniruq.
So then	he went to her	in the evening,	but no,	she went out.

Lawrence D. Kaplan is Associate Professor of Linguistics at the Alaska Native Language Center, University of Alaska, Fairbanks.

Animman   ittuallakkaluaġami,   aniruq.   Anivḷuni,   aŋatkuq
Since she had he stayed a while,   and went   He went out,   the shaman
gone out   out.

taamna   anivḷunitauq,   animman   taamna
that one went out too,   because she had gone out   that

niviaqsiaq kiuvvauna.   Tavra   kisununtai   igluŋnuktilaaŋa
young woman.   Then   to which house   she had gone

nalummigaa.   Tara   iḷitchuġivlugu   iñuŋniñ   uqaqtuaniñ
he did not know. So   he found out   from people   who were talking

tamauŋaqsaaqtuaq   imma.   Iḷitchuġigamiuŋ   taapkunuŋa   piviiñun,
she had gone down   earlier. When he found   to that   place she
that way   out   had gone,

isiqtuq.   Iḷisaġigamiuŋ   taavruma   niviaqsiam   isiġman,
he went in.   When she   that   young woman,   when he
               recognized him,   went in,

        aniruq,
        she went
        out,

niviaqsiaq taamna.   Taimma   animman,   malikkaġlugu   aniruq,
the young   that one.   Then   when she   following her   he went
woman,   went out,   out,

aasii   iñuŋnuguni   taamna   allanun,   niviaqsiaq.   Isiġman,
and   she went to   that one to others,   the young woman.   When she
        people   entered,

taavruma   aŋayuqagram   qanisani   paaġaa   taamna   niviaqsiaq.
that   old man   in the   he passed   that   young
                          entryway   her [going   woman.
                                       the other
                                       way]

Qimakkaluaqtaa niviaqsiam, paaġutiruk. Isiqsaġman sivulliglugu
Even though she the young they passed. When she he got in
had left him woman, started in, front of her,
behind,

qanisanuaniŋniqsuq. Paaġamiuŋ, utinmun aniruq. Allanun
for he had already gone When he turning back, she went At other
into the entryway. passed her, out. houses
    aasii
    too

iñuŋnulgiḷḷuni. Tainnaiḷiugaqsigaa isiqsaġman, paaġaġlugu.
she went to visit He kept doing this to her, when she started he passed
people. to enter, her.

    Kiisaimanna iniqtuuliutiaqsivaa taavruma niviaqsiam.
    Finally, she began to grow that young woman.
             tired of him,

      Talvauma
      Then he

siññiqsaġataġaa aŋatkum taavruma. Siñiguliqpan kiisaimma
made her fall the shaman this one. When she would finally
asleep, fall asleep,

qanuġisigaa samma. Tainnaiḷiugaqsigaa aigaluaġman qanisani
he would do something He kept doing this to even when she in the entry
to her then. her went home,

paaqpakkaa taamna aŋayuqagraq. Aigaluaġmata
she met him that old man. Even when they
went home,

    tainnaiḷiugaqsigaa
    he kept doing this to her

allanullu isiġman paaqtaliġlugu tuġruuŋni.
to other [houses] when she entered he would pass her in the entrance
tunnel.

Kiisaimanna   uiṅġaliqpuq   uiḷuaqtaq.   Uiṅġaliġami
Finally   she grew sleepy the woman who   When she grew
                                 wouldn't marry.   sleepy

         taimma,
         then,

aivḷuni.   Siñaaqsiruq.   Taamna kii   iḷisimaruq kii
she went home.   She began to   That one   knew
                    sleep.

         qanuġlaŋniġmik
         what to do,

aŋatkuq.   Suŋiñmigaa,   iññaqiniaŋiñmigaa,   aglaan   allamik
the shaman.   He did   he didn't even lie   but   something
                nothing to her,   with her,   else

         piñiaġaa
         he would do

tasamma.
then.

Unnuapak   aaquaġniqsuq   niviaqsiaq.   Kigutait
Overnight   she aged,   the young woman. Her teeth

kataŋmivḷutik   akisaanun,   qiḷġiq una.   Iḷitchuġigamitku
fell out   onto her pillow, she turned gray. They found out
                                                     about it,

aanaakisa,   tainnaqsimamman   kigutaiġḷuni,   kigutait   akisaanun
her parents,   that she was that way losing her teeth, her teeth   onto her
                                                                      pillow

kataŋmivḷutik,   qiḷġiq,   aaquagraq   una   unnuapak
falling out,   gray,   the old woman   this one   overnight

         aaquaġniqsuq.
         had aged.

Aaquaqsimamman,   suŋitchuq   taamna aŋatkuq.   Tainna
When she became an   he did nothing   that shaman.   Thus
old woman,

nayuġaluaġamitku   aanaakisa   paniktik,   makitiqtilaagraa
they stayed by her   her parents   (their daughter)   to see if she could get up

aaquagraq ki una.   Niviaqsiaq imma,   unnuaq,   kigutait
the old woman, this one.   A young woman, before   last night,   her teeth

inmiŋñik,   kigutait   kataŋmivḷutik,   qilġiq.
by themselves,   her teeth   were falling out,   [she was] gray.

Taimma   uqallautigaa   aġnaqtik,   "Aggiuŋ amna,   aŋatkuq
Then   he said   to his wife,   "Bring that one,   the shaman

taamamna.   Iluaqsiḷugu   nuliaġukkumiuŋ,   nuliaġisigaa   tasamma
that one.   He shall make   if he wants to   he shall marry   then
        her right   marry her,   her

uiñigukkumiuŋ.   Taamna aaqualliq   iḷuisimakpan   uiñiguliġniaġaa."
if she will have him   That being an old   if it is   she will want him
for her husband.   woman,   unpleasant   for her husband."

samma paniktik   tainna   pigaa   aapaŋan,   iluaqsiḷugu,
so [to] their daughter   thus   he said,   her father,   that by making
                her right,

        iluaqsiḷugu
        by making her right

nuliaġuŋmagaa.   Aaquagrauŋaiġḷugu.   Aigaa   aakaŋan.
he would marry   By making her no   She fetched   her mother
her.   longer be an old   him,   did.
        woman.

        Tainnakii
        This way

tavra   iliuqpalgiññiqsut   taimani   sivulliit   makua,
then   they really used to   back then,   the old time   these,
    shamanize   people,

    uiḷuaġman
    when [a woman] wouldn't marry

tainnaqpaksimalgitkai.   Isiqtuq   aŋatkuq,   isiġami
they really would do this   He entered,   the shaman;   when he
to them.   entered

    niviaqsiaŋusugauq
    the one who had been a young woman

kanna,   aaquagraq   kanna.   Iḷitchuġigaak   kigutait
was down   the old   there.   They found out   her teeth
there,   woman

    kataksimammiut,
    had fallen out, and

qiḷġiq.
[she was] gray.

    Isiġman,   aquvinman   aŋatkuq,   qanuŋiñmiuq.
    When he   and sat   the shaman,   she did nothing.
    entered   down,

    Aŋatkulaŋiñmiuq.
    He didn't shamanize.

Tainnaitchaqtillugu,   aumisaiñiñ una   puugraaŋniñ,   natchiq
Remaining thus,   from her bedding,   from her   a seal
                                      sleeping bag,

    paamġuaq
    a baby

(qaŋa imma,   uqaluktuaġmiraġa   uvva   paamġuaq,   tainnasikii
(long ago,   I told about,   you see,   a baby seal,   like this

Nanmaŋmik   paamġuaq.)   Iġlaŋagaluaqtuq   niviaqsiaq,
Nanmak   baby seal.)   She made a face,   the young
                                              woman,

   anilġ'ataġman
   it finally went out

inmiññiñ   puugraaŋniñ,   natchiq paamġuaq.   Paamġuġluni
from her,   from the   the baby seal.   Crawling,
            sleeping bag,

   iġlaŋagaluaqtuq
   she made a face

niviaqsiaq,   qanuġniaŋitchuq   makinniaŋitchuq   anigami
the young   she couldn't do   couldn't get up   when it went
woman,   anything,   out
   tarvaŋŋa
   from there

ilaaniñ puugraaŋniñ   aniruq   tainnasiq   quiññakkaluaqtuq
from her sleeping bag,   it went out   this thing,   even though it tickled

qanuġniaŋitchuq.   Aniqqaaġluni   aasii   utinmun   isilgiḷḷuni
she could do nothing.   After going out   then,   turning back   it went in
                                                                 again

niviaqsiamun.   Isiġman   taimma   aapaŋan   uqallautigaa
to the young   When it went   then   her father   said to
woman.   in
   aŋatkuq
   the shaman,

taamna,   "Tainnaiḷḷuni,   inniaŋitchuq   tasamma   uiñigukumisin,
that one,   "This way   she won't remain   so   if she wants you
                                                            for a husband,

uiñigniaġaatin,   taavrumiŋa   aglaan,   piqaŋaiġḷugu.   Ataramik
she will take you   that one,   though,   you must remove   Forever
for a husband;   from her.

itchuŋitchuŋnaqtuq   inmiñi.   Ititquŋitchuŋnaġaa   panimñuk.
she does not want to   herself.   She doesn't want to   our daughter.
be so   be kept this way,

Iluaqsiḷugu,   uiñigukumisin tasamma   uiñiksaġaatin."
Make her right;   if she wants you   then she will take you for
                  for a husband,   a husband."

Tavra iluaqsigaa.   Aaquagrauŋaiqsuq.   Iviqtittuq.
So he made her   She stopped being an She had been
right.   old woman.   turned back.
        Nuyaiḷḷu taatchaatun,
        Her hair [was] dark,

niviaqsiaq   una.   Aniaqsigami,   "Qanuq,"   qanuuġaa,
the young   this.   As he was   "Well,"   he said "well"
woman,   going out,   to her;
        maliksaġaaguuq.
        she said she would follow him.

Anusinŋuqsautim   paqisimagaa.   Niviaqsiamun   anusinŋuqsaun,
Punishment   had found her.   To the young   the punishment
                                       woman
        inmiñun
        to herself

tikittuaq.   Uqallautigaaguuq   talva niviaqsiam   maliksaġaaguuq.
had reached.   She spoke to him   then, the young   said she would
                                     woman   follow him.

Tavra animman,   malikkaa.   Aŋayuqagraq   niviaqsiamik
So when he went   she followed   The old man   the young woman
out,   him.

nuliaġataqtilgitchuq,   talva uvva!   Talvaguuq,   iviqtillugu,
finally took for a wife,   right away!   So it is said,   by changing her back,

iviqtillugu,   aggisigamiuŋ,   iviqtillugu,   niviaqsiaŋuġlugu.
by changing   he took her home,   by changing   and making her a young
her back,   her back,   woman again.

Siġvanaguuq,   tavra,   taapkuak   paniak,   tainnaqtuaq.
Siġvana, it is   then,   those two   their daughter,   she did this.
told,

GLOSSARY OF NAMES AND TERMS

Numbers in parentheses refer to story numbers.

NAMES

Aġviqsiiña (Frank)	Tikiġaq storyteller, circa 1875–1945.
Aliŋnaq	The spirit of the moon, *tatqim iñua* (2).
Anaugraq	Trading partner of Aniŋatchaq (8).
Aniŋatchaq	Tikiġaq shaman (8).
Aniqsuaq	Son of Quliuq and murderer of Ataŋauraq (20, 22).
Aniqsuayaaq	Diminutive of Aniqsuaq; Tom Lowenstein's given Iñupiaq name.
Aqsaqauraq	Paniunayuk's rival (15).
Aquppak	Tikiġaq shaman, also called Kattuaq (12).
Asatchaq	1. Jimmie Killigivuk, Tikiġaq storyteller, 1891–1980; 2. nineteenth-century shaman (19).
Ataŋauraq	Tikiġaq shaman and "chief" (22).
Aviq	Dinah Frankson, Tikiġaq storyteller, born 1908, and wife of Umigluk (David Frankson) (23, 24).
Ayagiiyaq	Tikiġaq shaman (23).
Iḷaŋiaqpak	Kivalina man (3).

Imaġliq	Little Diomede Island.
Iñupiaq (pl. Iñupiat)	"Real person"; north Alaskan Inuit.
Ipiutak	Proto-Inuit site at Tikiġaq.
Iqiasuaq	"The lazy one" (5).
Itivyaaq	Group of spirits and place where they live (8).
Kavisiġluk	Niġliq's brother (14).
Kayuktuq	Son of Quliuq (20).
Kiḷigvak	"Mastodon"; father of storyteller Asatchaq.
Killigivuk	Anglicized version of "Kiḷigvak."
Kinnaq	"Fool, idiot, crazy" (6).
Kivaliñiq	Modern Kivalina, Alaska.
Kunuyaq	Paternal grandfather of storyteller Asatchaq (20).
Kuukpak	"Big river"; about ten miles east of Tikiġaq.
Kuuvak	"Big river"; modern Kobuk.
Maġuan	Nephew of Qipuġaluatchiaq (7).
Masiiñ	Tikiġaq's last shaman (24).
Niġliq	"Brant goose"; Kavisiġluk's brother and rival of Suuyuk (14).
Niġuvana	Mother of storyteller Asatchaq.
Noatak	River south of Tikiġaq.
Nuliayuk (Sedna)	Mother of the Sea Beasts (1).
Nuyagruaq	Stranded hunter (18).
Paniunayuk	Aqsaqauraq's rival (15).

Pisiktaġaaq	Kobuk shaman and rival of Ayagiiyaq (23, 24).
Qaagraq	Kobuk shaman (8).
Qaġmaqtuuq	Tikiġaq qalgi.
Qalgiiraq	Tikiġaq qalgi.
Qaŋiḷiqpak	Tikiġaq qalgi.
Qaunnaiḷaq	Marmot spirit shaman (9).
Qayaqtuġuŋnaqtuaq	"One who always goes by kayak" (4).
Qikiqtaġruk	Modern Kotzebue, Alaska.
Qilugiuq	Trading partner of Qaunnaiḷaq (9).
Qipuġaluatchiaq	Tikiġaq shaman (7).
Quliuq	1. Tikiġaq man, murderer of Suuyuk the Elder and slain in turn by Kunuyaq (20); 2. Protective name given by Kunuyaq to his son Kiḷigvak (Asatchaq's father).
Samaruna	Storyteller Asatchaq's maternal uncle.
Saugvik	Tikiġaq qalgi.
Siġvana	1. Woman terrorized by shaman (11); 2. Niġliq's sister (14).
Sisualik	Site of annual trade fair near Qikiqtagruk.
Suuyuk	Niġliq's rival (14).
Suuyuk the Elder	Great-grandfather of storyteller Asatchaq, murdered by Quliuq (20).
Suuyuk the Younger	Paternal uncle to storyteller Asatchaq and subject of a shamanic attack by Ataŋauraq (21).
Taŋnaaluk	Tikiġaq hunter (17).

Tatqim iñua	Spirit of the moon, Aliŋnaq (2, 3).
Tigguasiña	Boy shaman (10).
Tikiġaq	"Point of land" (lit. "something like an index finger"); modern Point Hope.
Tikiġaġmiu (pl. Tikiġaġmiut)	Tikiġaq person.
Tukummiq	1. Carol Omnik, translator; 2. Shaman woman (22).
Tuluŋigraq	"Something like tulugaq [Raven]": trickster-creator (1).
Uivvaq	Modern Cape Lisburne.
Ukuŋniq	Shaman trickster (4).
Umigluk	David Frankson, Tikiġaq storyteller, born 1900, the son of Aġviqsiiña.
Uŋasiksikaaq	Tikiġaq qalgi.
Utkusik	Tikiġaq shaman (10).
Utqiaġvik	Modern Barrow, Alaska.
Utuaġaaluk	Abused young man (16).
Utuqqaq River	River about two hundred miles north of Tikiġaq.

TERMS

aana	Grandmother.
aġviqtaq	Whale amulet.
alġaġuun	"Warning" story.
anaq	Excrement.

aŋatkuq	Shaman.
atiq	1. "Name"; 2. "namesake"; 3. element in human three-part soul structure.
avataqsiun	Song for the whale float.
igalaaq	Iglu skylight.
iglu	Earth house.
iġmaġun	Packet of choice meat wrapped in skins.
iġñiruaqtuqtuq	One of two amulet groups; literally, "has an amulet empowered by birth things."
ii	"Yes."
iḷiappaq	"Orphan"; usually a child shaman.
iḷitqusiq	"Personal soul" or "spirit"; element in human three-part soul structure.
iñua	1. Resident spirit or spirit owner; 2. animal's human part-soul.
iñuusiq	"Life force" or "soul"; element in human three-part soul structure.
katak	Iglu entrance hole (in floor).
kikituk	Shaman's power object.
kuyak	To have sexual intercourse.
maktak	Whale skin and blubber.
niġrun	"Animal"; alternate name for Tikiġaq.
niŋau	Sister's husband.
niulu	"Twisted tooth," usually shamanic in connotation.

niviaqsiaq	Young woman.
nuġlu	Buckle made of bone or ivory.
nuna	"Land, inland"; territory of *nunamiut*, inland people.
nunamiu (pl. *nunamiut*)	Inland Iñupiaq.
pisiktaġvik	Area where men practice archery.
qalgi	Ceremonial house.
qanitchaq	Iglu entrance passage, typically made of whalebone.
qataŋun	Exchange sibling.
qattaq	Waterpot.
qattauraq	Little qattaq.
qiḷa	Shamanic power.
quġvik	Waste pot.
qulliq	Oil lamp.
quŋuqtuqtuq	One of two amulet groups; literally, "has an amulet to be activated by grave goods."
siñiŋnaq	Sleep song.
siññiktaq	Supernatural sleep; dream.
tulugaq	Raven.
tupitkaq	Shamanic practice involving reconstruction of dead animal or sending out of power object.
tuttu	Caribou.
tuuŋġaq	Shaman's helping spirit.

ugruk	Bearded seal.
uiḷuaqtaq	"Woman who won't marry."
umialik	Skinboat owner.
umiaq	Eight-man skinboat.
unipkaaq	Old story, myth, legend.
unipkaluktuaq	"A story that comes to life"; also explained as synonym for *unipkaaq*.
uqaluktuaq	"The things that were said of them"; ancestor chronicle.
usuk	Penis.
utchuk	Vagina.

Aldrich, Herbert L. 1889. *Arctic Alaska and Siberia; or, Eight months with the Arctic whaleman.* Chicago: Rand, McNally.

Allen, Arthur James. 1978. *A whaler and trader in the Arctic.* Anchorage: Alaska Northwest.

Bailey, Alfred M. 1971. *Field work of a museum naturalist: Alaska–Southeast; Alaska–Far North, 1919–1922.* Museum Pictorial, vol. 22. Denver: Denver Museum of Natural History.

Beaglehole, J. C., ed. 1967. *The voyage of the "Resolution" and "Discovery" 1776–1780.* Cambridge: Cambridge University Press.

Beechey, Frederick William. 1831. *Narrative of a voyage to the Pacific . . . in his Majesty's Ship "Blossom" . . . in the years 1825, 26, 27, 28.* 2 vols. London: Colburn and Bentley.

Birket-Smith, Kaj. 1936. *The Eskimos.* Trans. W. E. Calvert. London: Methuen.

Boas, Franz. 1888. *The central Eskimo.* Sixth Annual Report of the Bureau of American Ethnology for the Years 1884–1885. Washington, D.C.

———. 1889, 1894, 1897. Eskimo tales and songs. Journal of American Folk-lore 2:123–31; 7:45–50; 10:109–15.

———. 1902. The Jessup North Pacific Expedition. In *Proceedings of the Thirteenth International Congress of Americanists,* 91–100. New York.

———. 1910. *Kwakiutl tales.* Columbia University Contributions to Anthropology, vol. 2. New York.

Bockstoce, John R. 1976. On the development of whaling in the western Thule culture. *Folk* 18.

————. 1977. *Eskimos of northwest Alaska in the early nineteenth century: Based on the Beechey and Belcher collections and records compiled during the voyage of H.M.S. "Blossom" to northwest Alaska in 1826 and 1827.* Pitt Rivers Museum Monograph Series, no. 1.

————. 1977. *Steam whaling in the western Arctic.* New Bedford, Mass.: Old Dartmouth Whaling Society.

————. 1986. *Whales, ice, and men.* Seattle: University of Washington Press.

Bodfish, Hartson H. 1936. *Chasing the bowhead.* Cambridge: Harvard University Press.

Bogojavlensky, Sergei. 1969. Imaangmiut Eskimo careers: Skinboats in Bering Strait. Ph.D. diss., Harvard University, Cambridge.

Bogoras, Waldemar G. 1902. The folklore of northeastern Asia, as compared with that of northwestern America. *American Anthropologist* n.s. 4:577–683.

————. 1904–9. *The Chukchee.* Memoirs of the American Museum of Natural History, vol. 11. New York. Rpt. 1975. New York: AMS Press.

Briggs, Jean L. 1970. *Never in anger: Portrait of an Eskimo family.* Cambridge: Harvard University Press.

Brower, Charles David. [1945.] "The northernmost American: An autobiography." Microfilm of typescript, University of Alaska Archives, Fairbanks.

————. 1950. *Fifty years below zero: A lifetime of adventure in the Far North.* London: Travel Book Club.

Burch, Ernest S., Jr. 1970. The Eskimo trading partnership in north Alaska: A study in "balanced reciprocity." *Anthropological Papers of the University of Alaska* 15, no. 1:49–80.

———. 1974. Eskimo warfare in northwest Alaska. *Anthropological Papers of the University of Alaska* 16, no. 2:1–14.

———. 1975. *Eskimo kinsmen: Changing family relationships in northwest Alaska*. Monographs of the American Ethnological Society, no. 59. St. Paul, Minn.: West.

———. 1979. The nonempirical environment of the Arctic Alaskan Eskimos. *Southwestern Journal of Anthropology* 27, no. 2:148–65.

———. 1981. *The traditional Eskimo hunters of Point Hope, Alaska: 1800–1875*. Barrow, Alaska: North Slope Borough.

Campbell, Joseph. 1959. *The masks of god: Primitive mythology*. New York: Viking.

Chowning, Ann. 1962. Raven myths in northwestern North America and northeastern Asia. *Arctic Anthropology* 1, no. 1:1–5.

Collier, Arthur J. 1906. *Geology and coal resources of the Cape Lisburne region, Alaska*. U.S. Geological Survey Bulletin, no. 278. Washington, D.C.

Collins, Henry B., Jr. 1951. The origin and antiquity of the Eskimo. In *Annual Report of the Smithsonian Institution for 1950*, 423–67. Washington, D.C.

Curtin, Jeremiah. [1898] 1969. *Creation myths of primitive America*. New York: B. Blom.

Curtis, Edward S. 1930. *The North American Indians*. Vol. 20. Norwood, Mass.: Plimpton. Rpt. 1970. New York: Johnson.

Czaplicka, M. A. 1914. *Aboriginal Siberia: A study in social anthropology*. Oxford: Clarendon.

Douglas, Mary. 1966. *Purity and danger: An analysis of concepts of pollution and taboo*. New York: Praeger.

Driggs, John B. 1892. Dr. Driggs' work at Point Hope, Alaska. *The Spirit of the Missions*, March, 88–104.

————. 1905. *Short sketches from oldest America*. Philadelphia: George W. Jacobs.

Dumond, Don. E. 1977. *The Eskimos and Aleuts*. London: Thames and Hudson.

Dundes, Alan. 1988. *The flood myth*. Berkeley and Los Angeles: University of California Press.

Eliade, Mircea. 1964. *Shamanism: Archaic techniques of ecstasy*. Princeton, N.J.: Princeton University Press.

Foote, Don Charles. [1959–62.] Field notes from Point Hope, Noatak, and Kivalina. Foote Collection. University of Alaska Archives, Fairbanks.

————. American whalemen in northwestern Arctic Alaska. *Arctic Anthropology* 2, no. 2:16–20.

————. 1965. "Exploration and resource utilization in northwestern Arctic Alaska before 1855." Ph.D. diss., McGill University, Montreal.

Garfield, Viola E. 1953. Contemporary problems of folklore collecting and study. *Anthropological Papers of the University of Alaska* 1, no. 2.

Giddings, J. L. 1952. *The Arctic woodland culture of the Kobuk River*. University of Pennsylvania, University Museum Monograph, no. 8. Philadelphia.

————. 1961. *Kobuk River people*. University of Alaska, Study of Northern Peoples, no. 1. College, Alaska.

————. 1967. *Ancient men of the Arctic*. New York: Knopf.

Golder, Frank A. 1909. Eskimo and Aleut stories from Alaska. *Journal of American Folk-lore* 22:10–24.

Grinnell, George Bird. [1892] 1962. *Blackfoot lodge tales: The story of a prairie people*. Lincoln: University of Nebraska Press.

Gubser, Nicholas J. 1965. *The Nunamiut Eskimos: Hunters of caribou*. New Haven, Conn.: Yale University Press.

Hall, Edwin S., Jr. 1975. *The Eskimo storyteller: Folktales from Noatak, Alaska*. Knoxville: University of Tennessee Press.

Hawkes, Ernest W. 1913. *The "inviting-in" feast of the Alaskan Eskimo*. Canadian Department of Mines, Geological Survey Memoir, no. 45, Anthropological Series, vol. 3. Ottawa.

————. 1914. The dance festivals of the Alaskan Eskimo. *University of Pennsylvania, Museum Anthropological Publications* 6, no. 2:5–41.

Healy, Capt. Michael A. 1887. *Report of the cruise of the Revenue Marine steamer "Corwin" in the Arctic Ocean in the year 1885*. Washington, D.C.: U.S. Government Printing Office.

Himmelheber, Hans. 1938. *Eskimokünstler: Teilergebnisse einer ethnographischen Expedition in Alaska von Juni 1936 bis April 1937*. Stuttgart: Strecker and Schröder.

Hrdlička, Aleš. 1930. Anthropological survey in Alaska. In *Forty-Sixth Annual Report of the Bureau of American Ethnolology for the Years 1928–1929*, 19–347. Washington, D.C.

Jenness, Diamond. 1924. Eskimo folk-lore. In *Report of the Canadian Arctic Expedition 1913–18*, vol. 13. Ottawa.

Jochelson, Waldemar I. 1905–8. *The Koryak*. Memoirs of the American Museum of Natural History, vol. 10. New York.

Kaplan, Lawrence. 1975–1990. Personal communications on the Iñupiaq language.

Kleivan, Inge. 1971. Why is the Raven black? *Acta Arctica 17*. Copenhagen.

Koenig, Franz Heinrich. 1887–1900. Papers in the Koenig Collection, University of Alaska Archives, Fairbanks.

Krause, Aurel. 1956. *The Tlingit Indians: Results of a trip to the northwest coast of America and Bering Straits*. Monographs of the American Ethnological Society, no. 26. Seattle: University of Washington Press.

Kroeber, Alfred L. 1899. Tales of the Smith Sound Eskimo. *Journal of American Folk-lore* 12:166–82.

Lantis. Margaret. 1938. The Alaskan whale cult and its affinities. *American Anthropologist* 40:438–64.

————. 1947. *Alaskan Eskimo ceremonialism*. Monographs of the American Ethnological Society, no. 11. New York: J. J. Augustin.

Larsen, Helge E. 1969–70. Some examples of bear cult among the Eskimo and other northern peoples. *Folk* 11–12:27–42.

Larsen, Helge E., and Froelich Rainey. 1948. *Ipiutak and the Arctic whale hunting culture*. Anthropological Papers of the American Museum of Natural History, vol. 42. New York.

Lewis, I. M. 1989. *Ecstatic religion: A study of shamanism and spirit possession*. 2d ed. London: Routledge and Kegan Paul.

Lowenstein, Tom. 1981. *Some aspects of sea ice subsistence in Point Hope, Alaska*. Barrow, Alaska: North Slope Borough.

————. 1993. *Ancient land: Sacred whale*. London: Bloomsbury.

Lowie, Robert H. 1918. *Myths and traditions of the Crow Indians*. New York: American Museum of Natural History.

MacLean, Edna Ahgeak. 1976–80. Personal communications on the Iñupiaq language.

————. 1981. *Abridged Iñupiaq and English Dictionary*. Fairbanks and Barrow: Alaska Native Language Center and Iñupiat Language Commission.

Mauss, Marcel. 1950. *Seasonal variations of the Eskimo: A study in social morphology*. London: Routledge and Kegan Paul.

Moore, George W. 1966. Arctic beach sedimentation. In *The environment of the Cape Thompson Region, Alaska*. Ed. Norman J. Wilimovsky and John N. Wolfe. Oak Ridge, Tenn.: U.S. Atomic Energy Commission.

Muir, John. 1892. *The cruise of the "Corwin": Journal of the Arctic expedition of 1881 in search of De Long and the "Jeannette."* Boston: Houghton Mifflin.

Murdoch, John. 1892. Ethnological results of the Point Barrow expedition. In *Ninth Annual Report of the Bureau of American Ethnology for the Years 1887–1888,* 19–441. Washington, D.C.

Neihardt, John. 1932. *Black Elk speaks: Being the life story of a holy man of the Ogalala Sioux.* New York: Morrow.

Nelson, Edward William. 1899. The Eskimo about Bering Strait. In *Eighteenth Annual Report of the Bureau of American Ethnology for the Years 1896–1897,* 3–518. Washington, D.C.

Nelson, Richard K. 1969. *Hunters of the northern ice.* Chicago: University of Chicago Press.

Norman, Howard A. 1976. *The wishing bone cycle: Narrative poems from the Swampy Cree Indians.* New York: Stonehill.

Oesterreich, T. K. [1930] 1966. *Possession, demoniacal and other, among primitive races in antiquity, the Middle Ages, and modern times.* Secaucus, N.J.: University Books.

Oswalt, Wendell H. 1967. *The Alaskan Eskimos.* San Francisco: Chandler.

Pulu, Tupou L., Ruth Ramoth-Sampson, and Angeline Newlin. 1980. *Whaling: A way of life.* Anchorage: National Bilingual Materials Development Center, University of Alaska.

Radin, Paul. 1937. *Primitive religion: Its nature and origin.* New York: Viking.

———. 1956. *The trickster.* New York: Schocken.

Rainey, Froelich G. 1940–41. Field notes from Point Hope. Rainey Collection, University of Alaska Archives, Fairbanks.

———. 1947. The whale hunters of Tigara. *Anthropological Papers of the American Museum of Natural History* 41, part 2:231–83.

Rasmussen, Knud. 1927. *Across Arctic America: Narrative of the fifth Thule expedition.* New York: Putnam's.

----. 1930. *Intellectual culture of the Iglulik Eskimos*. Report of the Fifth Thule Expedition 1921–24, vol. 7, no. 1. Copenhagen.

----. 1931. *The Netsilik Eskimos: Social life and spiritual culture*. Report of the Fifth Thule Expedition 1921–24, vol. 7, no. 1. Copenhagen.

----. 1952. *The Alaskan Eskimos, as described in the posthumous notes of Kund Rasmussen*. Report of the Fifth Thule Expedition 1921–24, vol. 10, no. 3. Copenhagen.

Ray, Dorothy Jean. 1961. *Artists of the tundra and the sea*. Seattle: University of Washington Press.

----. 1967. *Eskimo masks: Art and ceremony*. Seattle: University of Washington Press.

Rink, Hinrich J. 1875. *Tales and traditions of the Eskimo: With a sketch of their habits, religion, and other peculiarities*. Edinburgh and London: Blackwood.

Shirokogoroff, S. M. 1935. *Psychomental complex of the Tungus*. London: K. Paul, Trench, Trubner. Rpt. 1980. New York: AMS.

Simpson, John. 1855. Observations on the western Eskimo and the country they inhabit, from notes taken during two years at Point Barrow. In *Arctic Geography and Ethnology*, 233–75. London: Royal Geographical Society.

Simpson, Thomas. 1843. *Narrative of the discoveries on the north coast of America, effected by the officers of the Hudson's Bay Company, 1836–39*. London: R. Bentley.

Spencer, Robert F. 1959. *The North Alaskan Eskimo: A study in ecology and society*. Bureau of American Ethnology Bulletin, no. 171. Washington, D.C.

Stefánsson, Vilhjálmur. 1909. The Eskimo trade jargon of Herschel Island. *American Anthropologist* n.s. 11:217–32.

----. 1919. *The Stefánsson-Anderson Arctic expedition of the American Museum: Preliminary ethnological report*. Anthropological Papers of the American Museum of Natural History, vol. 14, part 1. Washington, D.C.

———. 1921. *The friendly Arctic: The story of five years in polar regions.* New York: Macmillan.

Swanton, John R. 1909. *Tlingit myths and texts.* Bureau of American Ethnology Bulletin no. 39. Washington, D.C.

Tedlock, Dennis. 1972. *Finding the center: Narrative poetry of the Zuni Indian.* New York: Dial.

Thalbitzer, William. 1914–41. *The Ammassalik Eskimo: Contributions to the ethnology of the East Greenland natives.* Meddelelser om Grønland, nos. 39–40, 53.

Thompson, Stith. 1929. *Tales of the North American Indians.* Bloomington: Indiana University Press.

Vanstone, James W. 1958. Commercial whaling in the Arctic Ocean. Pacific Northwest Quarterly 49, no. 1:1–10.

———. 1962. *Point Hope: An Eskimo village in transition.* Seattle: University of Washington Press.

———. 1968–69. Masks of the Point Hope Eskimo. *Anthropos* 63–64:828–40.

———, ed. 1977. A. F. Kashevarov's explorations in northwest Alaska, 1838. *Fieldiana: Anthropology 69.*

Weyer, Edward M., Jr. 1932. *The Eskimos: Their environment and folkways.* New Haven, Conn.: Yale University Press. Rpt. 1962. Hamden, Conn.: Archon.

Worl, Rosita. 1980. The North Slope Iñupiat whaling complex. In *Alaska Native Culture and History.* Ed. Y. Kotani and W. B. Workman. National Museum of Ethnology, Senri Ethnological Studies, no. 4. Osaka, Japan.

Zaehner, R. C. 1957. *Mysticism, sacred and profane: An inquiry into some varieties of praeternatural experience.* Oxford: Clarendon.

The text of this book is composed in a digitized version of Monotype Bembo. The last in a series of classic type design revivals, Monotype Bembo (270) was issued in 1929 under the guidance of Stanley Morison, type director for the Monotype Corporation. Monotype Bembo is based upon types punch cut by Francesco Griffo for Aldus Manutius for a text entitled De Aetna, *written by Cardinal Pietro Bembo and published in 1495.*

One of the advantages of Bembo over many other typefaces currently in use is the readability of the italic font, in which, for example, this colophon is set. The font owes its existence neither to Griffo nor Aldus, however. The model for Bembo Italic can be found in a typeset book published in the late sixteenth century by the Venetian writing master Giovanni Tagliente.

The display font for this book is Lithos, a typeface currently popular in advertising but rooted historically in the lapidary inscriptions of the early Greeks. Issued in 1989, Lithos was designed by Carol Twonby for Adobe Systems.

The Things That Were Said of Them *was designed by Steve Renick of the University of California Press. The maps were drawn by Megan Allen. The production coordinator for the project was Fran Mitchell, and the book was typeset, printed, and bound by the Maple-Vail Book Manufacturing Group.*

Library of Congress Cataloging-in-Publication Data

Asatchaq, 1891–1980.
    The things that were said of them : shaman
stories and oral histories of the Tikiġaq people /
told by Asatchaq ; translated from the Iñupiaq by
Tukummiq and Tom Lowenstein ; introduction
and commentaries by Tom Lowenstein.
        p.   cm.
    Includes bibliographical references.
    ISBN 0-520-06569-7 (alk. paper)
        1. Eskimos—Alaska—Point Hope—Legends.
        2. Eskimos—Alaska—Point Hope—Religion
and mythology.   3. Shamanism—Alaska—Point
Hope—Folklore.   I. Lowenstein, Tom.
II. Title.
E99.E7A766   1992
398.2′08997107987—dc20   92-6319

Canadian Cataloguing in Publication Data

Asatchaq, 1891–1980.
    The things that were said of them

    Includes bibliographical references.
    ISBN 1-55054-035-1
        1. Inuit—Alaska—Legends.   2. Legends—
Alaska.   3. Shamans—Alaska—Folklore.
I. Tukummiq.   II. Lowenstein, Tom.
III. Title.
E99.E7A83 1992   398.2′089′971   C92-091307-5